Build your own
Motorcaravan

Author: John Wickersham
Project Manager: Louise McIntyre
Copy editor: Peter Nicholson
Page build: James Robertson

First published 2006
Reprinted 2007, 2009 (twice) and 2011

Published by: Haynes Publishing,
Sparkford, Yeovil, Somerset BA22 7JJ, UK

A catalogue record for this book is available from
the British Library

ISBN 978 1 84425 221 3

Printed in the USA by Odcombe Press LP,
1299 Bridgestone Parkway, La Vergne, TN 37086

**Readers are strongly advised that all
electrical and gas installations should be
carried out or inspected by properly
qualified engineers.**

**While every effort is taken to ensure the
accuracy of the information given in this
book, no liability can be accepted by the
author or publishers for any loss, damage
or injury caused by errors in, or omissions
from, the information given.**

John Wickersham

Build your own
Motorcaravan

A practical manual for van conversions, coachbuilts
and major renovation projects

Contents

THE CHALLENGE

Thousands of people wonder if they could build a motorcaravan; many go on to achieve their dream.

It's a great feeling! Driving towards a holiday destination in a motorhome you've built yourself – the long hours engaged in constructional work have brought a special reward.

This is a book about fulfilling the dream. Having spent 15 years building five vehicles in a garden at home, I've learnt a lot in the process. So now it's time to help others as well.

To begin with, I hope that *Build Your Own Motorcaravan* is a source of inspiration. On the other hand, I make no secret of the fact that projects like this should never be taken lightly. In fact, there is one quality that is especially important: determination. Once you've taken the very first step, you must continue right to the end.

However, before starting out on this constructional journey, bear in mind that the term 'motorcaravan' embraces a number of different types of vehicle. For example, a leisure vehicle which started life as a panel van and was subsequently equipped with comfortable living accommodation is often referred to as a 'campervan'. In contrast, if a living 'pod' is built on top of a bare chassis, the resulting vehicle is typically called a 'coachbuilt motorcaravan'.

Not surprisingly, there are many variations on this theme. Some campervans have elevating roofs, others have a replacement high-top roof fitted. Coachbuilt models vary, too. Some are built around the original commercial cab whereas the 'A-class' has a purpose-made full-width cab which combines with the living space.

At one time, both A-class and large American 'recreational vehicles' (RVs) were referred to as motorhomes, but that has changed. Nowadays, the words motorhome and motorcaravan are interchangeable and act as generic terms for all types of leisure vehicle offering on-board accommodation. This convention is adopted throughout the book.

If you want to find out more about different types of motorcaravan, these are discussed and critically compared in *The Motorcaravan Manual*, also published by Haynes.

Terminology aside, the key point in the enterprise is the fact that *you* take the opportunity to create your very own motorcaravan – irrespective of type. Its size, internal layout, aesthetic embellishment and overall design will be chosen by you, the originator. In consequence, the finished vehicle will not only meet your particular needs; it reflects your personal tastes and vision for a smart but functional 'holiday home'.

Not that you will necessarily carry out all the constructional work yourself. The extent of a person's involvement depends on their spare time, financial resources and command of particular skills. Sometimes you will find it necessary to enlist the help of others – just like the manufacturers do in the course of their constructions.

The task in context

It's an exciting challenge but let's make no mistake about this; building your own motorcaravan is a task of considerable involvement. In fact, you might reasonably ask yourself why you should bother at all when there are so many professionally built models on the market.

The fact is there are hundreds to choose from, and to prove the point, I recently made a count of all new models currently on sale in this country. This is what was found:

- There are around 260 different British-built motorcaravans currently on sale.
- In addition, there are approximately 400 European and 85 American imported models being sold by specialist dealers.
- This makes a total of more than 750, which is a huge number of vehicles by anyone's reckoning.

And don't forget that this calculation doesn't include all the pre-owned, older models presently offered for sale by private owners and traders.

AN EXAMPLE OF INDIVIDUALITY

Above: Motorcaravans are seldom built to carry canoes and sailboards *inside* but not everyone wants a rack on the roof…

Left: …so this model was built with a facility for loading outdoor sports equipment through a purpose-made hatchback door.

When you reflect on this startling fact, you might conclude that there are more than enough models on the market to meet your particular requirements. So why bother to build your own?

Personal aims

This is really a personal thing. For my part, I decided as a teenager that if I couldn't afford something, I could always try to build it myself. I started by making a pair of skis. Hours were spent bonding thin layers of wood and applying varnish in a bathroom, to achieve a truly dust-free finish, but all to no avail. The left ski snapped on its first downhill outing.

A tenacious teenage spirit wasn't dampened though, and later self-build projects were more successful. These included several rough water canoes, a sailing dinghy, furniture, kit cars and a self-build house. However, in 1986, I discovered motorcaravans.

Lessons were learnt from these DIY projects and several of the techniques described in this book come from first-hand experience. However, it must be emphasised most strongly that you don't need mastery of a wide range of skills to complete a motorcaravan. Nor do you need an incredibly well-equipped workshop.

Similarly, you should always be prepared, where necessary, to enlist the help of others. This doesn't diminish the feeling of accomplishment and successful do-it-yourself enthusiasts, seldom do it *all* themselves.

The quest for individuality

If my early projects were born out of financial necessity, as time passed, equally potent driving forces also came into play. For example, there may be hundreds of shining motorcaravans displayed at exhibitions and sold in showrooms, yet the strange thing is that none meet my particular needs. And I'm not alone; many DIY builders come to the same conclusion.

In addition, I am often asked to test professionally built motorhomes for magazine reports. Some are noteworthy, others reveal surprising design flaws and are very poorly built. These are more reasons why a self-build approach is tantalisingly tempting.

Professional construction techniques

In some people's eyes, 'DIY' means second-rate and sometimes that view is justified. However, in other instances this presumption is mendacious propaganda. Many self-built motorcaravans exemplify the highest standards of workmanship. It is also an indisputable fact that a number of well-established

Technical Note

CONSTRUCTIONAL CONSIDERATIONS

- Fitting out a shell: Most self-builders find that it is less involved to fit-out a pre-built shell. This might be the goods section of a panel van, or a moulded glass reinforced plastic compartment mounted on a chassis-cab vehicle. The only time-consuming matter in this type of project is the fact that you're dealing with multiple angles inside rather than flat sides. A similar challenge faces the boat builder who is fitting-out a cabin cruiser.

- Coach-building from scratch: This would be a feasible alternative were it possible to purchase bonded sandwich panels shown overleaf in the construction of the Compass Avantgarde. That's not easy, but some self-builders have worked traditionally by constructing a timber skeleton framework, cladding it on the inside with ply, placing insulation in the core, and bonding sheet aluminium on the outside using adhesive sealant. Until recently, this constructional technique was employed when Carlight Caravans were built as shown page 10.

How a manufacturer converts a panel van

The prices of converted light commercial panel vans are often surprisingly high. This is partly because there is no speedy way to convert a van – and time is money. For instance, there's seldom room inside to allow more than two builders to work simultaneously. It is also evident that production-line practices are difficult to implement although pre-assembled furniture modules can be built in a joinery shop and installed in the vehicle later.

This photo-sequence shows some Bilbo's van conversions in progress. Bilbo's is an award-winning manufacturer from Godstone, Surrey whose quality of workmanship is well respected. An invitation to visit the factory was accepted with considerable appreciation.

1 The Bilbo's Celeste is a smart rising-roof campervan, and like most of this manufacturer's products, it is built using a VW base vehicle.

2 One of the first tasks in a van conversion is to insulate and line the interior. Here, a light, flexible, carpet-like material is fixed in place with adhesive.

3 Prior planning has dictated where all electric cables need to be installed and lengths of wire are drawn along specially placed ducting.

4 The ribbed, carpet-like lining material is used on backing boards, and as a cover fabric for lightweight, hollow panels made from plywood.

5 Experienced manufacturers like Bilbo's construct furniture assemblies separately in a workshop, for installation later.

6 The rear of this kitchen unit has been pre-shaped to fit in close register with the contoured side walls inside the VW van.

High-quality Carlight caravans have been constructed using traditional coachbuilt bodies. Similar techniques could be adopted by a DIY motorcaravan builder.

manufacturers were originally started by enthusiastic amateurs.

All-in-all we can learn from each other and some manufacturers have responded to my published test reports and have carried out the suggested alterations. Conversely, I find it invaluable to look at the way professional manufacturers construct their products and often embody similar features in my own projects.

It is helpful to look beneath the skin and to see things taking shape. That's why there are two sets of photographs alongside which show professional examples of both van conversions and coachbuilt models being built. These help to 'demystify' different methods of construction.

Summary

To round off this chapter, the point is made again that there are different types of 'motorcaravan'. Bearing this in mind, it would be unhelpful if this book were to focus exclusively on just one type of self-build project. So instead of proceeding down a single path, this manual presents a broad spectrum of information applicable to any type of vehicle.

Then, to show where specific building techniques are employed, examples of different projects are used throughout the text. Step-by-step photographs are presented in abundance,

too. However, no book is able to provide all the answers and there will always be occasions when a builder has to show personal resourcefulness.

It's perfectly true that letters are sometimes sent to magazine editors asking if there are working drawings and a step-by-step guidebook on how to build a motorhome. Frankly, that approach is too prescriptive. Moreover, there's a feeling voiced in magazine responses that if you need that amount of hand-holding, a project like this might be rather too ambitious. It is not like painting by numbers.

There are also a number of references to supporting material in *The Motorcaravan Manual* which is now in its second edition, and has chapters devoted to specific topics including:

■ General maintenance and repair
■ Chassis, suspension, towing and tyres
■ Electrical systems
■ Gas supply systems and heating appliances
■ Water supply and waste systems
■ Refrigerator servicing

While aspects of these subjects are repeated here, *Build Your Own Motorcaravan* is more concerned with constructional issues. In contrast, topics like 'servicing absorption refrigerators' are covered in the complementary maintenance manual, to which occasional reference is made.

How a manufacturer builds a coachbuilt

You can purchase a very much larger coachbuilt model than a van conversion for a similar price. This is because construction methods adopt production-line techniques. For instance, the walls are sometimes added when the furniture's in place, which means that several builders can complete assembly tasks together without getting in each other's way

These photographs show work in progress at the Explorer factory in Co. Durham and permission to photograph the operation was gratefully appreciated. Seen under construction is a 2002 Compass Avantgarde 200, a smart, well-equipped, compact coachbuilt vehicle.

1 Even though the external graphics and windows are still to be added, the distinctive shape of this model is already evident.

2 Construction work commences: a bonded sandwich floor panel is fixed to the Peugeot chassis and a glass-reinforced plastic moulding has been mounted over the trimmed cab.

3 Elsewhere in the factory, flat side panels are assembled. These are made from rigid polystyrene block foam bonded to an aluminium skin on the outside and a decorative plywood liner for the interior.

4 When the side walls are prepared for bonding, sections of galvanised sheet are placed within the sandwich to provide sound fixing points for the furniture that is to be added later.

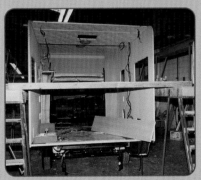

5 The side walls and the roof are assembled on the floor panel, but note the pre-constructed furniture and the rear section, which is left for access.

6 Once the cabinets are added they perform an important bracing function within the structure as a whole. Both walls and roof panels gain security from shelf units and furniture carcases.

THE REALITIES

If the idea of building a motorcaravan has a compelling attraction, what does it mean in practice?

While this book aims to present an inspirational picture, it never loses sight of important practical issues. Self-build projects are exciting in prospect, but there may be problems along the way that put you to the test.

There's no place for misconceptions about the task that lies ahead. For example, it is appropriate to keep in mind all the advantages offered by a self-build motorhome. On the other hand, the information panel opposite lists some disadvantages, too.

There are also key issues about the cost and time involved. Similarly, there will always be questions like: 'Will I need to purchase many specialist tools?' Let's take these topics in turn.

Financial matters

One of the obvious questions is: 'How much will it cost?' Unfortunately, there's no easy answer to that simple enquiry as the following case histories will show.

Example One: My first project was described in a brochure as 'a motorcaravan kit'. Prices started at around £1,800 but this only covered the supply of a steel chassis, and some brackets. A second payment led to the delivery of body components which consisted of seven untrimmed GRP (glass reinforced plastic) body panels, some panes of glass and their accompanying rubber surrounds.

It fell on the builder to buy a 'donor' Ford Cortina which was needed for its engine, cab and axles. On present day values, the finished campervan, known as a Starcraft, cost around £6,500 when fitted-out with the usual complement of fixtures and fittings.

Example Two: In this project, the builder wanted to convert an old vegetable van which he'd bought for a 'clearance price' through the classified advertisements in a local newspaper. Unfortunately his enforced early retirement from work meant that he didn't have the resources to buy a new refrigerator, cooker, sink unit and so on. On the other hand he *did* own an elderly touring caravan – and that provided an answer.

It was decided to dismantle this completely, and he recommissioned the appliances, and subsequently installed its beds, upholstery, furniture and kitchen appliances in the van. When the conversion was finally complete, the vehicle was repainted by hand and it subsequently provided several years of enjoyable motorcaravanning. On present-day values, this budget-building exercise had cost around £4,800. It certainly demonstrated that it *is* certainly possible to build a motorcaravan without having to spend a king's ransom.

Example Three: In contrast, my most recent DIY motorcaravan was built to achieve a particular standard; there were fewer constraints on costs. The finished vehicle is intentionally very different from mass-produced motorhomes. On the other hand, it followed the popular strategy of using a Fiat Ducato 2.8 Turbo Diesel chassis cab as its base which was purchased new.

The finished coachbuilt was fitted-out with many high-quality accessories at a total cost around £34,000. A professionally built vehicle fitted-out with similar equipment and non-standard 'extras' costs around £48–50,000.

These three case histories help to explain why it is impossible to answer the question: 'How much will it cost?' It all depends on the project

This low-cost van conversion used the furniture and appliances from an old caravan that was being scrapped.

Technical Note

Owning a 'self-designed' vehicle brings many benefits although it doesn't always work in your favour. Here are some points you need to consider:

ADVANTAGES

- Only a self-designed, self-built motorcaravan is likely to meet all your individual needs.
- Your own flair and design skills can be put into practice.
- You can create your ideal layout inside.
- Interior styling, colour and the choice of upholstery can be self-selected.
- Costs can be controlled at every stage and spread out over the building period.
- Interior appliances and accessories can always be upgraded at a later stage if you find you're running short of funds.
- DIY maintenance and repairs are much less daunting on a vehicle that you know intimately as the builder.
- There's an immense sense of achievement when you complete an involved project like this.
- The self-builder doesn't have to absorb costs that affect manufacturers, such as advertising expenditure, marketing strategies, wages and factory overheads.

Some production motorcaravans are very ornate inside, like this Auto-Sleepers model above…

…others are comparatively plain, such as this Murvi Morello to the left. But in a self-build model, you select your preferred styling.

DISADVANTAGES

- It is often difficult to get hold of motorhome components and purpose-made constructional materials.
- Domestic DIY stores seldom stock the lightweight materials that are so important when working on caravans and motorhomes.
- Selling or trading-in a self-built motorcaravan isn't always easy.
- Some DIY builders are blissfully unaware of important safety elements laid down in European Standards, Norms and Directives.
- Creative exuberance can overlook the all-important Maximum Technically Permissible Laden Mass and the Maximum axle weight limits of a base vehicle. Exceeding the limits stated by the vehicle's manufacturer is an offence for which you will be prosecuted.
- It is sometimes difficult to find an insurance company willing to insure a self-built vehicle.
- Legislation is becoming more onerous and the present freedom enjoyed by self-builders may be affected by increasing restrictions.
- If the design of a vehicle is bizarrely different from more conventional motorhomes, some proprietors might be unwilling to allow you to use their camping site.
- If a base vehicle is radically altered in the course of construction, the completed motorcaravan may have to pass the Single Vehicle Approval (SVA) inspection test. This is discussed later.

and its builder. *You* set the budget, you define the objectives and you 'cut the cloth' to suit your planned intentions.

Pay as you go

Since the building work can extend over many months – or even longer – one of the benefits of self-build is that you don't necessarily need to start with all the money 'up front'. As long as you have sufficient funds to get started, you thereafter 'pay as you go'. If this enables you to avoid arranging a loan, so much the better. You then don't pay interest to a finance house.

Also important is the fact that you can often use a vehicle in an incomplete form while the building fund accumulates. For instance it is not essential to have a sophisticated leisure refrigerator installed in the vehicle. Some campsites offer fridge/freezer facilities and in parts of warmer mainland Europe, a number of sites have ice-making machines. That's one example where the purchase of an appliance which might cost several hundreds of pounds can be deferred until more money is available.

Similarly, if you start using a part-finished vehicle during the summer months, you probably won't need a heating system in the living area. That's another item which can be added at a later date.

Of course, if the prospect of life without a fridge and a space heater seems utterly intolerable, you can always fit re-claimed items

To spread out expenditure, you can defer the installation of items like a heater or a refrigerator until funds become available.

bought from a caravan breakers as a temporary measure while saving-up for new appliances. That might have been the intention in Example Two cited above, except that the old fridge worked so well that a new one was never actually purchased.

Don't presume that this pay-as-you-go idea is the sole preserve of the self-builder. Some small-scale motorcaravan manufacturers operate similar schemes and Young Conversions based in Bletchley, Buckinghamshire calls this a 'Stage build' service. Arguably, it isn't an example of self-build so much as an owner-managed project, but it's worth keeping in mind. It works as follows.

From the outset, a customer discusses with the converter what he or she wants and the specification of the proposed vehicle is then noted down. Mike Young, the co-owner of the company then puts a suggested 'build-package' together. The package is made up of distinct constructional tasks, each of which represents a specific phase. Here is a typical example.

Phase One might include the installation of a high-top roof, the fitting of double-glazed windows and the addition of a timber floor. At this point the vehicle would be perfectly legal to use as a means of transport. Phase Two might involve the installation of beds, seats and furniture units. Phase Three could focus on the appliances and involve fitting a fridge, a hob, and grill. Phase Four might focus on the water supply system, a sink, wash basin and toilet installation. Phase Five would involve final completion jobs.

Taking this example further, if the total fitting-out operation were to be priced at £15,000, this sum would then be broken down into specific costings for each separate phase. The prices are then guaranteed for 12 months.

In the event of a project extending into a second year, a small start-up charge is then applied to each of the remaining phases. That's a fair way of recognising price rises in materials and the fact that it always takes a little time to re-establish a building operation that has been put on hold.

All this is negotiated at the beginning and there's always scope for flexibility. For instance, some clients might want the construction to run as five separate paid-for projects with a break in between, while others might want Phases One and Two to be completed in 'one hit' in early spring so that the part-finished vehicle is driveable and equipped with rudimentary sleeping facilities. Then the client might find further funds to book a return date in the winter, thereby taking care of the remaining three phases in one final operation.

This facility for spreading out payments can be a great benefit as it enables some prospective owners to defer or even avoid taking out a bank loan.

How long does a 'conversion' take?

Again, there's no simple answer to this question. In Example Two above, the builder and his wife had taken an enforced early retirement. Work began in the summer when the evenings were light and progress was only held up by bad weather. With the benefit of long days in summer and few interruptions, the van was duly finished after 12 busy weeks.

In Examples One and Three, the situation was completely different. I was working in full-time employment which meant that motorhome construction had to fit into odd moments and weekends – subject to good weather. The Starcraft took two years to complete and it was clear that fitting-out an unusually shaped interior to a high standard was extraordinarily time-consuming. In fact, I had previously completed a four- bedroom self-build house – albeit with the help of a bricklayer, plasterer and plumber – in something like half that time.

If two years sounds a long time, Example Three extended over four years. Note that the motorcaravan didn't take four years to build: it was just that the project extended over a four-year period. In reality, the vehicle was used for rough overnight accommodation after only four weeks. At that time it had no windows, no furniture and the experience was rather like camping in a GRP tent. Moments of hardship like this quickly sharpen the mind...

Delays also occurred because this project vehicle was used as a test bed by several component manufacturers. For instance, it was the first coachbuilt motorcaravan in the UK to be fitted with an Eberspächer oil-driven space and water heater whose running fuel is taken from the vehicle's fuel tank. Since then, oil-fired systems have become widely accepted as an alternative to gas appliances.

Similarly, the vehicle was used to test the installation and operation of a prototype Status 530/10 elevating television aerial, now widely fitted to new motorcaravans built in the UK. Inevitably, experimental installations take time to conduct, but opportunities to work with component manufacturers was wholly

consistent with an aim to create a radically different motorhome. Time was never an issue.

Since these three self-build projects took 12 weeks, two years and four years respectively, you can see why it is difficult to comment on how long it takes to build yourself a motorcaravan.

Space and equipment

When it comes to the matter of space and equipment, we all realise how helpful it would be to have access to an indoor heated workshop and a huge array of machines and tools! Regrettably few self-builders have a facility like that at their disposal. I've always had to work outdoors with one eye on the weather.

As regards the tools required, this depends on what work you intend to carry out yourself. If you're interested in woodwork for example, you will probably already own a reasonable number of hand tools with some portable electric machines as well. I would merely add from

Still awaiting its graphics... it took four years before this self-build project was completed.

Many DIY builders have to work outdoors and poor weather hinders progress.

When renovating a professionally built model, an owners' club can often offer advice if you encounter problems. This group get-together took place at one of the outdoor shows.

personal experience, that I started saving a lot of time and achieved better results when I purchased a small precision table saw. More recently I've found how useful a router can be as well.

In my tool collection there's also a cheap arc welding set but my skills are just not good enough to tackle safety-critical jobs. I also own a DIY compressor paint-spraying outfit which was purchased for use on a wind-free, fly-free, dust-free summer day to paint a kit car. That's when I learnt that you never get wind-free, fly-free, dust-free summer days and the finish was not as good as I'd hoped. Now a local specialist does the painting, although I'm allowed to do all the preparation and paper-masking tasks in his workshop to cut down on labour charges.

We'll come back later to this business of using professional help. As regards space for building a motorcaravan, it is obviously very important not to upset neighbours. Moreover, I once lived in an open-plan housing estate at which the parking of caravans wasn't permitted within the deeds. That's a possible restriction that always needs to be checked.

It would also be inappropriate to allow a front garden to become a building-yard. As a useful tip, I found that a local caravan storage specialist was willing to store all my GRP body mouldings during the long wait for delivery of a Fiat Ducato chassis cab. The fee was certainly reasonable.

Seeking help

As a conclusion to this chapter, it is appropriate to look a little more closely at areas where a self-builder often needs help.

Rather than starting from scratch, a number of self-builders decide to purchase an older motorcaravan which they plan to renovate

completely. Indeed, it's quite true that many motorcaravans are scrapped prematurely because the cost of professional repairs is greater than their actual market value. Labour rates are high these days and experienced craftsmen are thin on the ground.

This is where a determined and competent do-it-yourself enthusiast can reap rewards. You don't count your hourly rate when engaged in labours of love. Equally, some of those disadvantages of self help listed in the panel earlier may not arise. For instance, an insurance company is more likely to give a quotation for a motorcaravan which was originally built professionally than for one which was built completely by an amateur.

When rebuilding a pre-owned motorcaravan, you might have problems associated with its original construction or have difficulties tracing original fittings. That's where an Owners' Club can help. Address lists of owners' clubs are published in monthly magazines and these groups have regular get-togethers – especially at outdoor shows. If you need specialist parts, particularly if the original manufacturer is no longer in business, an owners' club can often lead enquirers in the right direction.

Professional work

While I like to try my hand at most things, certain skills are beyond my grasp. For instance, the five vehicles I have built to date have all had magnificent upholstery. That's important because the upholstery is one of the first things you notice. And the reason? Most of it has been professionally made to order.

Unless you have access to an industrial sewing machine and the skill to use it correctly, vehicle trimming and the creation of seat/bed cushions in the living section of a motorcaravan are best undertaken by a specialist supplier.

However, bespoke products are usually

Technical Note

OTHER SOURCES OF HELP

Practical articles published in motorcaravan magazines are another useful source of guidance; addresses of owners' clubs are also included now and again. The practical articles in *Motorcaravan and Motorhome Monthly (MMM)* and in *Motor Caravan Magazine (MCM)* are especially detailed.

The Motorcaravanners' Club is another source of information. The Camping & Caravanning Club and The Caravan Club both have a policy of discouraging major DIY projects. However, the 50 or so technical leaflets available free to members of The Caravan Club are especially informative.

Far left: To make a good job of the upholstery, you really need an industrial sewing machine – and the skills to use it.

Left: Some DIY work with fabrics is often undertaken by owners – like making zip-on seat covers.

costly and if you're working on a tight budget, you sometimes see surplus items for sale when attending outdoor shows. Equally, an inexpensive stretch cover can be run-up to hide grubby seats and new curtains can be made on a normal domestic sewing machine. It is also fairly easy to make up decorative padded panels using thin foam, a cover fabric, contact adhesive and a staple gun. But that's as far as most DIY builders will go. Preparing shaped foam and covering it with a high-quality fabric is a job for an upholstery specialist.

In the same way, it is strongly recommended that work involving a chassis should only be undertaken by experienced engineers. For example, some motorcaravanners want to be able to tow a trailer – and that means a tow bracket is needed. To the surprise of most owners, many professionally built coachbuilt motorcaravans cannot be fitted with a towing bracket. Even brackets designed for specific panel van models cannot be fitted once they've been converted into campervans. This is because items like under-floor tanks often hide the designated mounting points.

At the time of writing, there is no obligation to fit only Type-Approved towbars to light (or heavy) commercial vehicles. In contrast, light passenger vehicles first registered in the UK on or after 1 August 1998 which have a European Whole Vehicle Type Approval (EWVTA) Certificate of Conformity can only be fitted with a type-approved tow bracket. This legal requirement also applies to 'people-carriers' which are sometimes converted for overnight use.

Nearly all motorcaravans fall into a different category and it is legally permitted to have a one-off tow bracket designed and installed for a vehicle. However, the bracket must be structurally sound and the design and fit operation is *not* a DIY job.

Watling Engineers is one of several specialists which designs, builds and installs bespoke brackets for motorcaravans, unless the

work poses insurmountable technical problems. If there are any doubts about the safety of a proposed installation, the company won't proceed with the work.

To summarise, these are just two constructional tasks that should not be tackled by unqualified amateur builders. Other operations which should only be carried out by qualified personnel, receive mention in subsequent chapters. Gas installation work is a case in point.

Self-building doesn't mean that you should endeavour to do everything yourself. Even major motorhome manufacturers sub-contract important tasks to others and it is worth noting that all converters in this country buy-in the upholstery items.

When building on a budget, remember that surplus cushions are often sold at outdoor motorcaravan shows.

Designing a tow bar and fitting it to the chassis is a job you must entrust to a specialist company.

THE STRATEGIES

There are a number of approaches that you can follow when building a motorcaravan. Here are some of the options.

The point was made in the previous chapter that DIY and professional builders both use outside help. As a rule, manufacturers order specially made wiring harnesses, re-upholstered cab seats, modified chassis components and prefabricated doors.

In a similar way, a DIY builder can also buy-in products and skills. Without doubt, this is a logical way to proceed, but you still have to have a basic knowledge about practices and procedures. After all, it is essential to create a vehicle which is safe on the road and safe inside the living space. Comfort is also important.

To fulfil these objectives, you need to have an understanding of water services, electrical circuits, gas systems, heating, and refrigeration.

These topics are discussed in *The Motor Caravan Manual* and its content helps to underpin the practical procedures presented in this book. Even if you've gained experience from carrying out DIY work around the home, bear in mind that many of the practices and products used in motorcaravan construction are substantially different.

Once a basic understanding has been acquired, you are then in a position to decide which jobs you're prepared to tackle yourself and which ones you will get others to carry out for you. At that point in your pre-planning, it's time to find out about the services available from specialists, and to reflect on different building strategies.

Strategy One: rebuilding an older model

If you choose the refurbishment route to ownership, be prepared for problems in tracing replacement parts. Sometimes you'll find broken plastic mouldings on the exterior like a split body panel on a coachbuilt and it is often impossible to buy a replacement. These problems become especially acute when the original manufacturer is no longer in business. So how can you solve a problem like that?

Should you have a difficulty replacing unavailable body panels, a specialist like V&G near Peterborough can come to your rescue. This company has skilled staff who are able to repair badly damaged panels and can also recreate replicas. Let's suppose that an acrylic-capped ABS plastic side skirt on a coachbuilt model is badly split and is beyond normal repair. The strategy adopted by V&G staff is to create a GRP mould from the remnants. Using this mould, they can then cast a copy moulding in GRP which is all ready to fit. By applying a colour-matched paint, the replacement will look like new. (See the accompanying Tip box)

In a lot of cases, internal components can similarly be replaced with recreated copies that V&G will build to order. Items like a shower tray, a moulded bathroom cabinet or a plastic kitchen sink can be built in GRP as a

Most professional builders commission upholstery specialists to make the seating.

Wiring loom manufacture and electronic installations are usually entrusted to outside specialists.

Technical Note

TERMINOLOGY

- A mould is used to make plastic components such as a motorcaravan's external panels and internal items like shower trays.
- The product created from a mould is referred to as the moulding.
- GRP stands for glass reinforced plastic although many people use the imprecise term fibre-glass. This type of moulding is easy to identify because its reverse face is normally quite rough and fibres of chopped-strand glass mat can be seen.
- An acrylic-capped ABS moulding is usually shiny on both faces and it's a completely different material. Many modern cars have ABS mouldings for parts of the body such as the wings. However, some mouldings are created with a relief finish and these are commonly used for vehicle bumpers.

A GRP mould is being prepared for the manufacture of a high-top roof moulding.

direct replacement for cracked units. What is more, these replacements are often more robust than the original components.

Strategy Two: using part-build specialists

In Britain, many different types of manufacturer are involved in the construction of motorcaravans. These range from the major manufacturers like Auto-Sleepers, Auto-Trail, Auto-Cruise, the Explorer Group, and the Swift Group, whose annual output accounts for hundreds of motorhomes, to the small-scale manufacturers who might build no more than a dozen vehicles a year; these specialists are important.

It is the small-scale operators who are often willing to help self-builders and you will see advertisements for their services in specialist motorcaravan magazines. Several of these constructors offer what is described as 'part-build' assistance to DIY enthusiasts.

This service can prove invaluable so it is helpful to get in touch with companies such as Rainbow Conversions in Cambridgeshire, Leisuredrive FG in Bolton, Magnum Mobiles

in Grimsby, Middlesex Motorcaravans in Edgware, Young Conversions in Bletchley, and many others who can carry out tasks that you don't feel qualified to tackle yourself.

The extent of assistance varies, of course, and you need to discuss your requirements with as many specialists as you can find. For instance, you might only want a GRP high-top roof fitted to a van. Several small-scale manufacturers will do this for you. Alternatively, if you want an elevating roof assembled, fewer companies offer this service, but Middlesex Motorcaravans is a manufacturer which can install one of these for a client.

When contemplating fitting-out the inside, many different tasks are involved. Let's imagine a self-builder who is a qualified gas engineer by trade and whose daily work often involves installations with LPG (liquefied petroleum gas). A person like this would have

The part-build specialist, Young Conversions, tackles personalised projects for clients.

In this part-build operation, some of the cabinet work is being carried out by Young Conversions.

no difficulty fitting a gas cooker or connecting up the gas supply to a refrigerator. However, faced with the prospect of designing, constructing and installing cabinets, they might be seriously challenged. That's when part-build specialists can take that weight off their mind. So look at the advertisements in motor caravan magazines and find what services are currently offered.

Strategy Three: self-build kits

A rather different approach to ownership is to construct a motorcaravan from a kit. At the time of writing, the UK companies who used to sell kits are no longer in business and it is fair to state that the term 'kit' was also rather misleading. A potential customer might have presumed that a kit would contain a full complement of parts which would fit together with the ease of a jigsaw. Far from it! That's why many car kits are started, but

the product never gets finished.

The one which came closest to the idea of an easy-to-assemble package was the Rancher manufactured by Rickman in Hampshire. After success building and racing motorcycles, the Rickman brothers, Don and Derek, manufactured accessories like scooter top boxes and fairings. Then they launched the Rickman Ranger which resembled a 4x4 off-road vehicle even though it used the engine and running gear from a Ford Escort Mk 2. It was a delight to build and once all the donor parts had been cleaned and refurbished, I completed a Ranger in just a few weeks.

Shortly afterwards, a revised version was launched which was called the Rancher. Its front was much the same as its forerunner, the Ranger, but behind the cab was a large shell to be fitted out as a campervan. Optional items included GRP moulded lockers, kitchen units and bed bases. It was an excellent vehicle for two people and the builder could decide whether to use a refurbished Ford Escort 1.6-litre engine or to install a 2.0-litre engine from a Ford Cortina.

The GRP shell was supported by an exceedingly robust galvanised chassis and the vehicle was pleasant to drive. Although more than ten years have passed since the company ceased production, Rickman Ranchers are often advertised for sale in the classified advertisements in motorcaravan magazines. As long as you recognise that these are self-built vehicles, there are still a number around which are in very good shape. There is also an owners' club for all the

Both the Rickman Ranger and the Rancher kit projects used running gear from the Ford Escort Mk 2.

Above: The Rickman Rancher was a well-conceived GRP-bodied camper-van kit.

Below: Various convenient features were built into the Rancher and many models are still in active service.

Right: To speed up the build process, Rickman offered a number of GRP cabinets and cupboards, including the kitchen.

The unusual Starcraft was a challenging kit and the finished vehicle is certainly unusual.

Right: Most of the donor car Cortina items of running gear were reassembled on the Starcraft's new chassis.

Below: Once the dismembered cab had been mounted on the new chassis, GRP panels were fitted over the original Ford doors.

Rickman kit cars.

A camper-van kit which preceded the Rancher was more radical in design, and far harder to build. It was known as the Starcraft.

One of these took me two years to complete, but it taught many useful lessons. The concept was certainly unusual. The builder needed to purchase a Mk IV Cortina which was then cut apart in order to use the driving compartment, the two seats, the windscreen, front doors and the original dashboard. This was subsequently lifted on to a steel chassis which was fitted with Cortina running gear and transmission including the original suspension, brakes, propshaft, back axle and so on.

The external panels of the doors were then covered with GRP skins to disguise their original styling. GRP sections were also built around the re-mounted engine and a large shell was installed to the rear. This stretched so far rearwards that two extra wheels had to be mounted on non-driven, non-braked Indespension units. These rubber suspension assemblies are usually used on trailers.

The habitation section was supplied untrimmed, with no windows, no door and no floor. Needless-to-say, the builder had to carry out a lot of work on both automotive elements and the external body as well. However, for many constructors, fitting-out the interior was even harder on account of all the multiple angles and was just as

Loading the main bodyshell of a Starcraft was a tough task; it had no floor, windows or door.

demanding as fitting-out the hull of a cabin cruiser.

Completed Starcrafts display varying standards of workmanship and the majority make no secret of their DIY heritage. It was undoubtedly a difficult motorhome to build well, but its lively owners' club has always been an invaluable point of contact for technical guidance and encouragement.

Occasionally, Starcrafts are offered for sale but a potential purchaser should look most carefully at the standard of build. The rear suspension is often running in a grossly over-laden state and the Indespension trailer units – which were not designed for this application – were sometimes prone to failure.

Driving a six-wheeler around tight corners leads to tyre scrubbing at the rear and this undoubtedly provoked some of the problems. Moreover, only four of the six wheels were fitted with brakes – a situation that wouldn't be permitted in a vehicle built today. Not surprisingly, braking wasn't one of its more notable features.

In spite of its faults, my Starcraft provided ten years of enjoyable touring and it taught many lessons along the way. Moreover, the person who subsequently purchased the vehicle wrote for several years afterwards about the pleasures it provided.

If the Rancher and Starcraft motorcaravan kits are no longer in production, the Athano is

a smart looking A-class vehicle sold in Germany. Built on a VW base vehicle, this was exhibited at the 'Caravan Salon', a huge annual show held at the Messe Exhibition Centre in Düsseldorf. The vehicle has been offered in various stages of build to suit customers' requirements. Smart furniture modules have also been developed for builders who don't want to construct their own lockers, units and cupboards.

The Athano has been sold by Pleitner PS Wohnmobil GmbH and the manufacturer has confirmed that kits can be dispatched to UK customers. In reality, it is doubtful if that has

Multiple angles inside the bodyshell made the fitting-out process very involved but patience could lead to smart results.

Above: The VW-based Athano A-class kit from Germany was exhibited at the Caravan Salon, Düsseldorf.

Right: To help the self-builder, the Athano kit includes optional self-assembly furniture packages.

ever happened although enquiries confirmed that at the time of writing, this kit is still available in Germany. As the accompanying photos show, it's a bold way to enter the world of motorcaravanning, so let's hope that this kit doesn't suffer the fate of its British counterparts.

Strategy Four: fitting out a van with modular furniture

A later chapter looks more specifically at van conversions and one of the strategies worthy of consideration involves the use of modular

furniture. Anyone engaged in a fitting-out exercise should get a copy of the Reimo catalogues. These German publications are available in English and products advertised can be ordered through Motor Caravan Conversions in Cheetham, Manchester, which is a UK Reimo agent.

The accessory catalogue contains over 450 pages of products while a second catalogue contains nearly a hundred pages of modular pre-assembled furniture units and work-tops to suit a wide range of modern panel vans.

This is another build strategy which is reminiscent of flat-pack assembly products we buy for our homes. Clearly it's the answer for anyone who doesn't want to build furniture from scratch. And the results can look as good as a professional product.

Strategy Five: taking full charge

In a sense, taking full charge is an element that is ever-present in all the strategies mentioned above. You initiate the project whereupon you are in charge and you direct the way forward.

Even though some operations may be carried out by others, you have to manage the work and pay the bills. You will also need to acquire a knowledge about construction and procedures and pay due regard to standards, norms, codes of practice and numerous regulations.

Later chapters go into constructional details, so it's appropriate here to reflect on the work ahead.

Overview: the jobs that have to be done

As a guide to anyone contemplating a self-build project as opposed to a refurbishment exercise, here are some of the tasks that you will need to address.

☐ On a coachbuilt model constructed on a bare chassis cab, outrigger supports may be needed before the floor is added. Similarly, if major suspension upgrades are required, now is the time to do this work. Also give thought to the way a step might be fitted.

☐ Fresh and waste water tanks need installing at an early stage and on some models, both are fitted below the floor. Others situate the fresh tank inside to ensure it doesn't freeze in winter. Think about this at an early stage.

☐ Before a shell is fitted out, windows need to be fitted. Whether it's a van conversion or a coachbuilt model, planning the window positions is important. A window conveniently placed inside can sometimes look rather odd when viewed from the outside.

☐ On a van conversion, there may be preparatory work to do on the roof. Installing a high-top replacement roof or fitting an elevating roof system needs to be undertaken at an early stage in the project. There may also be roof ventilators to fit.

☐ Irrespective of the type of motorcaravan you're building, the addition of thermal insulation around the living space must be done with particular care. It is important to retain heat in winter but to prevent it getting like an oven inside on sunny days in summer.

☐ In most cases a vehicle's cab will need little work. However, it makes sense to allow this to become part of the living space whenever you stop for the night. This may involve fitting swivel turntables to the seats and checking the height of the floor.

☐ Deciding on the location of a leisure battery and establishing where to construct a gas cylinder locker are tasks to consider from the outset. If heating and cooking appliances are on one side of the vehicle and the gas locker is on the other, where will the gas supply pipe be routed?

☐ Wiring runs need working out before the van is lined with ply. This has implications for where the battery is located, the positions of the 12V charger/supply unit, the 230V consumer unit and the 12V fused control panel. Similarly, plan fresh and waste water pipe runs.

☐ What type of lighting is preferred and where will the units be located? Will some lamps be mains units? Where are the best places for reading lamps? And where would you like to have mains 13-amp sockets fitted in your motorcaravan?

☐ The position and installation of appliances needs careful consideration. A hob can get hot so check flammable surfaces. Most refrigerators necessitate the installation of external vents. What type of water heater will be fitted, and where will it be mounted?

☐ A sink, hand basin, toilet and shower tray all need a well-planned system of plumbing. Where will the water pump be fitted to offer access if there's a filter to change? What type of taps will be used and how will an electric pump be switched into action?

☐ Storage is a subject in its own right. Will there be any storage facilities externally? Under-floor lockers? Roof storage? A rack for a bike or two? And what about indoor storage? A small wardrobe, drawers, cupboards, a bedding locker and shelves for books?

☐ What about seating for meals? Will there be a place to lounge in comfort? And what about the all-important bed – or beds? Will there be a major upheaval when changing a lounge to a place for sleeping? If some of the seat cushions aren't used for the bed(s), where will you put them?

☐ Have you a clear vision of the upholstery and soft furnishings? What about cushions, mattresses and curtains? Will there be a living space with plush carpet for the slipper-wearer? Or will the floor covering have to cope with muddy boots or sand-filled beach shoes?

This overview has to be kept in mind when contemplating your vision of an ideal motorhome. Representing it as a tick-off list can also help a DIY enthusiast to choose their level of involvement in different constructional jobs.

Now let's look at different types of project before getting down to building details.

CONTRASTING PROJECTS

Some people convert existing vehicles; others decide to start from scratch.

Having looked at specialists who can help the DIY constructor, it is now useful to compare different types of projects.

One approach, which has been popular for many years, is to convert an existing vehicle. This is certainly very different from building a motorcaravan from a bare chassis.

On balance, the conversion approach is a less daunting undertaking, although it does mean that the design as a whole is limited by an existing structure. This is clearly not the case if you're starting from scratch. No-one claims this will be a problem-free enterprise – far from it. On the other hand, building on a flat chassis certainly offers more scope.

Converting existing vehicles

AMBULANCES AND DELIVERY VANS

Many enthusiastic builders have converted former ambulances into leisure vehicles. The fact that they originally carried heavy medical equipment means that the permitted weight limits are likely to be generous. As long as lightweight furniture is constructed as described in Chapter 15, it shouldn't be difficult to end up with a generous payload for your personal possessions.

Whether the engine is still in fair condition when an ambulance is finally sold is open to

question. Some builders might fit an overhauled power unit as a matter of course, just to be on the safe side. After all, accident and emergency vehicles are typically driven hard and therein lies a potential problem for a future owner. Breaking down on holiday is something you need to avoid.

Although the mechanical elements of former ambulances need close consideration, the body itself is likely to be sound. The trouble is, of course, that the finished project usually retains the look of a converted ambulance and even the addition of stripes and graphic embellishment is unlikely to hide its original function.

The rear doors of an ambulance can also be difficult to change, but at least they normally shut in a positive way. In fact, the one shown here has the thoughtful addition of a Fiamma roll-out sun blind, and rather than having an underfloor waste tank, water from the sink was taken to a portable container. That's an easy answer which follows the strategy used in touring caravans.

Clearly, this is a thoughtfully executed conversion and an advantage of this type of vehicle is that it can still be driven on a daily basis long before the interior alterations reach their final conclusion.

The same can be said of delivery vans and many people have fitted these out and created their own motorcaravans. For example, many of the Mercedes 508 and 608

Below: This converted ambulance has the addition of a rear-mounted awning; waste water is collected in a portable tank.

Below right: The motorcaravan here was based on a 1985 Mercedes-Benz van and these vehicles have been popular with DIY converters.

panel vans which were common in the 1970s were subsequently converted into leisure vehicles as the accompanying photograph shows. Diesel versions were particularly popular and motorsport owners used them, too. In fact, many Mercedes conversions are still in use some 30 years later.

BUSES AND COACHES

Conversion of a bus so that it can be used to transport a stock car in the back is another long-established practice. Add some simple accommodation in the forward section and you're ready to travel to racing circuits far and wide.

However, building a smart motorcaravan from a public transport vehicle is not an easy exercise, although the task is certainly achievable. The accompanying photo-sequence shows how a modern coach purchased at an auction was converted into a well-appointed motorhome.

Its designer, Mike Parker, is no stranger to the leisure industry and when he completed a Starcraft motorcaravan kit 20 years ago, he developed some night-time insulating covers for its windscreen and cab windows. Since those early experiments, his product, Silver Screens, has become an important accessory for thousands of motorcaravan owners. Not only does a Silver Screen help to reduce heat loss on cold winter days, its insulating properties also help to control interior temperatures when you park in the heat of the sun.

In addition to his mail order supply service, Mike sells Silver Screens at most of the outdoor motorhome shows and needs a capacious vehicle for transporting his stock. It also has to provide comfortable accommodation and to meet this need, Mike has converted a number of vehicles, including a former prison van. Drawing from these experiences, his most recent project has

This base vehicle was first registered in 2000 and it was offered for sale in an auction three years later.

One of the converter's objectives was to carry a small support car inside and the coach was suitable for this.

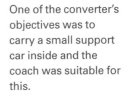

The tinted glass looked smart but it was very heavy and had to be removed. Steel panels were welded over the apertures.

When the vehicle neared completion it was painted metallic silver and finished with some attractive graphics.

Far left: Rear and side hatchback doors form part of the garage for the support car; a permanent bed is constructed above.

Left: A roll-out blind has been fitted on the near side and the original door affords easy access.

This 1994 British Telecom van was purchased for conversion into a two-berth motorcaravan.

involved the conversion of a large blue bus. From the outset, this was a striking looking vehicle but the tinted glass windows were remarkably heavy and had to be removed. Mike also wanted to construct a rear garage to take a small support-car.

Most of the interior work in this conversion project was carried out by Magnum Mobiles of Grimsby, but Mike Parker was closely involved with other practical work and created the overall design brief. The illustrations show what can be achieved when you're determined to build something notable. On the other hand, few bus-based motorcaravans are as aesthetically pleasing as this one.

BRITISH TELECOM GRP VANS

For a number of years, British Telecom (BT) engineers have been undertaking servicing work with the help of large, glass reinforced plastic-bodied vans. These vehicles are a familiar sight on Britain's roads and the purpose-moulded GRP monocoque shell is normally mounted on a Ford Transit diesel base vehicle.

As the accompanying photograph shows, the tapering over-cab roof is not dissimilar from those seen on purpose-designed coachbuilt motorhomes. The deeply profiled sides of the unit are different, of course, but the horizontal flutings give good rigidity to the walls. It is only the rear doors with their prominent stainless steel hinges which look disagreeably 'industrial'. However, these doors can be replaced.

Like many large companies, BT is constantly updating its fleet of vehicles and this type of 'Telecom van' is often sold with a moderate mileage when the vehicle is around five year's old. But that's not all; the vehicles are sometimes sold with a warranty and BT has also arranged finance packages. There is even a facility whereby servicing and maintenance can be carried out for a private owner in one of the 100 or so nationwide workshops.

Not surprisingly, the release of vehicles seems to be sporadic and a private purchaser needs to wait until a batch becomes available. Accordingly, potential owners should start by making enquiries at one of BT's regional offices. It is obviously difficult to quote prices since these are forever changing. However, in 2005, several T-registered vans with a mileage of 40,000 were being sold for £5,000 plus VAT. Little wonder, then, that several people have carried out successful conversions as the accompanying photographs show.

Technical Note

MONOCOQUE BODIES

This French word literally means a 'single shell'. In the aeronautic context it is used for a fuselage in which virtually all the structural loads are carried by the skin itself.

In the case of cars, the term has been used to describe a complete shell which also includes fixing points for the running gear and suspension. In other words, a monocoque vehicle doesn't have a separate chassis in the traditional sense because the shell has built-in reinforcement which meets the functional needs.

When the term monocoque is used in the context of coachbuilt motorcaravans, there's an important difference. The so-called 'chassis cab' base vehicle certainly does have a separate, traditional chassis. However, the well-known Auto-Sleepers 'monocoque' coachbuilt models have a single shell for the living compartment. This is clearly different from the coachbuilt Explorer motorcaravan depicted in Chapter 1 in which the separate walls, floor and roof were assembled as separate panels.

Like the Auto-Sleepers' product, the BT vehicles described here can also be referred to as monocoque vans.

EXAMPLE OF A CONVERTED BT VAN

Left: The BT vehicle shown here had been skilfully converted by a Yorkshire-based manufacturer.

Above: A mould was made from the sides to create an infill moulding at the back in place of the original workshop doors.

Left: Closing off the rear meant that lounge seating could be fitted at the back – and converted into a large bed at night.

Below left: On the driver's side, kitchen units were constructed to house a refrigerator, hob, grill and sink.

Below: As part of the conversion, the rear of the cab was cut away to create direct access to the living accommodation.

Converting a new GRP-bodied van

Some people would not relish the idea of purchasing a former maintenance vehicle, especially if its working life involved short journeys on a regular basis. Vehicle experts advise that high-mileage vehicles driven on long runs are usually in better mechanical order than low-mileage examples whose working conditions involve repeated stop/start routines. It is not just the engine which suffers. It stands to reason that a clutch is more likely to wear out prematurely if a vehicle spends most of its life 'stop-starting' in a traffic-congested town.

Even though a GRP-bodied British Telecom van has considerable potential for building on a budget, some enthusiasts might prefer to buy a brand-new body structure. But who sells monocoque shells? The author conducted enquiries and a plate on the body structure of a BT vehicle yielded the answer.

The converter of chassis cab vehicles such as BT vans is a commercial body specialist located at Neatishead near The Broads in Norfolk, known as Anglian Developments. Enquiries revealed that whereas BT vans are usually built on a Ford Transit, one-piece GRP bodyshells can be fitted to other vehicles such as the Vauxhall Movano Aero.

The first GRP shells were created at Anglian Developments in 1985 and since that date more than 17,000 GRP monocoque units have been manufactured and sold. Customers include British Gas, British Telecom, the Royal Mail, van hire specialists and many parcel delivery companies. Obviously, a GRP shell is completely leak-proof and repairs are usually easy, and in fact, the manufacturer also has an accident repair division.

You don't have to buy a white product either. A recent information sheet shows vehicles finished in signal red, yellow, silver and blue from a list of a possible ten colours which also includes black and white. The GRP body itself is colourised during manufacture by adding a pigment in the gel coat, which is the name for the outermost layer in a moulding. Many coloured GRP products such as kayaks, boats and kit cars are made in this way. The alternative is to spray the moulding with an etching primer and to use an automotive paint. Specialist GRP-bodied sports cars like the models from Lotus are usually painted. Similarly, anyone converting a pre-owned GRP van would have to paint the surfaces in order to cover any sign-written embellishments.

Other 'extra' items from Anglian Developments include deep side skirts which hide the chassis members and offer potential for the installation of under-floor storage lockers. The company can also undertake the construction of internal fittings and furniture – a task carried out for several of its clients. Previous projects which have included fitted interiors have been travelling veterinary surgeries and mobile workshops.

Understandably, the company's literature shows industrial items which wouldn't appeal to a motorcaravan converter. These include: rear roller shutters, commercial electric tail lifts and translucent roofs. However, the side door fitted on a van commissioned by the RSPCA would certainly suit a motorcaravan project. In the event, its lockable door offers considerably more security than some of those fitted on professionally built motorhomes.

Depending on your requirements, a GRP body installed on a long wheelbase chassis and supplied with side skirts, side door and coloured finish might cost in the region of £6,000–£7,000 (including VAT). That doesn't include the purchase of the base vehicle, of course. On the other hand, a professionally built motorhome of

Right: This monocoque GRP pre-used shell of the kind built by Anglian developments was a private purchase and would be ideal for a DIY coachbuilding project.

Far right: Roller shutters often fitted on vans would normally be replaced by a GRP panel when building a motorcaravan. This can be made by taking a copy mould from part of a side wall.

this size is likely to cost in excess of £30,000 so a keen builder could complete a DIY version for significantly less money.

Touring caravan conversions

In some respects, the quickest way to create a motorhome is to buy an old touring caravan, remove its chassis and running gear, and lower it on to the back of a flatbed truck. Bolt it down securely, add a few items here and there, fix up some steps to reach the door, and the job is nearly done. But is it?

Truthfully, some of these truck and touring caravan marriages are pretty grim. Done properly, the job involves a lot of work, particularly if you want your completed project to look like a motorcaravan rather than a mismatched partnership.

That's not to say that this sort of conversion isn't possible. For instance, Roy Webb is no stranger to unusual automotive extravaganzas. His three-wheel kit car called the Kindred Spirit was a head-turning, open-topped, road-legal racing car that started life as a Renault 5 hatchback. Surprisingly, it was remarkably straightforward to build – as I found.

With that kind of background, Roy wasn't too daunted by the prospect of taking a nearly new twin-axle Adria touring caravan and grafting it on to the rear of a Fiat Talbot base vehicle. By using his own specially created GRP mouldings, the integration of two completely separate road-going structures was cunningly achieved. To the untrained eye, the completed project could have easily been a normal production motorhome.

Another doyen of the kit car world is Barry Stimson who operates under the company name of Design Developments. His 1970s kit cars were also wildly bizarre, but his remarkable design and constructional skills have enlightened the marine industry, the builders of modern motorway coaches and the motorcaravan marketplace. The Romahome Campervan is just one of many masterpieces from his Portsmouth-based workshops.

No surprise then to find that Barry recently purchased a brand-new IVECO lorry and an equally new Swift 520SE Challenger caravan with a view to bringing them together. The commercial base vehicle was delivered in chassis cowl form, which means that it didn't have a cab. This type of base vehicle includes the instrumentation and fascia – but has no doors, no windows and no engine cover. These have to be fabricated by the converter and provide the starting point for the type of motorhome referred to as an A-class model.

There was much work to be carried out and the nearly completed vehicle is shown here. Deep side skirts hide the large steel members of the commercial chassis; clever design and construction ensured that the caravan looks at ease with the base vehicle.

Both the examples shown here were carried out by builder/designers who possess a wealth of experience. They had also demonstrated that 'two into one' *is* achievable without producing an incongruous result. On the other hand, whether many people possess the skills to follow in their footsteps is open to question.

Moreover, from a technical point of view the ultra-light nature of a modern touring caravan does not match the more robust structure found on a purpose-built motorhome. After all, a tourer isn't designed to take passengers when being towed because it's illegal. With that in mind, it could be argued that taking a touring caravan to form the body of a motorhome will not produce a particularly robust structure in which some occupants might choose to travel.

Building a coachbuilt from scratch

Purchasing a new chassis for a DIY conversion is yet another route to take. Since pre-built monocoque shells can be purchased, the prospect isn't as hard as it might seem. Furthermore, there are occasions when manufacturers sell prototype body components, and that is what happened here. At least three redundant prototype bodyshells were sold to self-builders, one of whom was the author.

Not surprisingly, parts were missing, sections of the GRP moulding were badly damaged and a lot of preparatory work was needed. That aside, many of the building tasks which follow are described throughout this book. Installing windows, insulating the walls, constructing furniture, designing a plumbing system and so on are tasks which have to be carried out irrespective of the model you decide to build.

When conceiving the design details, several objectives had to be met. These were listed as follows:

- The base vehicle had to have a powerful engine that would easily attain the maximum speeds permitted by law.
- The finished motorhome would need to be equipped to tow a trailer.
- Light furniture would have to be build in order to achieve a good payload.
- A rear hatchback door would be a required feature.
- Support transport would need to be carried inside the motorhome e.g. a motor scooter or a micro car and accessible via the hatch back.
- A computer reactive air suspension would be needed in place of conventional leaf springs to create a level ride, irrespective of load.
- The overhang at the back would be as short as possible in order to reduce the chances of exceeding the rear axle weight limits.
- Inside, a permanently made-up bed would be preferred, but without imposing a reduction in the normal day-time floor area.

In the light of these objectives, it was fortuitous that one of Barry Stimson's prototype body mouldings was about to be scrapped in order to achieve more space in his work area. Arranging to collect and transport the shell components posed problems but these were solved with the help of a twin-axle car trailer.

A brand-new chassis cab had to be purchased as well and that involved a considerable wait. A number of less common optional extras were ordered which contributed to the delay.

The author's Fiat Ducato 2.8 turbo diesel Maxi chassis cab was extended in the middle and fitted with air suspension in place of its springs.

Top left: Some of the body mouldings from a prototype project were purchased and transported on a car trailer.

Top right: With industrial lifting gear unavailable, the main body section was jacked on to trestles and the chassis was reversed under it.

Centre left: The over-cab moulding had a large flange to bolt it against the main body section, but first it had to be fitted.

Centre right: The branch of a mature oak tree and a pulley system enabled the over-cab moulding to be lowered into place from above.

Below: Details of building techniques used in this project are presented in several of the practical chapters which follow later.

The accompanying photographs highlight several of the elements involved in the construction. Later chapters include illustrations and constructional features in more detail, particularly fitting-out operations in the living space. Many techniques employed in this project are the same as those required in other conversions.

Conclusion

In summary, several contrasting approaches have been discussed here while later chapters add further examples, including a description of the task of fitting out a panel van. Irrespective of these differences, one thing remains common to all projects. You must ensure that the base vehicle provides the performance and driving characteristics you want from your motorcaravan. The following chapter offers advice.

THE BASE VEHICLE

Driving characteristics are important and once a motorcaravan is completed, you cannot go back to change its foundations.

CONTENTS

5

Cars as base vehicles

Light commercial vehicles (LCVs)

Heavy goods vehicles (HGVs)

Final advice

Motorcaravans are built on all sorts of base vehicles. As usual, there's compromise here; vehicles which drive like a car, seldom make comfortable, capacious motorhomes. Conversely, comfortable capacious motorhomes are unlikely to drive like a car.

As usual, the priorities in this matter will have to be resolved by the owner. What do you really want? Which feature of the vehicle is more important? On the one hand there's the lively engine option, the road holding, good cornering characteristics, agility in traffic and benefit of easy parking. On the other, there's the matter of living room comfort, storage potential, height, width and scope for expansive cooking, washing and sleeping.

Deciding how to achieve an ideal balance presents the biggest dilemma of all. To a large extent, the final compromise solution is determined by the base vehicle.

Cars as base vehicles

The earlier chapters have made reference to 'campervans' based on cars. Whether these merit the grander title of 'motorhome' is debatable, but I built a Ford Cortina-based Starcraft, for example, and used it for ten enjoyable years. A few hardy self-builders have repeated this circus act using a Ford Mondeo.

In some ways the driving characteristics,

Small motorcaravans can be parked much more easily in both urban and rural venues.

from the cab seat at least, were reminiscent of the donor vehicle. However, you can hardly load a huge living apartment on the back of a standard saloon car and expect it to retain its zest for the road. Nor are grossly increased back axle loadings likely to win the approval of automotive safety engineers. Perhaps it might be possible to construct wholly revised suspension and transmission arrangements, but there really are easier answers.

One is to follow the lead of Steven Wheeler. His manufacturing company, Wheelhome, is noted for building motorcaravans using multi purpose vehicles (MPVs). These car-like 'people carriers' are not only part of today's automobile landscape, they clearly offer conversion potential.

Most MPVs have a large interior and more than the usual number of seats, thereby providing plenty of scope for modification. Their driving characteristics are notably good and height barriers on most council car parks are unlikely to cause a problem. In addition, the entire internal space is already trimmed and insulated throughout – which is something you don't get when buying a panel van.

In some instances, the conversion of these vehicles is intended to provide a mobile office where executives can join for a meeting. A small kitchen makes it possible to prepare and serve simple meals and the availability of many types of compact compressor refrigerators

means that food and drinks can be kept cool.

By removing some seats and generally re-working the interior, it is even possible to create makeshift sleeping arrangements by tilting and reclining the remaining seats. The beds might not suit everyone, but if car-like driving qualities are a key requirement, Wheelhome has shown that MPVs can certainly be converted. The disadvantage of this approach is that these base vehicles tend to be expensive and perfectly good seats might have to be scrapped in order to increase the usable floor space inside. That is why the conversion of a light commercial vehicle is usually a more popular strategy.

For over a decade, Wheelhome has demonstrated that MPVs can be converted into motorhomes which drive just like a car.

There is no doubt that small minibuses and MPVs can be used as base vehicles for motorcaravan conversion projects.

Technical Note

BADGING

One of many confusing features of light commercial vehicles relates to the badges they carry on the front. For example, PSA made up of Citroën and Peugeot, together with Fiat created a consortium to produce European light commercial vehicles in 1978. Hence the Citroën Relay, Peugeot Boxer, and Fiat Ducato appeared around 1993 with near-identical elements. However, the engine options have not always been completely replicated.

In this group operation, the smaller Fiat Scudo which appeared several years later, was also badged as the Citroën Dispatch and the Peugeot Expert. Note that although vehicles might originate from the same production line, the marketing of different 'badged' models is keenly contested. Allegiances develop among converters, too. Recent models from the Swift group are Fiat-based whereas if Auto-Sleepers wants this base vehicle, it always buys-in its stock from Peugeot.

The Fiat Scudo was also 'badged' as the Citroën Dispatch and the Peugeot Expert.

These joint arrangements undoubtedly confuse newcomers to motorcaravanning – as does the practice of 'buying-in' major components. For instance, the Renault Master has sometimes been fitted with a Fiat engine although its gearbox was operated using a floor-mounted gearstick. Meantime in Germany, both the Mercedes Sprinter vans and the Volkswagen LT models were based on shared developments.

As regards LDV models, the Pilot and the Convoy are heavily revised versions of the company's former Sherpa, whereas the LDV Cub is a rebadged Nissan Vanette.

A joint venture was also developed between Renault and Vauxhall. The Renault Master and Vauxhall Movana were contemporaries and the recent Renault Trafic has been badged as a Vauxhall Vivaro.

Technical Note

FASCIA-MOUNTED GEARSTICK

When a motorcaravanner wants to move from the cab to the living quarters, or vice versa, the absence of a floor-mounted gear change is a considerable asset. Moreover, when you're driving, a well-placed fascia-mounted stick is easy to reach. After a short practice period, it is easy to operate, not that everyone shared this enthusiasm when Fiat announced the system in 1993.

The fascia-mounted Fiat gear selector falls easily to hand, regardless of the stature of the driver.

In spite of this dissent, a fascia-mounted control subsequently appeared in Mercedes Sprinter vans in 1995. It appeared, too, in 2002 versions of the Renault Trafic. Similarly, when the Volkswagen T5 first went on sale in Britain in October 2003, its fascia-mounted gearstick was noted with pleasure by VW motorhome converters. In 2005, the Maxus from LDV followed the trend as well.

When the VW T5 was launched, its fascia-mounted gearstick was noted with pleasure by motorhome manufacturers.

Light commercial vehicles (LCVs)

One of the most remarkable features of the latest LCVs is the way they perform on the road. Without doubt, the very smallest of the breed, such as the very compact panel vans, are just like a car to drive. Their cabs, as with larger LCVs, are also comfortable.

Even the largest models which fall into this broad classification are remarkably easy to control on the road. Once you have got over the fact that you can see over hedgerows and look down on the roofs of saloon cars below, the light power steering, the power-assisted brakes, and the (usually) easy gear changing come as a pleasant surprise.

So does the basic price of a brand new panel van if you're comparing it with an MPV. In truth, not many DIY converters start with a *new* base vehicle although this does bestow confidence. You have to be extremely careful when buying a pre-owned LCV as some have been subjected to a tough time in their capacity as commercial beasts of burden.

That said, the refinements that you find in modern LCVs are relatively recent additions. It is often suggested that 'car-like' innovations became more commonplace in commercial vehicles around the mid-1990s. Certainly, when the Peugeot Boxer and the revised Fiat Ducato ranges were unveiled in 1993, a large step was taken.

In addition to standard power steering, the fascia-mounted, cable-operated gear selector was a feature that motorhome converters viewed with pleasure. Movement between the cab and the living space no longer demanded slalom course agility around a floor-mounted gearstick.

Of course, Peugeot Boxer and Citroën Relay vans came from the same Sevel production line in the Abruzzo region of Southern Italy as the Fiat, so the gear selectors were identical, as were most things on the vehicles, apart from the badges. Engine options have been slightly different in the intervening years, too, but not a great deal else.

Prior to the arrival of the Boxer, Ducato, Relay trio, the consortium made up of Citroën, Peugeot and Fiat produced a van which British motorcaravanners knew as the Talbot Express. A rebadged version also bore the Fiat Ducato name, albeit in its pre-1993 incarnation. It also appeared bearing the names of Citroën, Peugeot, and Alfa-Romeo.

Left: The cabs in today's light commercial vehicles offer the comforts you find in a car.

Below: The price of this new 2005 LDV panel van was considerably lower than the cost of a similarly sized multi-purpose vehicle.

Left: At one stage, a Fiat Ducato could be purchased with a 2.8-litre engine whereas the largest capacity engine in a Peugeot Boxer was 2.5 litres.

Technical Note

FORD TRANSIT DRIVE CONFIGURATIONS

In the early 1960s, a joint programme involving Ford UK and Ford in Germany led to the 1965 launch of a European LCV which has always been referred to here as the Transit. There followed a facelift in 1978, a new generation vehicle in 1986, a facelift in 1995 and a completely new model range in 2000.

For many years, the Ford Transit range has been rear-wheel driven. However, at the launch of the third-generation 'New Ford Transit' in 2000, there was a mix of both front and rear-wheel drive models. The difference was broadly weight-related. All panel vans and chassis cabs listed with a maximum technically permissible laden mass (MTPLM) up to 3,000kg were front-wheel driven. Vehicles above this maximum weight and up to 3,500kg were rear-wheel driven.

It is often claimed that Ford Transits are the best-selling light commercial vans in the UK, but motorcaravan converters usually prefer front-wheel driven vehicles in order to gain a low floor. Owners are also inclined to load their motorhomes right up to the limit. With these points in mind, it is unfortunate that the only Ford Transits launched in 2000 with front-wheel drive were vehicles offering no more than 3,000kg maximum technically permitted laden mass.

Whereas motorhomes were built on these earlier Fiat Ducato bases from 1981 and onwards, along with the Talbot Express, the floor-mounted gearstick was far less convenient than the later fascia-mounted version. Peugeot made a special point of this when the first Boxer-based motorcaravans were shown at a UK press conference in 1994.

The advent of a fascia-mounted gear stick was one of several reasons why so many motorcaravans are built on the post 1993 Citroën/Fiat/Peugeot products made in Italy. Another important feature is that these three vehicles are front-wheel driven. This means that there isn't a prop shaft running down the chassis to drive the rear wheels and which is of particular interest to the coachbuilding manufacturers who want the floor of the living space to be as low as possible. The matter of floor height and chassis alteration is covered in the following chapter.

In contrast, rear-wheel drive has been a feature of many LCVs for a number of years including Ford Transits and Mercedes vehicles. Moreover, many drivers prefer the traction that this transmission system offers. There's no doubt that when manoeuvring a fully laden motorcaravan on a muddy camp

The diminutive Daihatsu Hijetta was used as a base vehicle for the micro motorcaravan built by Johns Cross Conversions.

Technical Note

VW TYPE 2 MODELS

The VW Transporter passed through many guises after its debut in the late 1950s. Rear-engined vehicles were finally superseded in 1991 when the T4 was introduced with its front engine, front-wheel-drive configuration. Not surprisingly, enthusiastic supporters of the archetypical rear-engined models were desperately saddened, but it wasn't the end of the road.

The original machinery was sold to a manufacturer in Brazil and near-replicas of the old Type 2 have been imported by Beetles UK, a partner company existing alongside Danbury Motor Caravans. The arrangement was established in 1998, two years after the owners had established similar rights to import early-style VW Beetles.

To comply with recent regulations, a few minor alterations had to be made to the original design of the T2, but to anyone other than the serious collector, the current model is just like the original. So it has been possible to build a motorcaravan on a new VW replica base vehicle. To see a professional conversion, look at the Danbury Rio Camper which is in production at the time of writing.

The New Rio from Danbury has been built on a new VW base vehicle imported by Beetles UK from Brazil.

---

site, a rear-wheel driven vehicle often achieves better traction, particular if it is towing a trailer.

Even a brief overview of light commercial vehicles should not just focus on European-built models; for instance the Toyota Hiace and Mazda panel vans are both used by converters.

The specialist, AVA Leisure has also made a name for importing and converting pre-owned Mazda SGL3 and SGL5 vans. In addition, the company sells unconverted imports to aspiring DIY builders for under £9,000. The SGL3 is a 2.5-litre turbo-diesel model and the SGL5 is a four-wheel-drive vehicle.

Like the Mazda, the Toyota Hiace isn't popular with many professional converters although it has been used by Devon Conversions. Another less-common vehicle is the Daihatsu Hijet which provided the base vehicle for JC Leisure's Hijetta motorcaravan.

Similarly, vehicles imported from the USA are seldom converted although pick-up trucks such as the Ford Ranger 2.5TD seem to be growing in numbers here. These make powerful partners for dismountable motorcaravans where the living 'pod' can be removed from its docking position on the platform at the back. However, the high cost of fuel in Europe inevitably turns converters away from most 'gas-guzzling' vehicles that are typically used throughout North America.

Heavy goods vehicles (HGVs)

Few self-build enthusiasts tackle projects involving large commercial base vehicles and with good reason. Models from the IVECO commercial range are occasionally used as base vehicles for Laika motorcaravans, but some owners have reported that they are cumbersome to drive. Base vehicles from IVECO can carry a maximum technically permissible laden mass far greater than that of an LCV, but whereas lorry cabs are infinitely more comfortable than they used to be, you won't experience 'car-like' driving.

Regulations also play a part, especially if you drive in other European countries. In Germany, for example, a vehicle weighing over 3,500kg is subject to:

■ Special speed restrictions.
■ Overtaking restrictions.
■ An autobahn speed limit of 80kmh (50mph).

Large A-class motorcaravans are often built on a commercial HGV chassis like this one from IVECO.

In Switzerland, drivers of a vehicle over 3,500kg have to pay a heavy goods vehicle tariff at border entry points in order to use motorways. Similarly in Scotland, there is a higher toll fee to cross the Tay road bridge for vehicles over 3,500kg.

On an administrative note, if you have a pre-1997 UK driving licence there are fewer restrictions when driving heavy vehicles in this country. Unfortunately the police abroad are not always aware of the position relating to those UK drivers whose full licence was issued before 1997. Since the changes made in that year, the minimum age for driving a vehicle over 3,500kg in the UK is 18 years (instead of 17 years) and an additional test has to be taken.

On reaching 70 years of age, when a UK licence has to be renewed, a special eyesight test is also required if an applicant wants to drive a vehicle over 3,500kg. This limit also plays a part in the procedures adopted by several of the vehicle recovery specialists; several companies will not assist motorhome owners if their broken-down vehicle exceeds 3,500kg.

These are just a few examples of the restrictions. Accordingly, this book tends to focus more on light commercial vehicles rather than HGVs.

Final advice

Since it is important to enjoy the driving part of motorhome ownership, a self-builder is strongly advised to try out as many base vehicles as possible beforehand. In addition, you can also hire motorcaravans for short spells and while this is usually expensive in the height of summer, the rates are notably cheaper in winter. Hire companies advertise in the specialist magazines, and the author has found this strategy extremely beneficial. Hiring a large, coachbuilt motorhome with an under-powered 1.9-litre non-turbo diesel engine was a distinctly pedestrian experience – never to be repeated.

When comparing base vehicles, don't overlook refinements like power steering, automatic transmission, ABS brakes and so on. In some instances, it is true that specialists can retrofit some of these products on certain vehicles – but not all of them, by a long way.

For example, TB Turbo of Lancaster has built up a good reputation for installing turbo chargers, intercoolers, power steering, auto-clutch systems, and alternative engine performance chips. However, many vehicles cannot be altered from the original specification. For instance, power steering can usually be fitted to a late 1980s petrol-engine Talbot Express, but the conversion cannot usually be carried out on the diesel engine model.

In particular, automatic transmission also needs careful consideration and a number of potential motorhome owners are disappointed that this is seldom found on light commercial vehicles. Of course, a true 'automatic' has a torque converter rather than a gearbox and some models in the current Fiat Ducato range sold in Italy can be ordered with automatic transmission. Unfortunately, however, this is only available on left-hand drive models. Fiat has stated that demand isn't sufficient to offer this option on right-hand drive vehicles.

On some of the post-2000 Ford Transits you will find that it is also possible to specify a Durashift EST system comprising a five-speed manual gearbox but featuring neither a clutch pedal nor a gear lever. An electronic gear shift mechanism and automatic clutch are fitted instead.

Also bear in mind that the Sprinter can be supplied with an optional Sprintshift system which is an automated gearbox as opposed to a torque converter. This is different from the VW T5 option in which certain models are fitted with a six-speed Tiptronic automatic gearbox with torque converter. The Tiptronic system includes a lever which can be pushed forwards or backwards to engage a particular gear, subject to the suitability of the engine revs.

All this adds up to the importance of carrying out thorough investigations before spending money. All-too-often, would-be builders see a vehicle being sold for 'a good price' which looks as if it would convert into a splendid motorcaravan. Then, after hours of work, and the addition of numerous heavy items, it eventually turns out that it isn't so good on the road after all. That's a mistake which must be avoided.

Technical Note

DIESEL VERSUS PETROL

For a long time, motoring journalists in this country have promoted petrol engines for their liveliness, but things have changed. Modern diesel engines are both more refined and more versatile than they were a decade or so ago. Certainly in the motorcaravan field, the popularity of diesel engines has been especially evident although this is partly due to the use of these power units by commercial vehicle operators.

At its launch, it was announced that the Volkswagen Transporter T5 range would include four turbo diesel options.

Without doubt, the addition of turbo assistance enhances acceleration, even if it does reduce the life of a diesel engine, as many automotive experts suggest is the case. In reality, few motorcaravanners undertake long and regular journeys, so engine longevity might not be an issue. Fuel price might be a more important consideration and anyone who tours regularly in mainland Europe will know that the price of diesel fuel is much lower than the cost of lead-free petrol. It is therefore little wonder that so many vehicles abroad have diesel engines. Unfortunately, this is not the case in the UK so there is less incentive to opt for diesel purely on running costs, especially if you spend most of your time on motorcaravanning trips in Britain.

In the end, it is up to the individual who's converting a vehicle to make the final decision.

Far left: Automatic gearboxes can sometimes be retrospectively fitted; the ZF GB automatic gearbox was fitted here on a Citroën Dispatch.

Left: On this automatic gearbox conversion, an indicator panel was mounted just behind the steering wheel.

CHASSIS, RUNNING GEAR AND WEIGHT LIMITS

A good chassis and an efficient suspension system are key foundational elements. They are also linked to the weight limits which builders and users must always observe.

A topic like chassis construction is unlikely to be of interest to someone who has decided to convert a panel van. Modern panel vans are not built on a chassis in the traditional sense of the word and that is where they differ from coachbuilt motorcaravans.

On the other hand, the section on suspension systems and brake operation has relevance to van converters and coachbuilder alike. Also important is the section on weights, weighbridges and related legal matters. This latter part of the chapter should be read by all self-builders; even people who already own a motorcaravan need to be ever-mindful of its loading limits. To overload a vehicle is potentially very dangerous; it is also a criminal offence.

Chassis base variations

THE CHASSIS CAB

Many motorcaravans are built on what is known as a 'chassis cab'. The term appropriately acknowledges the two principal components which make up the structure and a number of light commercial vehicle manufacturers sell their products in this form to conversion specialists.

The cab itself is usually complete in so far as it is equipped with seats, safety belts and all conveniences. There will be a covered engine compartment and front bumpers.

Sometimes the driving compartment is a wholly weather-proof enclosure; in other cases the wall behind the seats is merely covered by a temporary panel in recognition that a rear enclosure of some kind will be added later. A chassis cab is the base unit for delivery vans, small removal vans and, of course, coachbuilt motorcaravans.

The chassis itself is usually supplied with a spare wheel whereas items like a spare wheel

carrier and a numberplate board fitted with road lights are often optional extras as depicted. It all depends on what the converter plans to construct. In some cases, for example, the final structure might embrace its own means of storing a spare wheel.

A chassis cab can also be ordered by private customers through a commercial vehicle dealer and the base vehicle for the author's recent self-built motorhome was purchased in this way. Bear in mind that there are numerous variations in optional equipment and you may have to wait many months for the delivery of a base vehicle. Note, too, that if there are no rear lights, the vehicle is not road-legal. Come to that, a vehicle should be fitted with mudguards before being used on a public road.

In the case history project described later, it was arranged for a chassis cab to be delivered directly to a specialist for modification work. After this work had been carried out, the author would then have to drive the vehicle home, so a rear light panel was specified as one of the optional extras. In addition, arrangements had to be made for the vehicle to be insured, registered with the DVLA, licensed, fitted with numberplates and made road-legal. Makeshift mudguards were also installed. If it isn't possible to meet these requirements, a chassis cab would have to be moved on a trailer or transporter.

THE CHASSIS COWL

A different variation on this theme is the chassis cowl which lacks a weather-protected cab and has neither a windscreen nor side windows. The engine bay won't have a bonnet and no doors will be installed either. However, the engine, instrumentation and controls are supplied in the package.

A chassis cowl is specified by converters who want to build an A-Class motorhome or, perhaps,

a small passenger coach. This involves a great deal of skilled work including the construction of external doors to provide access to the driving compartment. It is easy to see why completed A-class motorcaravans cost so much more money than chassis cab conversions. Moreover, on many professionally-built models, access to the driving compartment is often via a door that lacks the rigidity of the ones supplied with a completed cab.

It is believed that there have been DIY builders who have constructed A-class motorhomes from a chassis cowl but the amount of work involved in a one-off project like this is more than most individuals are willing to undertake.

This platform cab has a ready-made floor pan and wheel covers.

THE PLATFORM CAB

Finally, there is the platform cab, which is rather like a panel van bereft of its sheet steel sides, rear doors and roof. These are not used often for motorcaravan conversions, which is surprising, because they already have a reinforced floor panel – called a floor pan – on which to build the living accommodation. There are also inner wings already in place at the rear to provide protection from the wheels.

However, platform cabs *have* been used by motorhome manufacturers. For example, these base units were used for the Mk1 Auto-Trail Tracker coachbuilt motorhomes, even though later ones were built on a chassis cab instead.

Platform cabs have also been used for Fiat-based low profile Chausson motorcaravans such as the Welcome and Odyssee models and the Globetrotter Advantage from Dethleffs. But these are exceptions, and there is no doubt that a builder doesn't have as much scope when building on a pre-fabricated floor pan. A traditional chassis is more versatile because it can fairly easily be adapted to meet the dimensional requirements of the different models in a professional motorhome manufacturer's product range.

Chassis alterations

A surprising array of regulations including type approval requirements apply to modern road-going vehicles across Europe and these also affect anyone intending to convert a commercial vehicle into a motorhome.

Regulations are just as applicable to a motorcaravan as they are to a box truck or flatbed transporter.

The constraints they introduce can be onerous so the manufacturers of commercial vehicles normally publish guidelines for companies (or individuals) engaged in the business of converting a van or a chassis-based vehicle. Fiat, for example, publishes a textbook on the subject entitled *Commercial Vehicles: Manual for conversions/special outfits.* As it states on the opening page: 'This publication aims to provide information on Fiat commercial vehicles required for designing and building vehicle conversions.' (Publication No. 507.006) It is an invaluable sourcebook.

Vehicle manufacturers recognise that any kind of conversion will entail the installation of new structures and that is why a converter is advised what alterations are deemed acceptable. There are also restrictions which apply to a wide range of the original components. In the case of Fiat Ducatos. For example, modifications to the exhaust system are not normally permitted unless there has been prior approval and testing.

Some modifications are permitted as long as the recommended methods are followed; for example, a converter is explicitly advised by Fiat to avoid welding chassis load-bearing structures without manufacturer authorisation. Drilling certain key members is not permitted either and ways to extend a chassis are also strictly prescribed, especially with regard to rear overhangs.

Professional converters need to be fully conversant with all these issues and have a clear duty of care to their customers. Recognising that adherence to a manufacturer's advice must be strictly followed, converters keep in close communication with vehicle manufacturers. It is of mutual concern that special conversions are carried out appropriately and with due regard to safety.

There is reciprocation, too, and vehicle manufacturers also know which chassis/suspension specialists have the knowledge and skills to undertake alterations that fall within the stated guidelines. For instance, you will see in some of the later photographs that very radical alterations are often made to a chassis – even to the extent of cutting it off from the cab, scrapping it and fitting a completely different replacement. Under no circumstances should unqualified amateur builders ever contemplate this kind of DIY modification.

Major alterations of that nature were not ad hoc innovations carried out on the whim of an amateur self-builder. On the contrary, they are structural alterations that have gained formal approval after lengthy dialogue, careful design work, computer analysis and extensive testing; safety on the roads is of paramount importance.

When the author's self-build coachbuilt was planned, it was recognised that in order to implement some of the unusual design features, several alterations would have to be carried out to the chassis and suspension. Accordingly, the chassis cab was delivered by the Surrey-based dealer directly to an approved specialist in Lancashire so that modifications could be made before the conversion-proper commenced. To create the features embodied in the design, it was necessary for:

- The chassis to be cut and extended.
- The rear leaf springs to be removed and replaced by computer-reactive air suspension units.
- The rear axle tube to be extended in length by 225mm (9in).
- The maximum technically permissible laden mass (MTPLM) of the vehicle to be upgraded from 3,500kg (7,718lb) to 3,850kg (8,490lb) (see panel alongside).
- The rear axle tube to be strengthened as part of the weight upgrading operation.

These modifications were carried out by Drinkwater Engineering in Leyland (now part of the TVAC Group), a commercial vehicle specialist which works in close co-operation with all leading truck and commercial vehicle manufacturers. Many motorhome owners are now using this specialist on account of its developing expertise in carrying out retrospective upgrades and alterations.

Only when this all-important preparatory work had been completed was the chassis cab finally collected by the author and driven 200 miles to the venue where the subsequent construction work would be carried out.

Of course, in some projects, it would be possible to purchase a short, medium or long wheelbase chassis cab to use exactly as supplied by the vehicle manufacturer. In practice, few motorcaravan manufacturers do this. At the very least, the chassis is normally lengthened to accommodate a larger living area albeit without losing sight of the stated MTPLM of the base vehicle. In some instances a completely different, purpose-designed motorhome chassis is fitted instead.

Ready for conversion after the wheelbase of this Fiat Ducato Maxi had been extended.

Technical Note

UPGRADING THE MTPLM

The uppermost maximum technically permissible laden mass (MTPLM) of most LCV-based motorcaravans is 3,500kg. In some cases you can have a motorcaravan upgraded to 3,850kg and re-plated by having a number of alterations carried out by an approved specialist. The work may entail fitting different tyres, strengthening the rear axle tube, altering the suspension, fitting larger brakes and so on. Sometimes, the work is too involved to be a feasible proposition.

Then there are several implications of running a vehicle which is plated with an MTPLM greater than 3,500kg. These include the following matters:

- Since January 1997, new driving licence holders in the UK are limited to driving vehicles up to 3,500kg (7,718lb) – or 4,250kg (9,371lb) with a trailer. To drive heavier vehicles an additional test has to be taken.
- Many motoring organisations in the UK will not recover motorhomes weighing over 3,500kg.
- In the UK, the minimum age to drive a vehicle over 3,500kg is 18 years of age instead of 17 years of age for lighter vehicles.
- There is an additional requirement for eyesight testing in the UK when a vehicle is over 3,500kg and its driver is applying for a new licence. This also applies when drivers reach 70 years of age and their earlier licences expire.
- People with certain medical conditions like diabetes are not permitted to drive vehicles over 3,500kg.
- In some countries, particularly Germany, a vehicle over 3,500kg is classified as a goods vehicle and is subject to a speed limit of 80kmh (50mph), different overtaking rules and even weekend restrictions of use.
- In Switzerland, a motorhome exceeding 3,500kg has to pay a heavy goods vehicle tax supplement at the border in order to use motorways.

CASE HISTORY: ALTERATIONS

In the conversion referred to here, the author had decided to build a motorhome with a rear hatchback door so that a large motorcycle or small microcar could be transported in a dual-purpose lounge/garage area at the back. Recognising that large overhangs at the back accentuate loadings being carried by a rear axle, the chassis extension was carried out *between* the axles. This increased the original wheelbase to accommodate a 6.68m (21ft 11in) bodyshell and had the effect of moving the rear axle further aft. That in turn meant that any heavy item carried at the back could be positioned directly over the rear axle rather than on a projecting overhang.

The operation carried out on the author's chassis has also been carried out on a number of chassis supplied to Lunar Motorcaravan manufacturers as shown here.

As regards the installation of a longer axle tube, the small increase of 225mm (9in) placed the rear wheels slightly wider apart thereby offering an opportunity for a small microcar to be carried in the back instead of being towed behind the vehicle. Towing a trailer is certainly possible behind most base vehicles but there are implications like special speed limits, restriction on the use of the outermost lane on motorways with three or more lanes, and the higher charges for ferries.

Few manufacturers have these types of alterations carried out because the conversions have to meet the needs of the 'typical' owner. Therein lies one of the advantages of the self-build strategy. Self-built vehicles can meet an individual builder's precise requirements, although the chassis alterations described here are *not* for DIY constructors to tackle. On the other hand, it is appropriate to point out to self-builders that alterations can be undertaken by specialists without contravening a base vehicle manufacturer's recommendations.

Technical Note

LENGTHENING THE WHEELBASE

Altering the wheelbase on Fiat Ducato vans of the type used in the case history project described here is permitted by the manufacturer, provided that certain procedures are followed. These are laid down in *Commercial Vehicles: Manual for conversions/special outfit*, (page 34). The maximum permitted lengthening limit is 4,200mm and the advised cutting point is shown in drawings presented in the manual.

Extending the wheelbase on a chassis cab

1 The motorhome chassis was cut at the point prescribed by Fiat.

2 With the rear supported, linking box section was prepared.

3 Extension pieces would be formed to match the original members.

4 Reinforcing box section is secured with rivets as specified by Fiat.

Rear overhangs

In order to maximise the size of a living space, most motorcaravan manufacturers extend a chassis by adding a bolt-on assembly at the rear. This supports the floor panel and the construction is referred to as the 'rear overhang'. Although the very latest European guidelines may lead to revised practices, two formulae have been used to calculate the permitted maximum rear overhang of a motorcaravan. The one generally cited is as follows:

The wheelbase is measured between the centre of the front wheels and the centre of the rear axle. The overhang measured from the centre of the rear wheel to the rear-most body panel (or add-on rack where this has been installed), should be no greater than 60% of the wheelbase measurement.

NB A second formula which is sometimes used to calculate the maximum permitted rear overhang is rather more involved. It draws on the fact that when a vehicle is driven forwards in a circle on full lock, the outward deflection of the rear-most part of the vehicle will extend beyond the path followed by the wheels. If the overhang is excessive, this 'out-swing' could pose an unacceptable obstruction so a limit is given in the formula.

Notwithstanding these limitations, some vehicle manufacturers give more precise measurements for different chassis cab vehicles in their ranges and permitted overhangs may amount to less than 60% of the wheelbase. On a vehicle with a low-line chassis, for example, there would be greater likelihood of it grounding at the back on certain road surfaces if the overhang was too long.

The point has already been made that the load of a motor scooter supported on a wall-mounted rack will impose considerably more downforce on the rear axle when there's a long overhang. Put into simple terms, an extension rearwards of the axle acts as a long lever. Regrettably, many owners do not realise that a long overhang can be acutely detrimental in respect of loading limits. Moreover, if the rear axle weight limit is exceeded on a vehicle being driven on the public highway, this can lead to prosecution.

Notwithstanding the attendant problem that may arise when owners add heavy items, most motorcaravan manufacturers extend a rear overhang and various methods are adopted to lengthen a chassis. To give an example, the

accompanying photograph shows a galvanised steel bracket fitted by the Swift Group on a 1998 Sundance coachbuilt.

On this model, brackets were attached to both the flat mounting plates at the back of a Fiat chassis and these plates are clearly shown in the first illustration of this chapter. Suitable fixings needed to attach the brackets are defined by the base vehicle manufacturer. For example, the nuts must have an approved type of locking facility so that they cannot come loose.

Other manufacturers bolt on a rectangular structure in steel box section to these mounting plates to create a rigid extension for supporting the floor. Bearing in mind that many owners fit racks, rear wall luggage boxes and tow brackets, it stands to reason that any add-on assembly has to be structurally capable of carrying loads far greater than the floor itself.

Two galvanised steel brackets supported this rear overhang.

AL-KO's chassis for the VW T5 has a complex configuration.

cars use this service. However, TUV approvals make it very difficult to have these modifications carried out on new vehicles.

Hence the AL-KO chassis designed for motorcaravans are principally used on the Fiat Ducato (and its Peugeot and Citroën counterparts as described in the previous chapter). It is true that an AL-KO chassis can also be fitted now to the latest front-wheel-drive Volkswagen T5 chassis cab, but the exhaust assembly to the rear of the cab necessitates having a prominent level change in the chassis rails. To date, the majority of conversions are carried out on Fiat/Peugeot/Citroën vehicles and the accompanying photographs show what the work entails.

AL-KO Kober chassis conversions

Recognising that a vehicle manufacturer's chassis is designed to suit a wide range of applications, AL-KO Kober Ltd produces a chassis which is designed specifically for motorcaravans.

The development of this product gathered momentum when light commercial vehicles were launched with front-wheel drive. Technically it isn't difficult to fit a revised chassis to a rear-wheel-drive vehicle such as the Mercedes Sprinter or a rear-wheel-drive Ford Transit even though its propshaft would need lengthening. A number of engineering specialists can extend prop shafts and many kit

Changing a chassis

After close co-operation with Fiat during development work, AL-KO started undertaking installations using a standard chassis cab or chassis cowl vehicle. As the photo sequence shows, the original Fiat chassis is removed, some components are retained and the remaining chassis assembly and leaf springs are scrapped.

Attachment brackets are welded to the remaining short chassis rails which project from the underside of the cab. The replacement AL-KO chassis is then bolted to these brackets.

On the grounds of economy, motorhome manufacturers wanting to have the AL-KO product installed usually purchase short-wheel-base (SWB) vehicles so that there is minimum chassis wastage. In other words, the least expensive SWB vehicle emerges from the metamorphosis with a much longer AL-KO chassis.

Not surprisingly, most conversions carried out at the Warwickshire factory of AL-KO Kober Ltd are for professional motorcaravan manufacturers. However, arrangements can also be made to convert a new vehicle purchased by a private client – hence the information given here. The sequence which follows shows how the job is done.

Twin cabs

Whatever the advantages of a purpose-designed AL-KO amc product for motorcaravan construction, scrapping an original and virtually brand-new chassis seems extraordinarily wasteful. In the case of a one-off conversion, this is unavoidable, but it is worth adding that Fiat is now able to supply major manufacturers with chassis-free base vehicles. The twinned cab units are a bizarre sight as the photographs show. They are delivered direct to AL-KO Kober's plants and once separated, they're moved around the factory using a temporary jockey wheel as shown alongside.

Accessory benefits

A particular benefit of building on an AL-KO chassis is the fact that a full forward-facing harness structure can be secured directly to the chassis. Increasing concern is being voiced about rear passengers not always having safety belt provision and this feature has influenced a number of professional manufacturers to opt for the AL-KO product.

Purpose-designed racks and towing bracket can also be directly attached but herein lies a problem. This is only achievable if the floor doesn't project any further behind the rearmost cross member. Regrettably, a number of British manufacturers design the body to oversail this cross member by around 250mm (10in) which immediately precludes the use of these options.

The photograph on page 51 shows an instance where an attempt was made to cut away part of a Bessacarr coachbuilt motorhome whose body structure projected too far

Above: Major manufacturers are now able to purchase pairs of cabs…

Left: …and a support leg is fitted before adding the AL-KO chassis.

The installation of an AL-KO motorcaravan chassis on a standard Fiat Ducato chassis cab

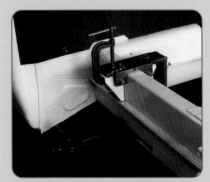

1 Taking full account of Fiat's recommended cutting point, AL-KO's specialist staff fit a cutting jig on the main chassis rails just to the rear of the cab.

2 When the cab has been fully supported, the cutting work is carried out using a hand-held sabre saw. The jig ensures that the cut is accurate and true.

3 The complete assembly is now severed from the cab; some items will be re-commissioned, but the original chassis, axle tube and leaf springs will be discarded.

CONTINUED OVER ▶

4 Components like the exhaust system, wheels, and spare wheel carrier are stowed on a purpose-made trolley pending reinstallation later.

5 At one time, angle brackets were always welded to the main chassis rails but in this instance a stepped coupling is being installed to the rear of the cab.

6 The coupling has now been painted and the AL-KO galvanised chassis connected. This is a *lowline conversion*; the finger points to the floor support height of the original chassis.

7 In this example a *standard height* chassis has been installed. Note the use of cross members which ensure that the floor panel is well supported.

8 In *double floor construction*, lowline longitudinal members are bridged by cross supports to create under-floor spaces for low-level lockers, service ducting and water tanks.

9 Compared with the original leaf springs, the inconspicuous torsion bar system is more compact. On an AL-KO chassis, outriggers support the floor at its outer edges.

10 Provided the floor of the living area doesn't project beyond the chassis rear cross member, AL-KO bolt-on accessories like the towing bracket and the cycle rack can be added.

Far left: A forward-facing harness bolts directly on to an AL-KO chassis.

Left: Here, the body extended too far at the rear to fit an AL-KO tow bar as designed.

rearwards of the cross member. While it proved possible to fit an AL-KO tow bar, a make-shift cut-out had to be formed in the rear skirt so that the hitch head of a trailer could be coupled to the ball. Of course, the articulation of a trailer's draw bar would be considerably reduced here. One can only hope that motorcaravan manufacturers will learn that considerable inconvenience arises if the body design extends too far beyond the rear-most chassis member.

Suspension variations

Now let's consider different types of suspension.

■ COIL SPRINGS

Probably the most common type of rear suspension on saloon cars employs coil springs on account of the smooth ride they provide. However, coil springs are seldom fitted on light commercial vehicles although VW vans are one of the exceptions. Their comfortable ride is often favourably reported by owners and several converters e.g. Bilbo's, focus most of their attention on manufacturing VW-based motorcaravans.

■ TORSION BARS

This system uses steel rods which twist as a vehicle rides over bumps. These have been used in the suspension systems of a number of vehicles including the early Renault 5. In some respects a torsion bar affords a similar twisting resistance as you get in a coil spring and can even be likened to a coil spring which has been straightened out. The ride quality it produces is usually good.

■ LEAF SPRINGS

These were quite common in vintage cars but have seldom been employed by manufacturers in the last 20 years although the Ford Escort Mk 1 and 2 were so fitted at the rear. Leaf springs are noted for coping with heavy loads and are unkindly referred to as cart springs on account of earlier applications. Not surprisingly, they are fitted to pick-up trucks, off-road vehicles and light commercial vehicles.

■ AIR SUSPENSION

For the smoothest ride quality there is air suspension and this is fitted on trucks which have to carry sensitive loads like aero engines.

Air suspension is also fitted to accident and emergency ambulances where injured persons need special attention. The system is also used on some light commercial vans and on an increasing number of luxury coaches. In these contexts the facility of 'dumping' air allows a loading platform to be lowered to afford an easier entry. For the motorcaravanner it can also be a useful fore and aft levelling facility when parking on a sloping pitch.

The AL-KO chassis conversion employs torsion bar suspension.

Right: Air suspension can be fitted to van conversions and ambulances.

Far right: The 'air dump' facility lowers the vehicle for easier entry.

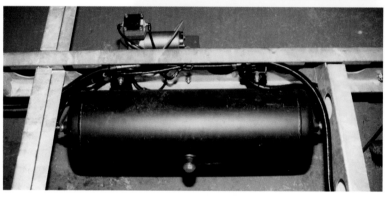

Full air suspension includes an air tank and compressor.

Below: This is one of AL-KO's air suspension products launched in 2004.

Below right: Air suspension on a vehicle assures a very comfortable ride.

As a further benefit, air suspension can be installed with a computer reactive automatic levelling system. Pressure in the air chambers is affected by the load being carried and a monitoring system automatically activates an inflation or deflation cycle. An air tank supplies the air and this is automatically replenished by an on-board compressor. In consequence a vehicle's ride height will be consistent, even when the owner adds or removes heavy personal effects.

■ **AIR ASSISTANCE**
This is a combined system in which auxiliary air chambers are fitted to augment the operation of leaf or torsion bar springs. In spite of claims made by some distributors, this is *not* an

example of air suspension. Nevertheless, air chambers supplied by specialists like Airide, AL-KO and Driverite are useful additions when steel springs become 'tired' and the rear end of a vehicle develops a noticeable sag. Vehicle handling and stability are likely to be improved as well. It is also important to note that air assistance units can be added retrospectively as shown alongside although it is essential that alterations are made to the braking set-up as described later. Moreover, the installation of air assistance products does not necessarily mean that more personal equipment can be carried. The stated rear axle load limit will remain the same as before and exceeding this can lead to prosecution.

Suspension on motorcaravans

The majority of coachbuilt motorcaravans have rear leaf spring systems and whilst an acceptable ride is achievable, this type of suspension is undoubtedly more suitable for the transport of ballast or crates of beer. Many owners of leisure vehicles prefer a smoother ride and this is one reason why the AL-KO chassis conversion has a torsion bar suspension. The rear wheels have three torsion bars apiece which are mounted, out of sight, within the rear axle tube. Regular lubrication is very important and grease nipples are mounted towards the outer ends of the axle tube.

In future, air suspension is certain to be used more and more by motorcaravan builders. These systems were being fitted to base vehicle chassis at Drinkwater Engineering as long ago as the late 1990s, and AL-KO has now launched two systems for its own chassis.

Known as Air Premium, the top AL-KO system, incorporates electronic controls and completely replaces conventional steel springs.

Fitting an AL-KO Air Top air-assistance system retrospectively

1 This Lunar Roadstar 720 with a cycle rack and large rear overhang needed air assistance units.

2 The AL-KO Air Top kit comprises two air chambers, plastic tubing and a pair of pressure gauges.

3 Available in 2004, the AL-KO Air Top air-assistance system can be fitted on existing motorcaravans.

4 The first task in this installation on a Peugeot chassis was to remove and discard the bump stop.

5 An AL-KO support plate is bolted to the chassis in the position previously used for the bump stop.

6 Each of the air chambers sits astride a leaf spring and couples to the plate that's fixed at the top.

7 The plastic inflation piping now has to be routed from the air chambers to the gauges.

8 On this installation the gauges were fitted inside the cab door for easy inflation with an air-line.

9 Brake compensation was originally activated by a bracket on the axle tube and a connecting rod.

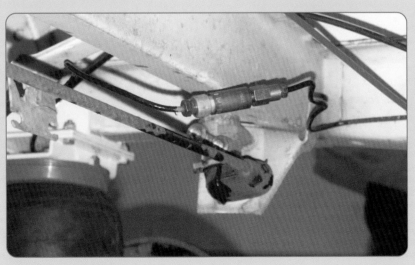

10 On vehicles without ABS brakes, the lever system is disabled and a brake limiting valve is fitted in the hydraulic pipes.

Air Plus is a similar system, but inflation of the air chambers has to be carried out using an external supply such as a garage air line. Neither system should be confused with AL-KO's third development, Air Top, which is a retrofit air assistance product.

Brake compensators

It was mentioned earlier that when a load-levelling device is fitted retrospectively, it is very important to recognise that an alteration will usually have to be made to the brake compensation set-up. This is not the case, however, if a vehicle is equipped with ABS brakes.

Braking on vehicles that don't have an ABS facility is usually controlled by a device (the brake compensator) which balances the operating level of the front and rear brakes to suit the load being carried.

This is often achieved, as in the case of Fiat LCVs, by a system of levers which operate a control unit in the hydraulic pipes serving the front and rear brakes. For instance, when the rear of a vehicle is heavily laden and riding low, this will be noted by the lever arrangement which in turn alters the hydraulic control unit. Conversely, if a vehicle is lightly laden and riding high, the apportionment of front-rear braking will again be altered.

This is why the addition of an air bellows to elevate the back of a motorcaravan sagging

through a heavy load and tired springs can upset the brake compensation facility. Lifting the rear activates the control levers to set the braking for light loading conditions – whereas the vehicle is actually heavily laden. In the case of the AL-KO Air Top system, a potential problem is overcome by disabling the lever arrangement altogether and installing a control valve in the hydraulic supply instead.

Case history:

SUSPENSION CHOICE
Anyone deciding to build a motorcaravan is clearly faced with a number of decisions regarding the chassis, suspension and running gear in general. Not only did the author's base vehicle chassis need lengthening, but the suspension system on the Fiat chassis needed changing, too. Apart from wanting the high comfort level afforded by full air suspension, a computer-controlled automatic levelling system was also needed to cope with widely dissimilar loads. Sometimes the motorcaravan would be lightly laden, while other times another vehicle might be carried in the back.

Drinkwater Engineering was thus commissioned to install an automatically controlled air-suspension system and this was probably the first to be fitted to a coachbuilt motorhome in the UK. Shortly afterwards, this option was being offered by Lunar Motorhomes. Five years later, AL-KO launched air suspension options for the company's chassis.

A self-builder could similarly arrange for one of these installations to be carried out by a specialist, but remember that the work has to be done at the chassis stage; unlike air assistance units, a full air-suspension system cannot be fitted retrospectively.

PLATFORM PREPARATION
When considering ways of fitting a body structure, I had noticed that several manufacturers of Fiat-based coachbuilt motorcaravans were supporting the floor panel solely on the main chassis members. On a number of models, no extension supports were added along the outer edges of the main longitudinal chassis members and this seemed to be an ill-judged omission.

When coachbuilt bodies are constructed on an AL-KO chassis, the well-designed outrigger supports shown in the photo of the torsion bar system earlier, ensure full-width support to a

Special outrigger brackets were made to fit a Fiat chassis.

floor panel. With that in mind, a design for outriggers was drawn-up which would bolt to the Fiat chassis side lugs and a local steel specialist made them up.

Rubber webbing was also obtained to be placed between the chassis members and the floor panel. Wooden boards mounted directly on steel members without a rubber cushion can develop annoying squeaks.

One last preparatory task followed. A chassis is built with a number of breather holes and these provide an opportunity to inject Waxoyl rust inhibitor into the structure.

In order to do this a local garage elevated the front of the cab on the end of a ramp so that the Waxoyl would flow through the labyrinth of steel sections. It was surprising to note, therefore, that as soon as the cab was lifted, a quantity of water seeped out of the rearmost chassis holes. Perhaps it is not unusual for rain to get inside chassis sections during outdoor storage, but this was a matter of concern that needs to be passed on to other builders. After that, a liberal quantity of Waxoyl was injected through all the holes.

Weight matters and weighbridges

Both caravan and motorhome owners have a tendency to fill every locker cupboard and crevice before taking to the road. For many years, very few people seemed to bother about the total laden weight of their 'van and even today thousands of caravans and motorhomes have never been taken to a public weighbridge. This is starting to change.

Road-side checks conducted by the police have revealed instances of gross overloading and while towed caravans appear to have come under the most scrutiny, attention seems to be turning to motorhomes as well. There are undoubtedly many people who fit a remarkable array of accessories to their motorcaravans without any concern for the additional weight that these impose. Equally, there are a lot of owners who transport motorscooters or bicycles, and there's no shortage of motorhomes which have large storage boxes mounted on the roof. This all adds up.

A related matter of concern is that some motorcaravans are constructed which are remarkably close to the vehicle's maximum

Above left: Waxoyl rust inhibitor was injected into all the chassis members. Note: The operator should be wearing a face mask and gloves.

Above: A Fiat chassis is built with a number of breather holes.

Technical Note

PAYLOAD
This is often divided into three distinct elements:

- Essential equipment – such as gas cylinders and toilet chemicals.
- Optional equipment – such as solar panels, bike rack and air-conditioning system.
- Personal effects – such as clothing and food.

In total, this adds up to the payload and the limit is often quite severe. It is a helpful discipline to enquire about the weight of any item of optional equipment that you might want to fit – especially heavy items like an on-board generator. Relate the item to your overall payload potential and then consider the product in terms of the equivalent weight in pairs of trousers, shoes, socks, shirts and warm wear. The more ancillary equipment that's added, the more personal effects you will have to leave behind.

It's advisable to call at a public weighbridge when it is not busy.

motorcaravan might fall within its maximum limit, but through thoughtless packing, most of the gear may have been stowed right at the back. This could easily exceed the weight limit of the rear axle which can lead to prosecution.

As far as the self-builder is concerned, this problem should be borne in mind throughout the build. Moreover, before starting the constructional work, your very first task is to find a public weighbridge. Addresses of weighbridges available for public use are normally held by your local authority. At one time these were available from the Weights and Measures Department although the addresses are often available by phoning a County Council Trading Standards Service.

Normally, a public weighbridge doesn't operate an appointment service although it is useful to find out when there are quieter periods. It is no fun joining a queue of heavy commercial vehicles whose drivers are running late.

Fees vary for EACH weight taken, and at present tend to fall between £5 and £10. A certificate of the recorded weights will be issued before you leave, and two checks are normally taken. The first is the weight of the entire vehicle, less the driver. Then you drive forward leaving just the rear axle on the weighing platform. That is recorded, too. You could also take a third reading for the front axle, but most people find that out by subtracting the rear axle weight from the total vehicle weight.

When going through this process it's worth noting down several key points.

- What was the state of the fuel tank?
- Was there any water in the fresh and waste water tanks? It's better to have them empty.

laden weight limit when the product leaves the factory. In other words, there's only a very small margin left to cover the personal possessions of the user, not to mention additional accessories.

On one hand there's the absolute maximum weight permitted for a particular vehicle when it is full of possessions and passengers and being driven on the public highway. On the other hand, there's the actual weight of the same vehicle when it leaves the factory empty. When this latter figure is subtracted from the maximum weight limit, you have what is called the payload and this can be divided into three categories as described in the panel on page 57. The payload refers to the capacity you have at your disposal, not forgetting your own weight along with that of your passengers.

The terms for these different figures are given in the accompanying panel and in parts of this chapter it has also been mentioned that the front and rear axles carry a maximum permitted weight limit as well. For instance your loaded

After weighing the vehicle, the back axle is weighed on the plate.

- Were there any gas cylinders on board and how full were they?
- Was there a toolbox and jack on board? And so on…

Obviously, on one occasion you should load everything up for a typical holiday and then go for a weight check to confirm that you haven't exceeded the limits. Many people get a nasty shock when they do this but being forewarned allows you to offload surplus items. It also gives some clues as to what scope there is to return from a trip abroad bearing bottles of wine or packs of beer.

In the context of building, the first thing I did when collecting a modified chassis from Drinkwater Engineering was to have the 'bare bones' vehicle checked on the weighbridge of Leyland Trucks next door. For the record, that first certificate for a Fiat Ducato 2.8TDI Maxi with long wheelbase and only a dribble of fuel in the tank read as follows:

Total weight	1.82 tonne
Front axle weight	1.32 tonne
Rear axle weight	0.50 tonne

From that point onwards every structure was kept as light as possible and careful thought was given to the positioning of heavy items. For instance the two 90ah batteries were housed in a compartment built on one side midway between the axles, on the opposite side was the freshwater tank, the gas cylinder locker was positioned one metre forward of the rear axle, and nothing heavy other than an addition tow bracket was fitted near the back.

Three further weight readings were made on a weighbridge before the final completion check was taken. Moreover, plans to fit an on-board 2.5kW generator were abandoned during the build. It would have simply reduced the payload by too much.

Summary

The purpose of this chapter has been to inform potential builders of different types of chassis, suspension, and the services offered by specialists. On account of the increasing constraints placed on the builders of vehicles, work on most of the elements discussed fall mainly in the domain of the engineering specialist. It is in the work which follows where there is opportunity for considerably more personal involvement by a self-builder.

Technical Note

LOADING TERMS
Weight is expressed in kilograms (1kg = 2.2lb)

Actual laden weight: The total weight of a motorcaravan including all personal contents being carried. This should be measured on a weighbridge to confirm it doesn't exceed the MTPLM.

Maximum technically permissible laden mass (MTPLM): This refers to a vehicle's gross weight, as defined by the base vehicle manufacturer. Note: this has previously been called 'Maximum Laden Weight' (MLW); 'Maximum Authorised Mass' (MAM); 'Gross Vehicle Weight' (GVW); and 'Maximum Authorised Weight' (MAW).

Mass in running order: This is the unladen ('ex works') weight of a vehicle which sometimes takes into account a full fuel tank and may include a weight allowance for the driver, often taken as 75kg (165lb).

Maximum user payload: The payload is a vehicle's maximum carrying capacity and it's calculated by deducting a vehicle's mass in running order from its maximum technically permissible laden mass.

Maximum axle weights: Both front and rear axles have maximum weights, too, and these figures must not be exceeded by the load. On vehicles with front and rear axles, their loading can be checked on a weighbridge by driving one axle at a time on to the weighing plate.

Gross train weight: This is normally given in a vehicle owner's manual and refers to the maximum weight permitted for the vehicle together with a trailer and the load being carried on the trailer. This is most important to note when towing heavy items like a support car. It is sometimes referred to as the combined weight.

NOTE:
Information plates: Data related to weights is displayed on a metal plate which is usually permanently fixed in the engine bay.
Weighbridge: To confirm a vehicle doesn't exceed its MTPLM, it is necessary to put a fully laden vehicle with full petrol tank and its full complement of passengers on a weighbridge.
Terminology: Since 1999, new motorcaravans are covered within BS EN 1646-2 which sets out the way that weights and payloads should be expressed.

A vehicle's maximum weights are shown on a plate in the engine bay.

7

CONTENTS

The cost

Labour saving

Damp testing

Places to take readings

Dealer damp checking services

Repairing areas of damp

Tracking down materials

Body repairs on vans

Rebuilding a VW T2 campervan

RENOVATING AND REBUILDING OLDER MOTORHOMES

One way to create your own motorcaravan is to embark on a renovation project. However, this approach to ownership isn't without its challenges.

There's no doubt that building a motorcaravan from scratch is a time-consuming route to ownership. Notwithstanding the obvious rewards, not everyone has the time to invest in such an elaborate enterprise.

That is why many self-builders opt for the alternative strategy of renovating an existing model. On the face of it the task merely involves purchasing an old motorcaravan and then spending time bringing it back to scratch. If the vehicle is purchased with an MoT certificate and some unexpired road tax, so much the better. This means you have a road-going motorhome so your subsequent expenditure in time and money can be spread over an extended period. You also have a vehicle which can be used to transport constructional materials such as large panels of plywood.

Some DIY enthusiasts take this strategy one step further and decide to recreate a historic vehicle. However, this type of project is often driven by a personal objective. Perhaps it is born from a wish to recapture memories of a vehicle

owned long ago, or holidays spent with parents.

When rebuilding a historic model, nostalgia usually plays a part and sometimes the finished project becomes a link with a past age rather than a van to use in the future. In fact, some owners carry out such a perfect rebuild that there's almost a reluctance to use their reborn vehicle in anything other than favourable weather.

Only the builder can decide the ultimate direction of their project and in the case-history VW renovation shown in the accompanying photographs, the intention was clear. Although the objective was to restore a 1973 Type 2 Westfalia-converted Volkswagen in a faithful and painstaking manner, the finished campervan was destined for regular use.

For that reason it wasn't slavishly rebuilt to replicate its original specification. Although the renovation work preserved the vehicle's character, this VW campervan was fitted with modern accessory items including a new gas heater, a 230V mains system and a separate leisure battery.

The 'split-screen' was the first VW Transporter and production ran from 1950 to 1967. This example looks almost too good to use in bad weather!

58 Build Your Own Motorcaravan

Steve Rowe, former editor of *Motor Caravan Magazine*, decided to purchase a renovated VW out of nostalgia as he had owned one during his days as a student.

Some readers will consider this a matter of common sense: others would regard it as an inappropriate way to treat a historic 'icon'. Celebration through preservation is usually part of their credo and fitting modern appliances is considered unacceptable.

The cost

Whether your intention is to renovate a conventional motorhome or to recreate a model possessing historical character, there are several common issues, starting with matters of cost.

Motorcaravan magazines quite often run a series in which a project van is purchased and a refurbishment programme is subsequently described in monthly reports. These projects usually afford inspirational editorial, and provide plenty of ideas for readers.

However, cost is a matter to keep in mind.

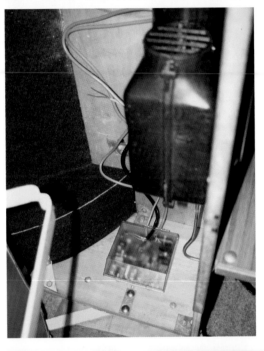

Left: Improved creature comforts were needed so the Westfalia-converted T2 was fitted with a compact Truma 1800E heater.

Below left: The completely enclosed Truma heater was inconspicuously fitted under the rear bench seat.

Below: Outlet vents and extension warm-air trunking were installed discreetly in the living compartment.

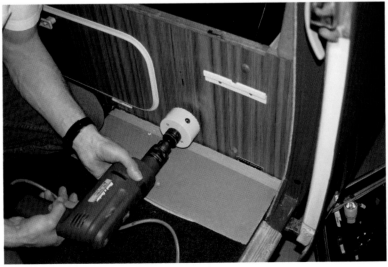

Above: Motorcaravan magazines often purchase 'project vans' like this Talbot Express Elddis 320 Autoquest which was the subject of a rebuilding series in *MMM* magazine.

Specialist magazines may have access to facilities which are not normally available to members of the public. Prices may include concessionary arrangements so it is important to carry out your own cost analysis during the planning stages.

To give an example, it may be beneficial to reupholster an interior which has born the marks of age quite badly and is looking tired. Fitting new upholstery can achieve a remarkable transformation. Unfortunately, the cost of a professional reupholstering operation is usually very expensive. Come to that, there are not as many motorcaravan reupholstery specialists as there used to be; even professional builders are presently facing supply difficulties.

Upgrading jobs like this call for a sizeable budget, so when carrying out pricing calculations, ask yourself if the proposed outlay might cause you to spend more than the vehicle is actually worth. If you decide later to sell the completed project, you could be disappointed by the return on your investment.

Right: On coachbuilt motorcaravans, leaks often start when sealant dries out behind trim strips and then starts to crack.

Labour saving

Savings can be achieved when rebuilding work involves your time rather than the purchase of expensive new products. A classic example of this occurs when the renovation work involves major reconstruction.

On many motorcaravans, damp creeps into the structure once the body sealant has

INTERPRETING DAMP READINGS

When a reading is taken with a damp meter, the damp content of a structure should be displayed as a percentage. Inexpensive meters which merely provide traffic light indicators, are far less useful. The measurement range of a good meter should be from 6% to above fibre saturation in wood, and its operating temperature range is usually recommended to be from -10˚C to +45˚C.

It also has to be recognised that materials such as wood have a natural damp content, so there is no cause for concern to find a reading of 8%. City & Guilds-qualified caravan and motorhome service specialists respond to percentage readings in the following ways:

0–15% – No undue cause for concern.
16–20% – Deserves further investigation.
21% and more – Evidence that remedial work is needed.

■ Elements which can upset the reading are examples of temporary condensation – perhaps a kettle has recently been left boiling inside the vehicle.

■ The internal temperature in the living area should be stabilised throughout, which means that all cupboard, locker, wardrobe, washroom and dividing doors are opened for as long as necessary before commencing the test.

Before conducting a damp test in a motorhome, all locker doors should be opened to stabilise the internal temperature and to ensure it becomes close to the workshop's ambient temperature.

■ The meter will react incorrectly in any region where there are metal plates in the core of a wall. These are often embedded by a manufacturer to provide fixing points for cabinets as shown on page 11.

---

become brittle and its flexibility lost. This is especially prevalent in coachbuilt models and a disintegrating body framework is often a serious threat to the structure, let alone the appearance inside.

To have this type of work carried out by a professional body repairer usually extends over a long period of time and the labour cost can be prohibitive. So this is one instance where a DIY repairer can make a noteworthy impact without spending large sums on materials. However, when you're comparing potential models for purchase you need to ascertain if a case of 'water ingress' is merely localised or whether it is affecting large parts of the structure.

Damp testing

When looking at motorcaravans suffering from water ingress, a damp test is needed. This is carried out using an electrically operated damp meter and its two sharp probes are pushed gently into the internal surfaces. If there is evidence of damp, a small current will track through the panel and the meter registers a reading.

Damp meters are available in DIY stores, but some of the cheap models are not entirely successful. Professional servicing staff normally use specialist instruments like those in the Protimeter range and which typically, cost more than £100. There is also a skill in using a meter and you need to know what to look for. The accompanying panel gives guidance on the way that readings are usually interpreted.

Left: The probes on this electric damp tester from Protimeter will identify areas where damp is a problem.

A check for damp always includes taking readings around windows and doors.

To avoid leaving tiny pinholes from the probes, a good service engineer will try to take readings *underneath* a window's rubber surrounds.

Places to take readings

Thorough checking is most important, especially where there are mildew stains on parts of an internal wall. Places where readings are normally taken during a service check are as follows:

- Around all windows.
- Around sky lights, ventilators and roof windows.
- Around the external door.
- On the inside walls in the region of external road light clusters and marker lamps.

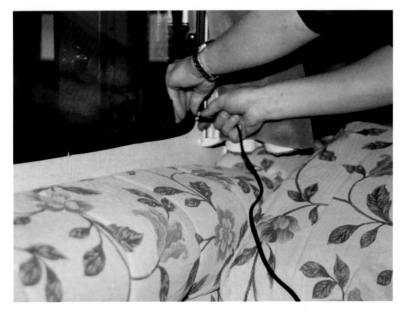

- Around flue outlets and fridge vents.
- In the region of trim mouldings and folded joins on an external aluminium skin.
- Around accessory items such as a TV aerial.
- In the vicinity of awning rails.

Checks are taken on the inside and effort must be made not to leave prominent pin pricks from the probes. This isn't always easy, but it is not difficult to peel back the rubber surrounds which border some types of opening window in order to ease the probes into a ply surface that's normally hidden.

Dealer damp checking services

Motorhome workshops offering servicing facilities will often carry out a damp check as a specific service operation. It isn't an expensive job and when completed you should be given a line drawing to show all the points where readings have been taken. These points should also be marked with each recorded percentage. Make sure that a diagram *will* be supplied by the dealer. A few dealers don't bother to issue these and since you're planning to repair zones where there's a damp problem, you must request a diagram of the findings.

Repairing areas of damp

In the opening chapter, photographs showed that the body structure of modern coachbuilt motorhomes is made using prefabricated panels. These consist of block foam insulant sandwiched between an inner skin of thin ply and an outer skin of aluminium or very thin GRP sheet. These three materials are bonded together with an adhesive, and that is how the panel achieves its impressive strength.

On the face of it, you might presume that rainwater is less likely to penetrate the core of a bonded composite panel than one of the old-style wall sections whose central core is merely a void filled with a quilt-like insulant. But that is not the case; water gets into the core just the same.

In many instances leaks develop where rusting screws used to attach decorative mouldings, awning rails, windows and ventilators provide a seepage point. These become exposed when the bedding layer of non-setting mastic loses its flexibility, dries out, cracks and then falls away.

Far left: When sealant fails on the external bodywork, rain often penetrates via screw holes – as these rusty fixings reveal.

Left: On some aluminium-skin coachbuilt models, tiny holes can sometimes be found.

Van conversions are less likely to suffer from water ingress, but don't imagine for one moment that leaks never occur. They do, particularly where components are fastened to a van's steel body panels. Windows and roof vents are classic weak spots; so are traditional panes of glass held in a rubber surround – especially when mounted in a GRP panel of inconsistent thickness.

Water has a remarkable facility for finding a fault in a motorcaravan. Even the smallest pin holes which sometimes develop in aluminium cladding provide the starting point for a damp patch.

Note: It is thought that an aluminium panel can suffer from this problem if the wooden struts used below the skin have been factory-treated with a cyanide-based preservative.

Of course, before embarking on a repair, you need to ascertain where the water is getting in. This might not be easy because it can track along points of weakness. In consequence an area of soggy, mildew-coated wood is sometimes a surprisingly long way from the point where water first penetrated the bodyshell.

On older coachbuilt motorcaravans where the wall panels have not been bonded, most repairers attack the problem from the outside. As the two accompanying photographs show, the skin is removed first so that soggy insulation material can be removed. If necessary, some of the wooden struts will be replaced, too. When the struts and the plywood internal skin are dry, the voids can be refilled with new insulation material and the aluminium panels rebonded using an adhesive sealant.

A product such as Sikaflex-512 Caravan sealant is particularly effective here. Then the attention turns to the interior wall and some of the internal 3mm plywood might need replacement if it's stained with mildew.

Finally, trim strips will be rebedded and fixing screws can be avoided altogether if Sikaflex 512 is used. The main reason why this adhesive sealant isn't used on a production line is the fact that components have to be held in place for around 12 or more hours; full bonding strength will take at least 24 hours.

Rain penetration damage on non-bonded walls

Above: The rear wall of this traditionally constructed coachbuilt motorcaravan was badly damaged by water.

Left: The front of the over-cab section was very damp, too; urgent repair work was needed.

Rain penetration repairs on a bonded wall panel

Above: Sections of wet ply were torn away inside where internal panels were badly stained.

Right: Damp and discoloured bonded polystyrene often has to be removed and replaced with new insulation panels.

be surprised if you have to remove cabinets and furniture units to reach the damaged areas.

The task normally involves ripping away sections of internal 3mm plywood followed by the contaminated areas of polystyrene block insulation. Small areas are dealt with individually and it's then a case of rebonding fresh boards of foam to the motorcaravan's outer skin, followed by new 3mm decorative wall ply.

Adhesive agents for this operation are manufactured by Apollo of Tamworth; however, this is a large chemical plant and there are no retailing facilities at the factory. For that reason, Apollo products have to be ordered from a motorcaravan accessory shop or from a wholesaler operating a mail order service, such as Leisure Plus.

On a related note, Apollo also manufacturers two-pack chemicals for injecting into floor panels whose facing plywood has started to lose its bond with the block insulation core.

This is referred to as delamination and if you find that a floor in a coachbuilt model creaks and has a spongy feel, a repair is urgently needed. Remedial work on delaminated floor panels is described and illustrated with sequential photographs in *The Motorcaravan Manual* (2nd Edition), pages 39–40.

Tracking down materials

Most materials needed in a rebuilding project are the same as those items required when you're building from scratch, so check the 'Seeking help' section in Chapter 2 and read Chapter 10, 'Tracking down materials'.

Also, see if there's an owners' club, especially if you're struggling to find parts for a historic model. For VW refurbishment, get the catalogue

When dealing with a modern motorcaravan built with sandwich-bonded wall panels, most repairers start from the *inside* instead, so don't

Right: Many of the re-bonding operations involved in motorcaravan repairs use purpose-made products from Apollo Adhesives.

Far right: When the layers in a composite floor start to lose their bond, holes are drilled, injected with a bonding agent, and plugged with dowel pegs.

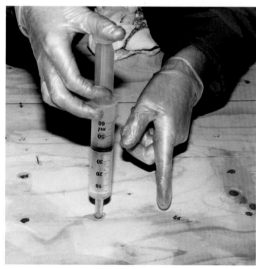

Sometimes parts are hard to find for models like mid 1960s Bedford vans, but help is often available from Adrian Bailey Classics.

from Just Kampers of Odiham, Hampshire, whose address is given in the Appendix. Keep in mind too, Beetles UK which is a partner company of Danbury Motorcaravans.

Other useful contacts include professional VW renovators like Andy Glazier who carried out most of the restoration work on the VW Westfalia shown overleaf and who now runs The Farnborough VW Centre. Alternatively if your preferred historic vehicle is the Bedford CF or its various derivatives, the main UK supplier for obsolete and used spares is Adrian Bailey Classics whose address is also given in the Appendix.

Body repairs on vans

The work shown in the photographs of the VW Westfalia conversion typifies the kind of reconstruction operations involved. It's true that modern polyester resin-based fillers can achieve smart results when dealing with small dents and localised deterioration. However, in most projects the only way to do the job properly is to weld in new sections of steel and to install replacement panels as shown here.

Before this work can begin, a badly corroded vehicle like this VW usually has to be stripped-out inside. In this project, all the furniture was removed and put to one side before welding work was commenced.

Most panels for VW campervans are still available and that is a great help when renovating one of these models. On other vehicles the situation might not be so easy, but don't forget that there are specialists like V&G near Peterborough which can patch a rotting panel, create a GRP copy mould and then create a brand-new moulding to install in its place. See panel "Creating a mould" in Chapter 14.

It might not be as good as being able to purchase a replacement steel panel, but it is structurally much better than applying filler paste in dozens of rusted areas. Filler eventually loses its bond, especially when the rusting process starts spreading.

The company's service also extends to reproducing obsolete interior items like shower trays, sinks and wash basins. The repairer will need the original product to make a mould, even if it is badly cracked and parts are missing. Both ABS plastic and GRP plastic products can be used for replication work. Then a new moulding is laminated in GRP, which is often stronger than the original.

As regards carrying out other reconstructional tasks, the procedures described in later chapters are equally applicable to refurbishment work.

Technical Note

With so many different vehicles used as the base unit for motorcaravans it is beyond the scope of this book to advise on repairs to the engine, transmission, suspension, bodywork and running gear in general. However, there are many relevant manuals in the current catalogue from Haynes Publishing. These include:

- Bedford CF Petrol (69–87) up to E: ISBN 1 85010 429 8
- Bedford/Vauxhall Rascal & Suzuki Supercarry (86–Oct 94) C to M: ISBN 1 85960 171 5
- Volkswagen Transporter 1600 (68–79) up to V: ISBN 0 85696 660 6
- Volkswagen Transporter 1700, 1800, & 2000 (72–79) up to V Classic reprint: ISBN 0 85696 614 2
- Volkswagen Transporter (air-cooled) Petrol (79–82) up to Y Classic reprint: ISBN 0 85696 638 X
- Volkswagen Transporter (water-cooled) Petrol (82–90) up to H: ISBN 1 85960 452 8
- Volkswagen Transporter Type 3 (63–73) up to M Classic reprint ISBN 0 900550 84 8

In essence these manuals focus on automotive elements but check content carefully. Information is not always included on diesel models or vehicles fitted with an alternative body – which includes camper conversions.

Other specialist manuals published by Haynes focus on specific tasks and include:

- *The Haynes Manual on Bodywork* by Martynn Randall: ISBN 1 84425 198 5
- *The Haynes Manual on Welding* by Jay Storer: ISBN 1 84425 176 4,

together with Haynes Manuals on Electrical Systems, Brakes, Carburettors, Diesel Engines, and Engine Management.

Manuals on the Talbot Express are available in the series by Peter Russek whose address is included in the Appendix.

Rebuilding a 1973 VW 'bay window' T2 campervan

1 *Before*: Some rebuilding work had already begun on this 1973 VW with its Westfalia conversion, but the vehicle was still in a pretty poor state.

2 *After:* Following many hours of painstaking work, the L-registered vehicle was a delightful example of a well-appointed campervan.

3 It may seem demoralising, but the interior has to be stripped completely before major welding work can commence.

4 Rotten sills and panels below the cab doors were replaced completely.

7 Little was left of the original front panel, but replacements are available from Just Campers.

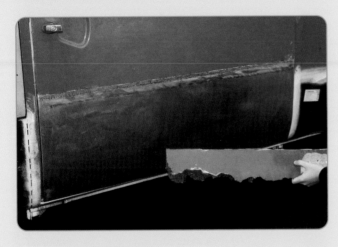

5 The lower section of the sliding door was badly corroded and had to be replaced.

8 When the new front panel had been welded into place, progress was clearly apparent.

6 New panels were installed around the rear wheels.

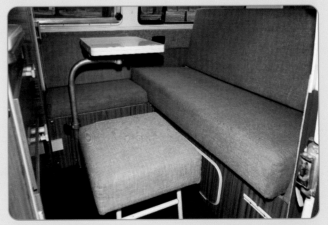

9 Although a new gas-blown air heater was fitted inside, the original furniture was retained.

VAN CONVERSIONS

Many people become motorcaravan owners by converting a panel van themselves. It's a rewarding undertaking and the cost of a self-built campervan is usually significantly lower than the price of a new one.

Outdoor enthusiasts often throw some spare clothes and an old mattress into the back of a panel van and head for the coast or the country. By including a sleeping bag, a lightweight stove, and a billy set, they know that a van can provide a very basic level of accommodation.

A van used in this way isn't very different from a tent – except that the roof is made from sheet metal rather than canvas. It will also be surprisingly cold inside and condensation soon starts to form on the exposed metal panels. You certainly couldn't call this a 'motorcaravan'.

Neither would the Society of Motor Manufacturers and Traders which has published clear criteria as to what constitutes a motorcaravan. Nor would the companies which arrange insurance for DIY leisure accommodation vehicles. For instance Shield Total Insurance states that before insurance cover can be considered, the following items of equipment must be fitted if a vehicle is to be deemed a motorcaravan:

1. At least one fixed bed up to 6ft minimum length.
2. A seating area with a fixed table.
3. A permanent installation for housing a water container.
4. Either a wardrobe or cupboards.
5. A permanently fitted gas or electric hob.
6. Windows installed on both sides of the habitation area.
7. A habitation entrance door – either sliding or opening outwards.

It is also worth adding that owners of panel vans which haven't been appropriately converted are often refused entry to campsites. This decision is not without reason, either. For instance, it isn't safe to operate a lightweight gas stove inside a van without having proper ventilation and the provision of low level gas escape outlets. If a vehicle is to be used as a campervan, its facilities have to be carefully planned, properly constructed and safe for both its occupants and anyone using neighbouring pitches.

Hence this chapter – which focuses on some of the tasks involved if you want to use a panel van for habitation purposes. (Incidentally, the term habitation is now being used in published documents setting out European Standards.) Moreover, after appropriately converting a light commercial vehicle (LCV), the end-product is now described in British Standards and European Norms as a 'leisure accommodation vehicle'. In this country, at least, we refrain from using the acronym 'LAV' for rather obvious reasons.

Cost saving and DIY van conversions

When compared with *coachbuilt* and *A-class* motorhomes, brand-new, professionally-built van conversions seem surprisingly expensive. This is because the conversion process lends itself neither to production-line building methods nor large-scale volume manufacturing.

The reason for this is simple. As mentioned earlier, campervans, as they're affectionately known, are usually quite small inside – which has serious implications for the conversion operation. At very best you're not likely to have the space for more than two operatives to work inside at the same time; there just isn't room to move about freely.

Then there's an array of composite angles inside a van which are created by the curving sides and the slopes of the roof. This means that furniture units have to be carefully shaped in order to reflect the various profiles embodied in the shell. It's so much easier for a manufacturer to install furniture carcasses in a box-like coachbuilt motorhome with its familiar flat, vertical sides.

With these points in mind, it is obvious that conversion work is a labour-intensive operation – hence the seemingly high price for the finished product. Enter the DIY builder for whom time is not such a critical element. Admittedly, if you're planning to use the Shield Total Insurance scheme for a self-build project described in Chapter 20, the principal conversion work has to be completed in 90 days. That can be onerous for anyone whose leisure time is limited, but it is still a long way from the output expectations of a manufacturer driven by commercial obligations.

In contrast, the self-builder is in a completely different position. His or her personal labour involves no wage, PAYE tax or National Insurance contributions. With a work force unlikely to exceed a total of *one* and none of the overheads involved in a factory operation, the DIY enthusiast is less likely to encounter the economic problems facing professional converters.

Notwithstanding the merits of small campervans, a coachbuilt motorcaravan offers a far greater opportunity to reap the benefits of production-line assembly methods. Presumably that is why some major manufacturers, such as the Swift Group, no longer include van conversion campervans in the product ranges.

Taking these points into account, it could be claimed that a self-builder is thus able to save more money by tackling a van conversion rather than constructing a coachbuilt. There are practical issues as well.

Fitting out a van is less involved than building a coachbuilt motorhome on a bare chassis. After all, the body of a van already has rigidity and affords full weather protection from the start.

Equally, for much of the project, the van can be driven around. We're presuming that it is taxed and insured of course, but this benefit is denied the amateur coachbuilder when a body structure is being assembled on an exposed chassis.

Of course, there are other advantages offered by campervans but we mustn't get

side-tracked into 'user issues' because these are already discussed in Chapter 1 of *The Motorcaravan Manual*. Different types of motorhome are compared and the appraisal includes a close look at subdivisions within the van conversion theme. Don't overlook the fact that there are also distinctly different types of campervan currently offered for sale.

Fundamental tasks

Since DIY campervan projects are especially popular, it might seem surprising that this chapter is fairly short. That's because key issues like choosing a base vehicle, insulating interiors, furniture-building, and locating specialist materials are dealt with in other chapters. So is the matter of weight.

In Chapter 6, vehicle weight limits were discussed in detail and these should be

Above: It can be cold sleeping in the back of an unconverted van; condensation is a problem as well.

Below left: Some campervans are very compact inside which poses a problem for converters.

Below: Compared with construction work in coachbuilt motorhomes, it is difficult for more than two operatives to work at once in a panel van.

The interior of this Fiat Scudo illustrates a typical unlined loading area.

The wheel boxes on this Scudo will have to be lined as well.

re-checked. A van is no different from a chassis cab in respect of its plating; there will be a stated maximum technically permitted laden mass (MTPLM), a gross train weight, and individual axle limits. Be ever mindful of these when installing appliances, self-built furniture, fixtures and fittings and make periodic visits to a

public weighbridge to monitor changes. Keeping the weight of fixed items to a minimum, will increase the scope for carrying personal possessions and 'extras' like a cycle rack, a towing bracket, a generator and so on.

Features of the original van

In Chapter 5, guidance was given about different types of base vehicle. Most DIY converters choose to purchase a pre-owned van although some self-builders purchase a brand-new model. Either way, the interior will bear little resemblance to the finished camper and the initial structure often looks very basic.

For instance, the brand-new 1998 Fiat Scudo shown alongside has exposed steel wall panels. The floor pan, too, is a ribbed metal panel and one of the converter's first jobs would be to install a ply panel on top, preferably with a layer of block insulation. The Scudo's wheel boxes over the rear wheels are painted, but otherwise exposed. However, that is quite normal in a light commercial van.

Different in a number of ways is the LDV 2005 Maxus Notice. In the example shown

Right: This LDV 2005 Maxus offers good potential for conversion into a motorcaravan.

Far right: Side panels in the Maxus are already protected with ply boarding; there's a wooden floor panel, too.

Right: The roof is robustly finished with several cross members adding rigidity.

Far right: Panels on the lower part of the rear doors are already in place.

here, the side panels are already protected with ply boarding. There are also flat ply panels with a surface finish already mounted on the steel floor pan. To reinforce the roof, notice all the cross members which could support ceiling boards and provide compartments for insulation. On the other hand, the headroom inside would not suit taller owners, so a converter would probably add a GRP high-top roof. Lastly, there are the rear doors. These are also fitted with plywood panels, thereby providing a good base on which to mount fabric-padded in-fills.

Approaches adopted by professional converters

Faced with a bare interior as shown here, a self-builder can learn a lot by looking at the different strategies adopted by professional converters. Some manufacturers, such as Young Conversions in Bletchley, arrange special open days. Even if you intend to carry out most of the conversion work yourself, many people will get a professional builder to fit a GRP high-top roof or to install additional windows. So it is useful to visit factories which arrange conducted tours and open days … as the accompanying photographs show.

Making decisions on services and equipment

Before commencing the building work proper, you will have to make decisions regarding the services and items of equipment that you want to include in your motorcaravan. For example, if you want to enjoy the flexibility afforded by a three-way absorption refrigerator which can run on mains electricity, 12V electricity, or gas, you will have to cut apertures in the bodyshell. These are needed for gas 'drop-out' escape vents, the flue, and ventilation of the appliance's cooling unit. Accordingly, the location of the unit is going to be important.

The photographs which follow are thus intended to highlight some of decisions you have to make – *before* commencing the installation work.

Learning from manufacturers

Bilbo's is a long-established, award-winning van converter and on this private visit it was interesting to note that one of the first jobs undertaken is the installation of several 12V supply cables.

Auto-Sleepers is one of the largest van converting manufacturers and fastidious preparation was especially evident on this high-top moulding which was about to be installed.

Young Conversions is a smaller manufacturer which often builds individual models to suit customers' specific needs. Young's part-build services for DIY enthusiasts were described in Chapter 2.

Not many manufacturers will fit an elevating roof for DIY builders; exceptions include EMC Warehouse at Knottingley, West Yorkshire and Middlesex Motorcaravans based in Edgware.

Some of the items you may wish to include

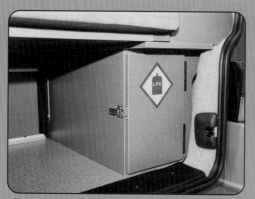

Give thought to the location of the gas cylinder – or preferably a *pair* of cylinders. Provided their locker is sealed from the living space, it is often constructed just inside the rear doors.

An input point for a mains socket should be mounted in a side wall. The installation of a face-fitted socket under a floor is no longer recommended because of likely damage by damp and dirt.

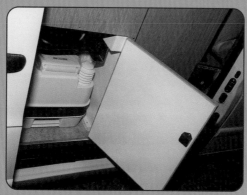

Is the interior large enough to permit the construction of a separate toilet cubicle? Or will you store a portable toilet in a locker and have some curtains to rig up inside when it's put into use?

Storage is always at a premium and designers adopt various strategies. Plastic crates can be useful and this system was tried out in the Cirrus, a prototype model made by Carlight.

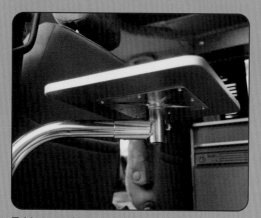

Tables are often a source of problems, especially if they need stowing when you're on the road. Swing-out tables mounted on arms are therefore installed by several professional builders.

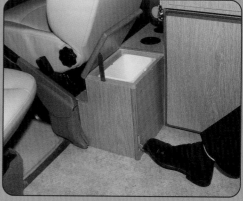

Few British-built campervans incorporate a waste bin near the kitchen, which is an oversight. A good designer will incorporate this important item although it needn't be as large as this one.

Space and water heating appliances

Another fundamental planning decision concerns the heating arrangements. Recognising that many users confine their touring trips to warmer times of the year, space heaters are often not included as standard items. On the other hand, if you plan to use your vehicle both winter and summer, a heater is very important.

Remember, too, that you must never use a gas hob as an alternative form of space heater; modern heating appliances are room sealed for safety. This means that combustion air needed for the room-sealed gas burner is drawn from outside – so oxygen isn't drawn from the living space. Equally, a flue arrangement returns the waste gases from combustion directly outdoors as well.

Whether you decide to fit a water heater or not depends on having sufficient space to install a shower in your campervan. As far as hot water for the washing-up is concerned, I've always made do by boiling a kettle.

Of course, our expectations and needs are all different – but the fact remains that you can't fit as many items in a campervan as you can in a coachbuilt model. Equally, wall-mounted space heaters are hardly suitable but there are efficient, compact, room-sealed, gas heaters on the market which can be installed unobtrusively in lockers. The compact Truma 1800E heater, for example, is illustrated in Chapter 7. In the accompanying photograph, the Propex Heatsource models offer similar benefits. In addition, several manufacturers are now fitting compact diesel heaters from Eberspächer or Webasto; these appliances draw fuel from the vehicle's tank.

Whatever your preferences, ventilation holes again have to be formed in the shell. As the creation of apertures is usually an early task in the conversion operations, you should choose your appliances before getting to work.

Decisions on the type of refrigerator

Some campervans, including modified people carriers manufactured by Wheelhome, are supplied with a portable refrigerated cool box rather than a fixed fridge. That makes good sense when space is very limited.

However, the more common preference of

The Propex Heatsource models are compact gas heaters that can be installed in a locker.

having an installed appliance raises another important question. Do you want an absorption fridge or a compressor fridge? As a point of interest, compressor fridges are compact 12V versions of the appliances we use at home.

- **Simple chemistry**. To achieve low temperatures in a cooling compartment, the most effective principle involves a chemical process. Chemicals are circulated around a complex labyrinth of pipes and as they change state from liquid to gas and back again, heat is drawn out of the food storage compartment, thereby lowering its temperature.
- **Other products**. You may also come across other types of cooling appliance. Cool boxes using the Peltier principle have a 12V fan. There are also water evaporative air conditioners which pass a flow of air across a wet filter to achieve low temperatures. Both serve a purpose and offer benefits; but they do not match the cooling performance of a refrigeration process in which chemicals are used.
- **Absorption refrigerators**. In these appliances, it is the application of heat which sends the chemicals around the cooling unit mounted on the back of the casing. Heat is supplied using a gas burner, a 12V heating element, or a 230V mains heating element. The operation is completely silent but the back of the appliance must be kept cool using air drawn from outside via purpose-made ventilators.
- **Compressor refrigerators**. In these products, the chemicals are circulated by an electrically driven compressor pump. This only operates when triggered by a thermostatic control switch and you will have heard the periodic hum from the motor in your fridge and freezer at home. In motorcaravans, compressor fridges use a 12V dc supply and require neither wall ventilators nor a flue outlet.

Right: A compressor fridge doesn't have to be mounted on a side wall.

Far right: This drawer-type fridge from Waeco is often fitted in lorries.

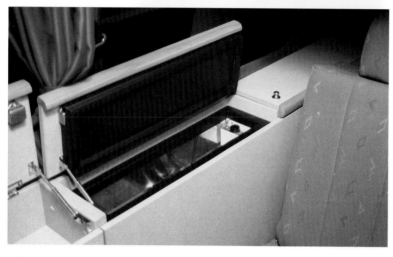

Above: Compact top-loading compressor fridges are made for installation in MPVs.

Below: The compressor fridge in this Bilbo's campervan looks just like an absorption model.

Choosing which appliance you prefer will be partly dictated by your style of holiday travel. If you want to travel in the wilds with little use of campsites offering 230V mains voltage hook-up points, an absorption fridge is better. The fact that the appliance will run on gas is particularly important. Remember that it will only run on a 12V supply while you're driving; your leisure battery would soon be flat if you re-wired an absorption fridge so that it continues running on 12V when the vehicle's parked.

The silent operation of an absorption fridge is especially welcome in the small space of a van conversion, but its disadvantage is the fact that you *must* mount it against a side wall and holes have to be cut as described above.

It is much easier to install a compressor fridge because it only needs a 12V supply – and no external ventilating apertures. As the photos show, there are designs to fit in long distance trucks, narrow units for MPV installations, tiny units for micro campervans, and larger models the size of absorption fridges. Like some other manufacturers, Bilbo's are particularly enamoured with this type of product.

The trouble is that they draw a considerable amount of current from a leisure battery. Of course, the pump only operates intermittently when the thermostat calls for action, but if you tend to park a campervan for extended spells and head off on cycle rides or walks, a battery can discharge surprisingly quickly. Equally, if you have installed a fan-driven heater, that will also be taking current from the leisure battery, too.

These patterns of use are not a problem if you stop at sites with mains hook-ups because the inbuilt battery charger will then be able to keep the leisure battery up to scratch. Nor is it so acute if you're regularly driving around in your motorhome because the alternator will be wired up to charge the leisure battery, too.

One upshot of this is that a compressor fridge enables you to keep the external appearance of a motorcaravan more attractive because it's uncluttered by plastic ventilators.

However, some users have written to magazines to report that their leisure battery can't cope with the demands placed upon it, particularly when they're camping in remote places. In such cases, they would be better served by an absorption fridge which can alternatively run on gas.

Variation on roof types

Another important element to consider is the type of roof you want on a van conversion. While you can use a van exactly as supplied without any intentions of altering the roof structure you might prefer to have the original roof replaced by a GRP moulding which offers increased headroom. Alternatively, you might opt for an elevating roof in order to reap the benefit of a low roof structure when you are driving and a high roof when you're parked and occupying the living area. Examples of different roofs are shown here.

Manufacturing GRP roofs

The altered roof structures shown below are achievable using a glass-reinforced plastic (GRP) moulding that has been specifically created to fit your base vehicle. At present, many of the GRP units are made by Reimo and these German products can be ordered in the UK through Concept Multi-Car (Reimo) in Hythe, Kent and Motor Caravan Conversions (Reimo) in Cheetham, Manchester.

Other manufacturers have been involved in the production of GRP roof mouldings and Euro Motor Caravans (EMC) used to offer many

Different types of roof

This fixed-roof model, called the Meteor (made by Murvi), might be low enough to pass under some height barriers. However, you cannot stand up inside and cooking has to be done while seated.

The Morello is another fixed-roof conversion from Murvi but even with its insulated floor and ceiling, this Fiat-based model still provides good headroom inside for the majority of owners.

Replacing the original roof with a GRP moulding is a popular way to gain headroom. The addition needs to be well-insulated for use in cold weather, and height barriers are a problem.

Models fitted with a canvas-sided elevating (rising) roof are also popular and seek to offer the best of both worlds. Inevitably, though, heat loss is a problem if you plan to use such a vehicle in the winter.

GRP moulded high-top roofs

The manufacture of a high-top GRP roof involves a mould which has been specifically made for a particular model. Laminating work is usually a manual operation and extractor ducting is needed.

While most elevating roof structures are constructed with synthetic fabric sides, the main 'lid' is made in GRP. Once again a mould is needed for its manufacture and an example is shown here.

When counting-up all the different vans sold in the last twenty years or so, it is no surprise that EMC needed extensive storage space for their daunting number of moulds and mouldings.

When mixing the polyester resin used in GRP lamination work, a colourising agent called a pigment can be added if required. Alternatively, the product can be painted at a later stage to create a perfect match.

different designs. Regrettably, this manufacturer has since closed although a new company operating from the same premises and called EMC Warehouse offers a fitting service.

The above photographs show more detail of their products.

Fitting a GRP high-top roof

As long as skilled fitters know exactly what they are doing, the installation of a GRP high-top roof is not as complicated as it might seem. Since the need for greater headroom is not uncommon, vehicle manufacturers often publish guidance booklets to describe body reinforcement requirements, together with diagrams showing the permitted cutting zones.

However, it stands to reason that severe distortion could occur once the main cross members of a roof are severed and the earlier photograph on page 70 of the LDV Maxus clearly shows these key structural items. That's why a publication from Fiat Auto (*Commercial Vehicles Manual for conversions/special outfit*) specifies that structural compensation is needed after a roof section has been removed

Installing a GRP high-top roof

1 Working closely to the cutting guidelines defined by the vehicle manufacturer, the original steel roof on this van has been removed in readiness to receive a GRP high-top moulding. Manufacturer's reinforcing struts are then installed.

2 To ensure that the new GRP roof is going to register exactly with the vehicle, temporary cross battens are used to hold it poised above the steelwork. There will be a generous overlap around the perimeter.

3 The bond between the GRP and the steel will employ an approved adhesive sealant and while the product is setting, lengths of webbing are used to hold the roof moulding in place.

4 Adhesive sealant will be applied to the overlapping flanges and left to set for 24 hours. The final application of sealant shown here is merely to cover any sharp edges left from the cutting work.

from a Fiat panel van. The manual explains that this is accomplished by installing an additional structural steel frame which has to be held in place around the aperture, using rivets or welds.

Suffice it to say, it would be misguided for an unqualified self-builder to attempt a job like this. Kit car enthusiasts will already know that cutting through a vehicle's steel panels is surprisingly easy. On the other hand, creating a safe, alternative roof structure on a van which achieves full structural integrity is best entrusted to an expert. The accompanying photographs show some of the stages of this operation being carried out by a professional installer.

Other preparatory jobs

Your decisions regarding the positions for a fresh water inlet, a cassette toilet access door, a water heater flue, a mains hook-up socket and so on, might enable you to carry out early cuts in the side panels. However, when building a 'one-off' campervan, it sometimes transpires that an appliance needs slight realignment, in which case a hole might be in the wrong place. This can cause a lot of repair work.

It is different for manufacturers who will have already built a successful prototype which is then replicated once full production commences. That was the case in the accompanying photo taken during a tour of the Auto-Sleepers' factory.

Note how this manufacturer applied a treatment to all exposed edges where cuts had been made in the steel panels. This mark of good workmanship should also be carried out by the self-builder. Since the rusting process needs oxygen, some builders treat cut edges with a generous application of an adhesive sealant as shown in the last photograph in the GRP high-top installation sequence.

As regards cutting apertures and installing windows in a van this is another service offered by small-output converters. Bear in mind that there are both single glazed automotive windows to consider as well as acrylic plastic double-glazed window units specifically designed for caravans and motorhomes. More information on the installation of windows is given in Chapter 9 where there are sequence photographs showing different types being installed in a GRP bodyshell.

On a different matter of preparation, there is also the business of bonding battens to the inside of a panel van in order to provide secure fixing points for appliances and furniture. Different manufacturers have their preferred bonding products but when working with timber and steel, Sikaflex-512 Caravan Sealant has been found to create a bond of formidable strength.

To achieve this, all contact surfaces must be scrupulously clean and Sikaflex supplies a product for ensuring that metal and GRP surfaces are suitably free of contaminants. Once the sealant has been applied, the components must be held in place for a recommended 24 hours. The use of cramps is not recommended because these are inclined to squeeze out sealant from the joints, and a band of at least 3–4mm should remain in the junction between the mating materials.

The accompanying photographs show how a small van was lined with 9mm ply sheeting in readiness for mounting some storage racking. This wasn't a motorhome conversion and you won't see any thermal insulation placed behind the ply. On the other hand, it adopts exactly the same procedures that you might follow when creating secure fixing points on which to attach furniture and appliances.

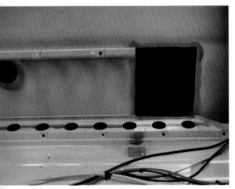

An anti-rust treatment should be applied to all apertures cut in the metal panels.

Lining the interior

The chapter on insulation describes how steel and GRP surfaces are often lined with an insulant and then covered with thin ply. Achieving a high level of thermal insulation in this way is certainly important if you plan to use a campervan in winter… or in really hot places where good insulation helps to keep excessive heat *out*.

It was mentioned earlier, however, that some van conversions are really only intended for warm weather use and their level of insulation is therefore more modest. In many conversions, the work involves protecting cold surfaces that might otherwise suffer from condensation simply by covering them with a ribbed head lining material. This type of product is also used in buses, coaches and kit cars.

Although it looks rather like ribbed carpet, this lining product is very light and sufficiently flexible to fix on curving components like a metal wheel box. It is usually installed using a contact adhesive which is sold in aerosol cans. A typical example is Delf Brand MP Spray Adhesive which is sold to furniture and carpet specialists. The product is obtainable from upholsterers, kit car trimmers and vehicle accessory outlets. The photographs on page 80 show lining work in progress.

Constructing furniture

There are probably four different ways to construct furniture for a campervan, as follows.

1. On a work bench using a product like Vöhringer faced plywood which is described in Chapter 15. When complete, the finished cabinet is installed as a pre-assembled unit and this approach is employed by Bilbo's. The strategy is particularly logical when there's a production run involving identical base vehicles. However, it can also be used for one-off conversions and Rainbow Conversions also assembles cabinets this way, even for customer orders where replication isn't involved.

2. By constructing a framework of battens in situ as shown in the Mazda DIY case history illustrated later in this chapter. After the skeleton framework has been installed in the van, it is then covered using lightweight, 3mm faced plywood. The strategy is usually good for keeping the weight down and it is a logical method of building for anyone involved in a one-off DIY conversion.

3. By cannibalising an old caravan and reassembling the lightweight units in a panel van.

1 This small van could undoubtedly be converted into a Micro Campervan. Here, it was being fitted out to carry tools and store items of equipment.

2 Since 9mm ply would be mounted on each side, only three battens were used for the fixing. A more elaborate framework would be built in a campervan.

3 A centre batten 30mm x 25mm (1¼in x 1in) was bonded to the steel frame using Sikaflex 512 and screws. A saw cut helped it to follow the curving member.

4 A difficult installation of battens at the rear was achieved using bonding adhesive; access was still left to reach the road light clusters and connections.

5 Twin-threaded Reisser screws were used for mounting the plywood board – checking length to ensure that they wouldn't hit the steel members.

6 The ply made a good mounting board. In a motorcaravan, only 3mm ply would be used so a more elaborate support framework would be constructed.

Installing head-lining material

In this conversion, the contact adhesive is used to affix lining material to the wheel box and along the reinforcing members within which some windows will later be fitted.

During a visit to Bilbo's factory, this lining material was being bonded inside the shell of a Volkswagen van. In this conversion, it was one of the first jobs to be undertaken.

Several companies will carry out this work for you and it is not as easy as it looks. Bedding down the material can be challenging; here the grips of a pair of scissors are being used.

Bilbo's constructs furniture on a bench using Vöhringer faced plywood.

Rainbow Conversions builds individual vehicles but often pre-assembles their furniture away from the vehicle.

This method was employed in the Renault Trafic conversion shown on page 82. Since the Renault was fitted-out in this way, a caravan breaker based near Pontypool, and known as The Caravan Centre has now started to supply van conversion packages using furniture units rescued from caravan write-offs.

4. It is also possible to buy modular self-assembly kits from Reimo and these are made to suit a large number of base vehicles. The wide range of different layouts is shown in a special catalogue which shouldn't be confused with Reimo's much larger accessory publication. A kit approach to furniture building is also adopted by LeisureDrive FG of Bolton although tailor-made products are not available for as many base vehicles as those covered by Reimo.

Two case histories

Many other tasks involved in construction work are described in the accompanying chapters. However, a helpful conclusion here is to look at two contrasting case histories.

PROJECT ONE – CONVERTING AN ELDERLY RENAULT TRAFIC. BUILDERS: JOHN AND ALISON FREAME

When you only have £2,500 available and want to build a motorcaravan, the dream is hardly likely to materialise. To be strictly accurate, this project was tackled some years ago and I suppose the budget in today's money would amount to something around £4,000, but it still sounded like 'pie in the sky'.

Surprisingly, there were very few professional converters who used the Renault Trafic although it offered good potential. This example came with a mileometer which didn't work, five previous owners and a mouse who'd taken up residence in one of the sills. In most of its Lincolnshire life, this working vehicle had been used to transport vegetables and there were still a few mouldy potatoes left in the back.

The Trafic delivery van was purchased through the classified advertisements of a local paper and it somehow managed to pass the MoT test. Then came the bad news.

When John Freame checked the price of kitchen appliances he found that an Electrolux refrigerator alone would cost nearly a quarter of the price of the van! However, determination can move mountains and it just so happened that John and Alison owned a leaking 1975 Elddis Shamal caravan which they hadn't been able to sell. So they stripped it apart, and reassembled its bunks, kitchen unit, stove, fridge and the ceiling lockers in their Trafic delivery van.

Fortunately, there was good headroom inside so there was no need to spend money on a high-top GRP roof. When there wasn't enough money in the kitty at the end to

Fitting a Seitz S4 window

On pages 94 – 97, Seitz framed windows are described and the illustrations show a product being fitted to a GRP ('fibre glass') coachbuilt motorcaravan. The sequence below shows some of the alternative strategies when a window is installed in a steel panel-van.

1 Using the window as a template, an internal structure is constructed using plywood and a softwood frame. The assembly is subsequently covered with interior fabric and offered-up temporarily. Pilot holes are then drilled in each corner through the metal panels.

2 On the outside of the vehicle these four pilot holes indicate where the aperture is needed. This is precisely marked and the opening's accurately defined using masking tape - which also protects the paintwork. Most DIY fitters cut out the aperture using a jigsaw.

3 After removing the panel and tidying-up the cut edges, trial fits are made holding the inner panel in place and inserting the outer window frame to ensure they coincide. When the alignment is confirmed, the frame's coated with Sikaflex 221 and bonded to the interior.

4 Normally this involves two people. Scrap timber is temporarily placed outside to protect paintwork while G-cramps secure the internal frame. When the sealant is fully cured, the window unit and internal rollerblind framework are put in place and screwed together.

Note: The illustrations on pages 95 – 97 highlight several additional issues involved when installing Seitz framed windows.

---

have the van resprayed, this indomitable team of two did the job themselves using paint brushes.

Even the windows on the van had been taken from the Elddis caravan, but that was a questionable strategy. Caravans built before November 1977 were not always fitted with safety-glass. The use of non safety-glass might not have been a source of concern in a 1975 towed vehicle,

but the reinstallation of this type of window in the habitation area of a motorcaravan could be potentially dangerous for anyone travelling in the back.

That said, a smart campervan was duly constructed which provided many happy holidays, albeit without the mouse.

PROJECT TWO – CONVERTING A MAZDA E2200. BUILDER: TONY BROOK

As a former woodwork teacher, Tony Brook is an accomplished cabinet maker, and several items of furniture in his house are a testimony to his well-honed woodworking skills. However, he is also experienced in a number of practical matters and Tony has converted several commercial vehicles including a large bread van.

In one of his later projects, pictured here, some interesting approaches to conversion work are demonstrated. As recommended earlier in this chapter, Tony enlisted the professional help of EMC at Knottingley, West Yorkshire, to have a high-top GRP roof fitted to a Mazda E2200 van which he'd purchased second-hand.

Once this was fitted, it was decided not to follow the common strategy of covering the inside of the moulded high-top roof using ribbed, carpet-like, head-lining material. Instead, a framework of battens was bonded to the roof in order to contain a generous layer of insulation material. Thin ply was used finally to cover the battens and it was only around the single-glazed roof windows that you could see how this had increased the original thickness of the high-top moulding. Without doubt this was a wise move because Tony and his wife enjoy ski-ing and their van is far better insulated for cold weather use than many professionally-built models.

The other point of interest is that Tony didn't follow the furniture-building strategy in which modular units are bench-built using Vöhringer 15mm faced plywood. Instead, the vehicle was parked completely level and plywood boards were then fitted on the metal floor pan. Battens could then be screwed to this level foundation after which frameworks for furniture were constructed in situ. Routine checks were made using a spirit level to confirm that the uprights were plumb and that cross members were truly horizontal.

Furniture units built in this way were then clad with 3mm decoratively faced plywood to produce smart, strong but surprisingly light furniture units.

Case history One – Converting a Renault Trafic

The project involved nine weeks of hard work during that part of the summer when evenings are light. The decision to reinstall existing materials seems entirely consistent with today's urgency to recycle as many things as possible. It was certainly a good way to extend the working life of a leaking caravan. As I've commented about old touring caravans on many occasions, some 'golden oldies' become site huts while others house hens. The reincarnation carried out by John and Alison Freame is a rather more noble metamorphosis.

This B-reg base vehicle was virtually purchased for pence rather than pounds and the new owners repainted it by hand.

Right: Even with an insulated ceiling, headroom inside was still 1,880mm (6ft 2in); ordinary wallpaper was used on the interior walls.

Far right: The bunk beds were taken from a scrapped 1975 Elddis caravan, together with all the original upholstery.

Right: The stove and the original Electrolux fridge were in good working order and this entire kitchen was reinstalled in the Renault.

Case history Two – Converting a Mazda E2200

Have a look at the different ways of fitting-out the interior of a van and then decide what is best for your particular project. As regards the construction of furniture you might adopt several of the approaches described here.

The high-top roof was made and installed by EMC before the company ceased manufacturing its own GRP mouldings.

Bonding timber support lugs to the metal panels takes time but compartments were thus created for insulation and facing ply.

The loading bay was completely covered with 12mm (1/2in) plywood to provide a floor on which to construct support frameworks.

Working from the installation instructions, an Electrolux three-way absorption fridge was securely mounted in the framework.

Far left: A framework was constructed for a seat with a hinged back to provide part of a bed base; there's good storage underneath.

Left: Several months later the interior had been completely lined-out to provide a comfortable campervan for Tony Brook and his wife.

9

CONTENTS

COACHBUILT MODELS

Enthusiasts wanting a more spacious vehicle than a converted panel van might decide to construct a 'coachbuilt' model. It's an ambitious undertaking but it brings special rewards.

Experienced motorcaravanners might question the use of the word 'coachbuilt' in this chapter when there isn't a further chapter devoted to A-class models. Suffice it to say, the term coachbuilt is used here to include *all* motorcaravans which are constructed on a traditional chassis. Descriptions of chassis and the associated running gear were given in Chapter 6.

When comparing models which use a chassis as the basic foundation, you will find contrasting methods of construction. For example, reference has already been made on page 28 to coachbuilt models which use a monocoque GRP shell as opposed to structures which are assembled using separate panels.

There isn't space, however, to dwell on all different variations; the main purpose of this chapter is to highlight some of the practical issues facing anyone embarking on this type of project. To meet this objective, a case history has thus been selected to exemplify some of the tasks confronting a self-builder.

The DIY motorhome used for this purpose has been in use for nearly three years. When it first appeared, many long-time motorcaravan enthusiasts were puzzled because they couldn't identify its origins. This aura of mystery led to its unique name which is now displayed in bold graphics on the sides. It's simply called: Mystique.

The Mystique – overview

It was mentioned that manufacturers and design specialists sometimes have to find fresh space in their factories by disposing of prototype projects. Old GRP moulds certainly take up a lot of space.

That was the case with the Mystique, which is a one-off self-build motorcaravan. Well, almost. To be accurate there's one other based on this bodyshell, owned by a self-builder in

Mouldings from former prototype projects take up space and are often destroyed or sold.

South Wales, while a third, part-finished and radically altered bodyshell is also privately owned.

The one pictured here was built using the original prototype shell which came in two pieces; it was unfortunate that parts of the door, a locker lid, the gas cylinder compartment and several other components were missing, presumed destroyed. That's when the author intervened.

Make no mistake about this; a self-build project of this kind can be a severe test of one's patience, determination and resourcefulness – a fact that was painfully evident from the outset. For example, the logistics of transporting large, heavy GRP mouldings is a challenge in itself. Still, there are usually solutions to problems and a Brian James twin-axle car trailer with its hydraulic elevating bed and winch system was usefully brought into service.

Several round trips of 220 miles were needed to convey the panels back to a local caravan storage centre for safe keeping. And that's where they remained for ten months or so while awaiting the delivery of a new Fiat 2.8 turbo diesel Maxi chassis cab. Things seldom progress as quickly as you would like.

Manoeuvring the mouldings

If you find yourself faced with similar problems of manoeuvring large sections, keep in mind the people who built the pyramids. Long before the advent of machine tools, hydraulic lifting systems and the internal combustion engine, ways were found to move huge blocks of stone. Rollers, pulley systems and levers all have a part to play.

THE MAIN MOULDING FOR THE LIVING SPACE

The fact that a 19mm plywood floor was already bonded to the main GRP body section meant that it was possible to elevate this moulding, stage by stage, until it could be supported on large blocks. Not wobbly piles of bricks, or the gas cylinders used by its designer, but huge, stable, hardwood chocks normally used to support ocean-going yachts. These were borrowed from a boatyard. Safe handling was crucially important here, as was a cheap trolley jack.

Two temporary trestles supported by large industrial castor wheels were constructed next

and bolted under the floor. The trestles made it possible for the entire moulding to be wheeled from its resting place and winched on to the car trailer. When the moulding was unloaded later, the temporary structures were then dismantled.

Builders' trestles and scaffold planks were used next to support the moulding whose floor had to be elevated *above* the height of the Fiat Ducato chassis. There was a reason for this. It was decided that instead of trying to lift the large living section on to the chassis, it would be simpler to elevate it so that the vehicle could be carefully reversed directly under the floor panel.

However, before this part of the exercise could be completed, locally made outrigger supports (shown on page 54) were bolted to the chassis fixing lugs. In addition, lengths of Pirelli rubber webbing (normally used in upholstery work) were stuck to all the uppermost faces of chassis members using

Large sections of bodywork are usually a challenging job to move.

To avoid heavy lifting, this GRP moulding was elevated so that the chassis could be driven directly underneath the floor panel.

Above: The upper faces of all chassis members were covered with strips of rubber.

Right: Apertures had to be cut in the floor panel to accommodate the rear wheels of the base vehicle.

Below: After its initial fitting, the main body moulding had to be advanced 12mm further forwards.

Evo-Stik contact adhesive. If this gets overlooked, squeaking noises often develop between chafing chassis members and the floor ply.

Equally important was to form cut-outs in the floor which would accommodate the rear wheels when the unit was subsequently lowered on to the chassis. Finally, a pre-moulded GRP bathroom cubicle and shower tray unit had to be stowed inside because it was too bulky to be passed through the entrance door at a later stage in construction.

Apart from this preparation, one of the difficulties in the coupling operation was ascertaining where to position the large body section, bearing in mind that an overcab moulding would be added later. Since the overcab section had been intentionally shaped to fit snugly on the roof of a Fiat cab, its position was dictated more precisely. Moreover, both of these large body components had connecting flanges that would subsequently be bolted together.

Recognising that 'fine tuning' of the locations might be needed later, the main section was bolted using only a few of the fixing brackets on the chassis. This was just enough to render it safe to drive two miles home from the caravan storage compound. It would almost certainly not be mounted in exactly the right position.

And it wasn't. Subsequent checking established that it needed to be advanced about 12mm further forward on the two longitudinal chassis rails. That wasn't the only thing as it also needed moving a few millimetres laterally towards the near-side of the vehicle. Back to the pyramid engineers of ancient Egypt.

After careful consideration it was decided that positional adjustments could be carried out using twist drills as miniature rollers. The floor was duly unbolted from the chassis brackets and then elevated in stages using the trolley jack and wood blocks. One by one, four twist drills around 10mm in diameter were laid on the main chassis members. These were slightly angled, too, in the hope that any longitudinal adjusting movements would also skew the large moulding to the nearside as well. Once in place, the unit was lowered on to the drill bits.

The result was amazing. One sharp shove at the rear of the moulding not only pushed this heavy item forwards and sideways: it even overshot a mark drawn on the chassis and advanced the body shell a full 25mm. Too far, but no matter; it had been proved that the principle of using rollers to transport blocks for a Pharaoh's tomb was equally relevant when constructing a motorhome today.

After final checking with a tape measure, holes were drilled for the high tensile 13mm (1/2in) bolts which secured the structure permanently to the chassis. The trolley jack was again used to ease up the four corners of the floor in turn – but only enough to retrieve each of the drill bits, one by one.

THE OVER-CAB MOULDING

The next challenge arose when the awkwardly shaped over-cab moulding couldn't be slid into place from the front. The cab's electrically controlled driving mirrors simply projected too much. An oak tree, a length of climbing rope, some washing line pulley blocks, a wife and a friendly neighbour provided the answer. This front moulding was supported in a rope sling, hoisted in the air using the branch of a large oak tree and gently lowered from above. The less strenuous role of the writer was to capture the operation with a camera.

Not that the moulding was allowed to make direct contact with the cab around its perimeter. That's what many professional builders do, subsequently squeezing out large beads of sealant to hide any ugly gaps. Instead, black 'P'-section plastic wing piping was inserted which had been purchased using Woolies mail order service. Alternatively, automotive trims like this can be bought at most kit car and classic car shows.

JOINING THE TWO MOULDINGS

A much smaller-gauge 'P'-trim finished in white was also purchased to mount between the junction flanges of the two body sections – on both sides and across the roof. It is scarcely possible to achieve a perfect register here, especially when a vehicle inevitably flexes as it is driven over uneven surfaces. As manufacturers of pre-war saloon cars knew all-too-well, a neater fit can be achieved between protruding wings and a vehicle's 'body tub' if piping is fitted to cover the junctions.

Of course, the use of piping gives a much neater visual appearance than an irregular beading of sealant, but it makes no contribution whatsoever to the bonding process. An all-important structural and weatherproof bond between the flanges of the two body sections, together with the coupling of the front GRP moulding to the cab itself called for a specialised product.

Above: The only way to fit the overcab moulding was to winch it into the air using the bough of an oak tree.

Left: Wing piping is useful for covering the junctions between adjoining panels.

Below: Hardly a safe way to get on a roof, although ropes held the structure together while the two main mouldings were joined.

This is where an adhesive sealant is needed to form a very strong bond. Many sealants are simply gap fillers and these are no good at all for this job. Not only must the product create unyielding adhesion to dissimilar materials; it also needs to retain a degree of flexibility without compromising its mechanical bond.

A product range widely used in several professional areas of construction is manufactured by an international company: Sika Ltd. Several versions of Sikaflex sealants are available and for this type of work, the use of Sikaflex-512 Caravan is ideal. Both black and white versions of the product were used on different parts of the body assembly.

Notwithstanding its remarkable bonding characteristics, Sikaflex-512 Caravan sealant takes around 24 hours before it achieves its full strength. Taking that into account, the section of the overcab moulding which had to be affixed to the metal sides of the cab was suitably braced against a wall using a series of timber struts as shown below.

It is also important to point out that the product loses its bonding capacity if squeezed out from adjoining surfaces. It is recommended that 3–4mm of adhesive sealant is always left between adjoining components.

This was less easy to achieve where the two mouldings were joined at the flange. More than two dozen bolts were fitted to hold the flanges

together and large 'penny' washers were also used with every fixing. These hardware items are usually on sale at kit car shows.

In this instance the mechanical connection between the sections was principally achieved using high-tensile bolts. However, Sikaflex-512 Caravan was liberally applied as well to add a weatherproofing element and when the bolts were progressively tightened, some of the sealant was inevitably squeezed out of the junction. This probably reduced it to around 2mm thickness, but that wasn't a problem. Here, the sealant was mainly used to keep out the rain whereas the bolts kept the flanges in register.

However, that wasn't the case where the over-cab moulding made contact with the roof of the cab. No mechanical fixings like rivets, self-tapping screws or bolts would be used there; instead, the bond was wholly achieved with adhesive sealant. Accordingly, the Sikaflex-512 Caravan was dispensed from a sealant gun all around the inside. This ensured there was a generous application between the GRP moulding and the steel roof of the cab.

Recognising the stresses imposed on a vehicle roof when driving into a headwind, I probably used more adhesive sealant than was needed. But it was also important to take account of the flange part of the 'P'-trim piping which had merely been anchored in place using Evo-Stik impact adhesive. This was now encapsulated completely within the bonding sealant.

As a footnote it is interesting to note that when Knauss launched the 2005 Sun Ti range of coachbuilts, the manufacturer similarly decided to tidy the junction between the cab and the GRP moulding above using wing piping rather than a tortuous line of sealant.

Wheelboxes

Another element that poses challenges even to professional converters is the provision of wheelboxes. For example a well-known ambulance builder encountered problems when the rear wheels fouled the wheelboxes through insufficient clearance. It would be imprudent to mention names, except to say that this allegedly happened to one of the leading UK specialists in this field.

Motorcaravan manufacturers can get it wrong, too. Again, no names, but there's one leading coachbuilt motorcaravan where it is exceedingly difficult to remove the rear wheels.

Sikaflex-512 Caravan sealant takes 24 hours to set completely so the forward moulding was held in place at the point where the GRP met the cab.

This is because the wheelboxes are mounted too closely to the tyres and it poses quite a problem when there's a puncture during a journey. No less surprising was the problem on a leading German manufacturer's A-class motorhome when it was being tested by one of our motorcaravan magazine editors. The test model was generously provided with optional alloy wheels, but on its first drive smoke started coming from the rear wheels. The reason? Once again the tyres were chafing against the wheelbox so the road test was brought to a halt.

Keep these instances in mind if you have to construct a wheel box around the rear wheels. Note, too, that if you achieve good clearance with steel wheels and later decide to fit alloy wheels, remember the story of the A-class motorhome. Carefully check profile dimensions and tyre details before spending money on alternative wheels.

On the project described here, the matter was even more complex because the chassis had been fitted with an air suspension system that incorporates a 'dump' facility for lowering the rear of the vehicle. When air is released and the body sinks at the back, the wheels create the impression of rising into the living area. In consequence, plenty of measurements were taken and re-taken before the size of the wheelboxes was finally established. Also remember that a finished vehicle fitted with all its equipment and carrying personal effects is likely to sink even lower on its springs than when the wheelboxes were first considered.

After Drinkwater Engineering had installed the air-suspension system on the Mystique, the Director recommended that clearances at the sides of tyres should never be less than 25mm. Get it wrong and you might not be able to tip a spare wheel enough when trying to lift it over the hub.

As regards the vertical clearance needed, seek the advice of the supplier of the chassis cab. For example, dimensions are given for what is referred to as 'rear wheel shake' in Fiat's *Commercial Vehicles: Manual for conversions/special outfits*. In practice, this information didn't help in the Mystique project because the original Fiat leaf spring suspension had been replaced by computer-reactive air suspension instead. Not surprisingly, different types of suspension create different degrees of wheel movement and it is obviously not possible to give a universal prescription in this manual.

Anyway, it pays to err on the side of caution

and for the record, the internal height of the wheelboxes shown here was 250mm (10in). This represents a clearance above the tyre of 112mm (4½in). Note that these measurements were taken *before* any equipment was fitted inside.

The wheelboxes were constructed using 9mm marine ply which is considerably more expensive than WBP ply (waterproof and boilproof ply).

The lining inside the ply box was formed using ABS plastic sections taken from a caravan wheelbox. Fitting this was quite involved and on reflection it would have been easier to have adopted a method used on an earlier conversion in which laminations of glass-reinforced plastic were built up on the inside of the plywood box.

With the chassis lowered on its air-suspension system, measurements were taken before designing the wheelbox.

The wheelboxes were made using 9mm marine ply and lined with an ABS skin.

When completed, longitudinal battens were screwed to the outside of the boxes so that they could be screwed down to the floor. The whole of the junction was then covered with several resin-impregnated layers of chopped strand mat so that road water couldn't penetrate the interior. Be diligent here. A tyre discharges a remarkable amount of water when you're driving in really wet weather.

Rear lighting

When the Fiat chassis was originally ordered, a tailboard for carrying the rear lights and a numberplate was specified in spite of the fact that this would only be a temporary fitting.

Once the body had been mounted on the chassis, the tailboard was no longer needed because the rear of the moulding incorporated mounting points for the registration plate and the Fiat tail lights. Fitting the light assemblies was a simple operation; the GRP body was drilled in the same way as the tailboard had been. The units were then bolted into place and there was no need to alter the supply cables in any way.

To introduce more variety in the lighting units, most manufacturers are now inclined to fit externally sourced lamps to add a more glitzy appearance. Some of the products look notably good although it means that quite a number of redundant Fiat lamp assemblies are then 'going spare'. One supplier who buy's up these virtually unused products for re-sale is Ken Carter at Magnum Mobiles. His company should be noted by self-builders and the products on sale are given a further mention in Chapter 10.

The steel roof of the cab was cut away quite drastically on this professional coachbuilt model.

Cutting away the back of the cab

When you've spent a lot of money on a new base vehicle, the radical cutting work shown here presents a rather daunting prospect. On the other hand, similar procedures are adopted by professional converters even though the purchaser sees a completely different picture when a vehicle reaches a showroom.

The key point to remember is that you must ensure that work is carried out within the guidelines laid down by the base vehicle manufacturer. The accompanying illustrations might suggest that the author adopted a 'gung-ho' approach when cutting out parts of the cab, but that's not really true. Assiduous checking was carried out long before the first cut was made.

Equally, the correct use of bonding adhesives is important since these help to create increased strength when bracing sections are added later. The success of these products is wholly dependent on the builder following the manufacturer's instructions to the letter. For example, surfaces need to be free of surface dirt and you will usually find that chemical cleaners are specially made for the job.

1 From a very early stage an access opening was cut in the rear panel using a jigsaw. Its sharp edges were covered using the reinforced edging strip sold by kit car accessory specialists.

2 It was much later in the conversion when it was decided to open up the rear of the cab. First, the glass panel had to be removed and it took just minutes to extract its rubber surround.

3 Like many DIY builders, I had no access to nibblers and other power tools used in this type of work. So it was necessary to use a hacksaw in order to increase the size of the access opening.

4 Then it was time to extend the window aperture sideways as far as a vertical seam. Again, a hacksaw was used; when it was decided to try a jig saw, the blades bent and snapped.

5 So back to the kit car builders' technique for cutting up donor cars. You merely grind the edge of a bricklayers' bolster until it is really sharp, whereupon it can then cut sheet metal with ease.

6 Bit by bit the cab was opened up to form part of the living space. Along the floor, battens were bonded on either side of the remaining metal lip and coated liberally with Sikaflex-512 Caravan.

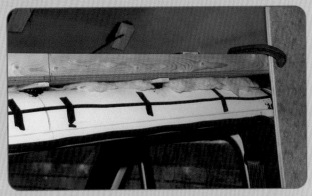

7 Over the cab, battens were bonded on to the roof panel and support a 9mm (3/8in) ply shelf. Plastic laminate-faced Vöhringer 15mm ply was then bonded to the cab on both side flanks.

8 Inevitably the conversion work looks quite crude when cutting a cab, but as work progresses, you can achieve a smart finish. Note how swivelling seats extend the size of the living space.

Cutting away parts of the cab

When it came to cutting away parts of the cab, guidance was checked in the Fiat Auto *Commercial Vehicles: Manual.* Understandably, there are certain elements which must not be touched, such as the seat belt attachments and the mounting pillars.

Of course, there's no problem removing the central wall panel at the rear of the cab; after all, chassis cabs intended for motorhome conversion are often supplied with just a temporary board here as depicted on page 43

It is also useful to look at professionally-built coachbuilt models, many of which seem to have very little left of the cab roof at all. The accompanying photo of a professional conversion reveals how the steel roof panel has been cut very close to the reinforcing cross member above the windscreen.

Bearing in mind that some cab doors have a nasty tendency to flex at the top, which leads to draughts, the author decided not to cut away the roof panel at all. In any case, this coachbuilt features a low-line front and offers insufficient headroom for an over-cab bed. So a cut wasn't made here on the presumption that the more you leave untouched, the better the overall bracing effect of the steel panels.

The rear section did have to be cut away, however, and the accompanying illustrations show how the job was accomplished.

Installing windows

The installation of windows in panel vans was mentioned in the previous chapter and it was also stated that further illustrations would be included here.

One of the interesting features in the Mystique is the fact that there are both safety glass *and* acrylic windows fitted in the living area. This is useful because it shows the reader two different types of installation.

In many ways the procedures shown here are not far removed from the operations involved when fitting windows in a panel van. However, metal panels are consistent in gauge whereas a glass-reinforced plastic laminated body is not only thicker; the thickness will often vary.

Bearing that in mind, let's start with the installation of the safety glass windows that were fitted just to the rear of the cab.

Fitting safety-glass windows in GRP

The prototype body had recesses on either side for two windows of non-standard shapes. However, it was far too costly to have double-glazed plastic 'specials' made to fit these recesses – hence the use of safety glass. This is how the job was done.

Acting on advice, the window was fitted without any weatherproofing sealant just to see if it wouldn't leak in heavy rain. But it did – right at the bottom on both sides. The help of a windscreen specialist was then enlisted and a proprietary sealant was applied. It took two attempts to get it completely right because the thickness of the GRP was not as consistent as it might have been. Since that initial hiccup, the windows have given no further trouble.

Obviously a single-glazed window doesn't have the thermal insulation afforded by double-glazed plastic panels. That's the case in the cab as well. However, Mike Parker of Silver Screens manufactures purpose-made insulated covers for cab screens and side windows. Nowadays he seldom makes 'specials' but in this instance he used the paper patterns to make covers which fit on the inside of these windows using suction pads.

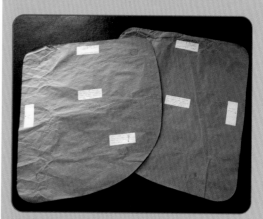

1 Two templates were made as a cutting guide for a glass specialist to use. On jobs like this, you cannot presume that a GRP moulding is identical on both sides – hence the need for two patterns.

2 Using glass for automotive use, an expert cut the pieces freehand. Since the rubber bead had a web section, a second pattern was now drawn to mark a cut-out about 4mm larger all round.

3 The two larger templates were taped to the GRP panel and a cutting line was carefully marked on the GRP body. It is crucial that you don't form a hole that is too large to accommodate the glass.

4 A power jigsaw running at slow speed and fitted with a blade to cut GRP was used to form the aperture. Wear safety eye protection while doing this because chips of plastic often fly into your face.

5 A rubber surround was purchased from a windscreen fitter; the groove on one side had to be wider than usual to fit the GRP panel. The rubbers used on cars and vans have a narrower groove to suit steel panels.

6 A pane of glass can be eased into the rubber groove without difficulty, then a 'key' insert is added to give rigidity. This can be fitted using coat hanger wire but it is easier if a proper tool is used.

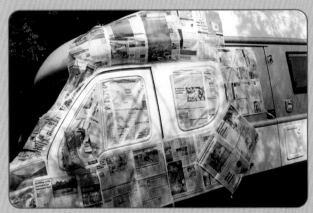

7 Once the window was in place, this area was masked up for painting. The surface was roughened gently and cleaned in readiness to accept satin black paint purchased in an aerosol can.

8 One of the endearing features of this vehicle is the fact that the living area looks as if it has always been part of the cab. The satin black which covers the junction helps to reinforce the illusion.

Fitting Seitz S4 and S5-framed windows

These excellent products employ a clever system of installation as the accompanying photographs show. The inner frame either houses a flyscreen and plastic sheet blind (S4) or a double concertina blind (S5). The concertina blind from Seitz is unusual because its unseen cross-section reveals a box structure which is silvered on the inner faces to achieve a high level of heat insulation. One of these was used in the kitchen of the Mystique

Both the outer and inner frame units of these products interlock so that when the internal screws are tightened, the two sections pull closer together. In effect this creates a firm grip around the prepared apertures. The bond thus achieved is weatherproof and experience has shown that these are the easiest types of double-glazed acrylic windows to fit – irrespective of whether the wall is made of GRP, bonded sandwich sections or the steel panels of a van. The downside is the fact that they are slightly more expensive than non-framed windows.

Normally the exterior plastic frames are finished in black but many manufacturers paint these to match other external body features such as white walls. In the event, it was decided that the standard satin black frames were fine for this particular vehicle. However, the internal frames supplied for the Mystique were cream and this matched neither the washroom sanitary wear nor the general décor in the main living space. So the ventilation holes in the frame were plugged to hide the rollers holding the sun blinds, the plastic was lightly rubbed over, and the frames were sprayed white using cellulose car paint purchased in aerosol cans. The results were excellent and the paint hasn't peeled off.

It is appropriate to point out that these framed windows are intended for mounting on flat walls. However, flat walls are seldom found on moulded shells or on panel vans but the introduction of packing pieces and an application of Sikaflex-512 Caravan enables a careful builder to install Seitz windows on curved surfaces. There are limits, of course, and a high-level window needed for the rear wall of the Mystique had to overcome considerable curvature where it met the rounded roof. It looked a doubtful operation, but ply packing and a generous application of Sikaflex-512 Caravan solved the problem and in four years the window frame has never leaked.

Also important to note is the fact that Seitz windows are sold for installation in walls of 26mm thickness. To fit wall thicknesses of 1–25mm, a supplementary frame has to be mounted around the aperture. For wall thicknesses of 27–42mm, the inner frame has to be trimmed. Lastly, for wall thicknesses of 43–53mm the outer frame has to be fitted with timber strips. These procedures are clearly explained in the installation instructions.

On the sides of the Mystique, the windows were top hung – in other words the hinges are at the top. The main rear window, however, was a fixed unit. It is also possible to purchase sliding windows from Seitz and one of these is often needed where a fully open entrance door would otherwise strike a hinged window left in its open position. The full range of products is of course shown in Seitz's brochures.

In the sequence photographs which follow, the window installation was carried out in conjunction with the insulation of the interior walls and the addition of 3mm vinyl-faced plywood. It stands to reason that you need to be absolutely clear where the windows have to be located. It is no good fitting a window which looks externally attractive but turns out to be far too close to a hob or an internal cupboard.

The manufacturer recommends that the screws fitted around the inner frame are tightened to a particular torque. Not everyone possesses a suitable torque wrench for this and in most instances you can manage without. If you under-tighten and subsequently find that rain creeps in at the head of the frame, the remedy is obvious. On the other hand, if you over tighten the screws you can damage the plastic coupling points in the outer frame. So tighten-up cautiously.

You will also find that there are tight-fitting caps for covering the screw heads and it is best to leave these in the packet until you have had several showers of rain – just in case adjustments are needed. Once inserted, they fit so snugly they're not easy to remove later. You normally have to prise them out using a sharp-bladed screwdriver and inevitably this leaves a mark.

Careful preparation is the keynote of a successful installation. Get that right and you will soon realise that this is a very good product to fit.

1 On this installation a framework was fixed to the GRP surfaces using quick-setting UPol B glass-reinforced car repair paste. Alternatively, Sikaflex-512 Caravan can be used to bond the battens.

2 When softwood frames had been secured, polystyrene block foam insulation was installed between the battens. On curving surfaces, Rockwool was used instead of polystyrene.

3 Once it had been confirmed that the inner frame would sit appropriately within the timbers, small pilot holes were drilled at the four corners of the internal framework.

4 Should it start to rain at this stage of the job, don't worry too much! A 3mm hole can soon be temporarily plugged – and that was often necessary when the weather sprung a surprise.

5 The next stage was to cover the battens with 3mm decoratively faced ply. This was bonded on to the battens using Sikaflex-512 Caravan sealant and left to cure.

6 As long as the internal frame is square at the corners and of the correct size, cutting lines can be confidently drawn on the outside of the wall. But don't forget the adage: 'Measure twice … cut once.'

7 The sole plate of a jigsaw often leaves marks so apply masking tape. Use a blade intended for cutting GRP, set a slow speed, and wear safety goggles when forming the aperture.

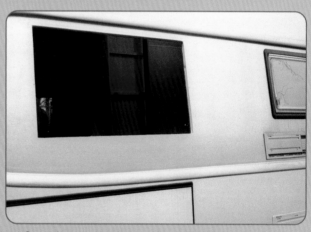

8 Once the aperture is complete, offer up the outer frame to check that it fits. Don't be too concerned if there is a small amount of movement as there are usually adjustments to make.

9 Barbed wood rasps are seldom seen, but are worth purchasing. One of these was used to take off high spots in the GRP, to round off the corners and to remove any wood if needed.

10 Ribbon sealant now had to be applied in the recess around the outer frame in accordance with the installation instructions. Depending on its thickness, several layers are usually needed.

11 Having carried out dummy runs *before* adding the sealant, it is now time to offer up the frame. Some sealants have vicious 'grab' characteristics, so try to position it correctly first time.

12 Moving inside, the inner frame with its blinds and fly screen are mounted next. The screws provided should engage with the holes moulded in the outer frame, but don't over-tighten them.

13 Gentle pressure is now needed all around the frame so that the sealant eventually makes continuous contact. On a flat wall, this is easier to accomplish, and avoid distorting the frame itself.

14 The manufacture asserts that the ribbon sealant and the fitted gasket are sufficient to provide weather protection, but on a curving wall you may want to mask-up and apply some extra sealant.

TRACKING DOWN MATERIALS

Purchasing materials for a self-build project isn't always straightforward and this chapter looks at ways of finding the parts that you need.

With so many well-stocked DIY superstores established in our towns, you'd imagine that getting hold of materials for a motorhome project would be fairly easy. But that is not the case. The problem arises because many of the products used for home improvement work are *not* appropriate for use in motorcaravans.

This usually boils down to the matter of weight. Take veneered chipboard, for example, which is frequently used by DIY enthusiasts. Here's a timber-based product which seldom twists or warps. It is readily available, surprisingly inexpensive, and chipboard panels can be found in cabinets, tables and shelves in our homes. However, this product should not be used in motorcaravans because it is heavy and that is why professional manufacturers use special lightweight plywoods instead.

Many years ago, hardboard was also used by caravan constructors, but that is comparatively heavy as well. In its place, the material used for lining interiors is 3mm faced plywood. The product is shown in the concluding photo sequence of the previous chapter as a lining for an internal wall before the installation of a Seitz S4 window. The material is incredibly light and on one face it carries a decorative finish. Sometimes a plasticised print resembling woodgrain is used; other times it is finished in a light pastel shade appropriate for walls or ceilings. Not surprisingly, it is a product used by virtually every caravan and motorhome manufacturer but you won't find it stocked in your local DIY store.

Looking for product suppliers

Finding the right products can be difficult and searches have to be conducted in many different directions. For example, you will find that some of the products used in boat building and coach conversion can also be used in motorhome projects.

Oddly enough, some motorcaravan manufacturers seem reluctant to pursue alternative supply avenues; others are more thorough in the search for components. Murvi Motorcaravans, for example, came across salt and water-resistant external TV fittings designed for boats that were ideal for installation in their award-winning Morello conversion. In the Auto-Trail 2006 range of coachbuilt motorhomes, domestic door handle assemblies have been fitted instead of the less-sturdy catches more commonly specified. Similarly, AutoCruise CH has recently been fitting brushed stainless steel taps normally only fitted in expensive boats.

It certainly pays to look far and wide for the parts that you want and one of the best ways to start is to attend a range of exhibitions and shows.

Exhibitions and outdoor shows

Exhibitions present more than an opportunity to see finished products like boats, motorcaravans, coaches or cars; they also draw attention to individual components. Here are some events to consider when your project is at its planning stage.

■ **BOAT SHOWS** present an excellent opportunity to see fixtures and fittings that can be used in motorhomes. Of course, keeping a close watch on the weight of accessories isn't such a critical issue when you're building a motorcruiser. There's no doubt too, that the prices of components used in the marine industry are often higher.

That said, there are still many items worth noting. For example, LED internal lights are starting to appear in motorcaravans but they have been fitted in boats for several years. Other products like water pumps, solar panels, chargers, power inverters, bunk bed systems and so on are also worth checking.

These are some of the obvious items; others are rather more subtle. For example, when the author built a Starcraft campervan, considerable time was spent searching for a flexible 'D' section to cover an untidy external join where the GRP roof moulding was bonded to the sides. Eventually, a black rubber moulding was found on sale at a marine suppliers. The trim was sold from the roll and used as a rubbing strip to fit on the gunwales of pleasure boats. In that context it protects the side of vessels that are moored against a quay; on the Starcraft, it effectively covered a join that had been poorly manufactured.

■ **KIT CAR SHOWS** are usually outdoor events and these are attended by a variety of component manufacturers. There's usually hardware on sale like door handles, stainless steel fixings, road lamps, upholstery trims and so on. Here are further examples of products worth noting.

In the previous chapter, reference was made to a flexible 'P'-trim material that's often called wing piping. This was used when the body of the Mystique was coupled to the cab. Then there's the paddle-type door catch used on the Mystique which was also purchased from Europa, a kit car component specialist. So, too, were the marker lamps which are mounted near the roof on the rear wall of the vehicle.

Also bear in mind that the owners of kit cars are usually allowed free entry to these shows. This concession brings them out in force and their parked vehicles are an attraction in themselves.

Accordingly, if you were to visit one of the larger shows, you might see examples of Rickman Rancher and Starcraft self-built campervans. A chat with the owners is often quite revealing.

■ **BUILDING EXHIBITIONS** like Interbuild are normally intended for members of the trade, but there's seldom any check on the credentials of visitors. The truth is that people seeking an entry to these kinds of events *are* likely to be potential purchasers in one way or another.

Perhaps there are fewer products here which have a place in motorcaravan conversion work and the issue of weight was discussed earlier. On the other hand, many of the sealants, adhesives and mastics made by

The door catch with its stainless-steel paddle-flap was purchased from Europa, a kit car component supplier.

manufacturers such as Hodgsons and Sika are used in both the construction of buildings as well as the production of caravans and motorhomes.

Security fittings are worth noting, too, and domestic window bolts can be used to secure doors or external locker lids on motorcaravans.

Owners' cars gain free entry at most kit car shows; look out for Starcraft and Rancher motorhomes and have a chat with the owners.

Using a domestic security bolt

To supplement the locking latch on this entrance door, two domestic security bolts were fitted as well.

Before insulating and lining the door, a hardwood block was bonded to receive the the bolt using UPol B glass-reinforced polyester paste.

Similarly, push-fit plastic plumbing components which appeared in the building industry in the 1960s are now being fitted in more and more motorhomes instead of flexible hose and clips.

Then there are the onerous expectations embraced in Part L of the Building Regulations which focus on the conservation of fuel and power in building. These regulations have led to the manufacture of many types of insulation materials. No surprise, then, to learn that several products principally intended for use in buildings are fitted in motorhomes, too.

■ **BUS, COACH, VAN AND TRUCK EXHIBITIONS** are also trade events intended for commercial vehicle builders. On the other hand, if you purchase a base vehicle and then embark on a major conversion project, many exhibitors will rightly regard you as a bona fide builder.

You will also find that some of the smaller bus and coach converters are willing to undertake projects for independent builders like fitting external lockers. As it turned out, the author built the hatchback door on the back of the Mystique himself but had there been doubts about tackling the job, a bus converter had been lined-up as well.

Then there are component suppliers like those who sell the ribbed, carpet-like material used for headlining and shelf protection in coaches. Many panel van converters purchase this covering fabric, too, and it is illustrated in Chapter 8.

When you look at some of the hardware items used on commercial vehicles, you will note that they are often more sturdy than components typically used on motorcaravans. For instance, the stainless-steel hinges used on the Mystique entrance door might look rather

Stainless-steel heavy-duty hinges for the main door were purchased from Albert Jagger.

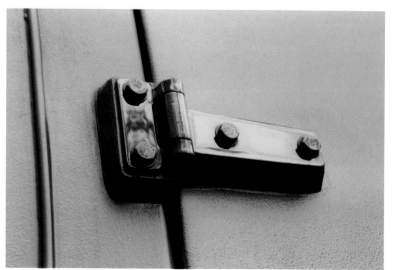

'industrial' – but they will neither rust nor fail prematurely.

Suppliers of commercial-grade mud flaps and items like the orange reflectors mounted along the side skirts of the Mystique were also tracked down at one of these shows.

Also present at this type of exhibition are the manufacturers of the adaptation equipment that is required if a vehicle is going to be used by persons with physical disabilities. Ramps and wheelchair lifts are often on show to converters.

Without doubt, the annual exhibition for bus and truck converters which is normally held at the National Exhibition Centre near Birmingham proved especially useful when the Mystique was in the planning stage.

■ **CARAVAN AND MOTORHOME SHOWS** come in two distinct forms. The indoor exhibitions held during the colder months of the year are where you will see the latest finished products, together with appliances, small components and so on.

Then there are the outdoor shows, many of which are held at venues like agricultural showgrounds. Not only are these useful for meeting owners of motorcaravans who stop overnight, but you will also find smaller accessory suppliers who cannot afford the high cost of stand space at indoor exhibitions. All kind of products are offered for sale at these events – from door catches to cushions.

Products sold at outdoor shows

In fact, it was at a show held at Peterborough Agricultural Showground where a specialist was found who agreed to make an unusual one-off awning to fit the channelling mounted on the lifting tail gate of the Mystique motorhome.

Clearly it is well worth extending your knowledge of products by attending a variety of exhibitions. This is especially true now that many traditional retail shops are disappearing and mail order suppliers are taking their place. Take ships' chandlers, for example. These are treasure troves where you can purchase unusual fixtures and fittings used on boats – many of which are also suitable for motorcaravans. However, if you visit coastal towns, chandlers' shops seem to be in decline, so that's why it's a relief to find that many mail order companies at least show their products at boat exhibitions.

Suppliers of surplus components

When looking at professionally built motorcaravans, remember that most manufacturers have a tradition of frequently changing the models. Whether it is economically wise to relaunch new models every 12 months is a point of debate, but the strategy does mean that components frequently become 'surplus to requirements' every time a production run comes to an end. This long-established practice has led to a lively enterprise in which surplus, end-of-line stock is bought up by specialists.

One of these companies is Magnum Mobiles and Caravan Surplus. The Company even produces van conversions for clients using its own off-the-shelf stock, hence the first part of the name. An example of a Magnum-built interior can be found in the bus conversion described in Chapter 4, although its principal activity is selling end-of-line products.

The owner, Ken Carter, is knowledgeable about caravan and motorhome construction because he used to work at the original Abbey Caravan factory in Grimsby. That was before its acquisition by the Swift Group in Hull. Indeed, Magnum Mobiles still operates from some of the old factory buildings where Abbey caravans used to be made. Today it is an Aladdin's Cave of components and the only problem faced by the author is the fact that it is a long way from home.

It has always been worth the trip, however, and no sooner had the empty shell of the Mystique reached a roadworthy state and a drive to Grimsby was arranged. For instance, you will find there, hundreds of sheets of 3mm ply in dozens of colours.

In addition to these raw materials there are complete caravan/motorhome doors, furniture sections, work tops, cupboard fronts, double-glazed windows and structural items that you might recognise from a number of professionally built products. The fact that the Auto-Trail factory is not far away either is no coincidence and there are other manufacturers just across the Humber Bridge in the Hull region.

MAGNUM'S SURPLUS PRODUCTS BOUGHT FROM MANUFACTURERS

All the decorative 3mm ply panels used to line the Mystique were obtained from this supplier, along with a ladder for the high-level bed, cupboard fronts, and general items of trim. Other builders might want to purchase double-glazed plastic windows, plastic sinks, shower trays, and even items of upholstery. In fact, so much stock is now held in the warehouses, the company doesn't attend outdoor shows like it used to as it would need such a very large lorry!

That's not the case with O'Leary of Beverley.

Above left: You will often find suppliers of small handles and catches attending outdoor shows, but they may not attend larger indoor exhibitions.

Above: End-of-the-run bargain cushions are the kind of products often sold at outdoor motorhome shows.

Below: A huge range of 3mm decoratively faced lightweight plywood is stocked at Magnum Mobiles and Caravan Surplus.

Right: At Magnum Caravan Surplus you will find double-glazed acrylic plastic windows of all sizes . . .

Far right: . . . standard-size caravan and coachbuilt motorhome doors . . .

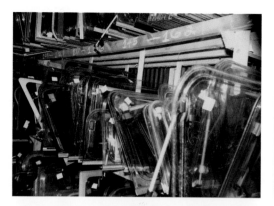

Right: . . . sinks and washbasins in a variety of materials, and . . .

Far right: . . . wooden cupboard door frames awaiting a plywood insert.

Surplus cabinet components are sometimes sold on the O'Leary stand at outdoor shows.

This is another supplier of new parts purchased directly from manufacturers and the company often has a covered space at outdoor shows to display a selection of products.

Of course, if you're refurbishing an existing model you might not find matching parts as quickly as you want. That's when a breakers might be a better place for components.

Caravan and motorhome breakers

While the surplus products sold by Magnum Mobile and O'Leary are new, components sold by breakers have of course already been used. On the other hand, they haven't always been *heavily* used.

For example, it is not unusual to see a caravan breaker dismantling a 'van less than a year old. It only takes a severe rear-end shunt to render a new caravan a write-off in insurance terms. The fact that its refrigerator is only a few month's old and undamaged doesn't help the case if it is uneconomic to rebuild the structure as a whole. That is why you will sometimes find fairly new fridges, cookers, and heaters offered for sale in a breaker's shop.

Members of the Caravan Club can obtain a free address list of caravan and motorhome breakers in the United Kingdom. However, it is not a long list. Even though the National Caravan Council has reported that over 500,000 caravans are in 'regular active use', and the '. . . useful life of a touring caravan is approximately 14 years', it is a matter of considerable intrigue to know where they all go when they reach the end of the road. Similar information regarding motorcaravans is less forthcoming. Either way, you won't stumble across many caravan breakers as you travel around this country.

However, one place where you will find a large breaker's yard with an accompanying accessory shop is near Pontypool in South Wales. The Caravan Centre, as it is known,

Far left: It is not only worn-out caravans which reach a breakers' yard; some much newer 'vans get scrapped after serious accidents.

Left: Low-voltage electrical distribution panels are often rescued and resold in the Caravan Centre's accessory shop.

Far left: If a washbasin is still in sound condition, this is another item that gets offered for sale – and it might have a tap still in place.

Left: Using products taken from dismantled caravans, staff at the Caravan Centre quite often build a van conversion.

dismantles many hundreds of caravans and motorhomes every year. Reusable parts are offered for sale and the company has even started a separate division in which it builds the occasional campervan using recycled parts.

THE CARAVAN CENTRE: SPECIALIST BREAKERS

Also interesting is the fact that the Caravan Centre is now preparing packages of products to sell to DIY motorcaravan converters. Don't forget that in many instances, the appliances and materials used in caravans are no different from the products used in motorhomes. That was brought home in the case history conversion of the Renault Trafic described and illustrated in Chapter 7. The only difference in that particular project was the fact that the builders dismantled their own caravan as opposed to buying the parts from a breaker.

It stands to reason, of course, that items sold by a breaking specialist are usually 'sold as seen'. Moreover, you'd be very unwise to re-install a safety-critical appliance like a cooker or a space heater without getting it serviced and recommissioned by a specialist qualified to work on LPG appliances used in leisure vehicles.

As long as you accept that caveat, there's plenty of potential for a practical person to use pre-owned and refurbished products, especially when building on a budget.

Structural plywood

Notwithstanding the usefulness of second-hand items, there are times when new products are needed. That's the case when you want structural plywood.

Since veneered chipboard is considered too heavy for use in motorcaravans, many manufacturers use a German product called Vöhringer plywood; the UK importing agency is given in the Appendix address list. The company doesn't sell direct to individual builders but provides enquirers with the addresses of their nearest dealer, some of which will send you off-cuts to show examples of different colours of laminates.

In the Mystique project, Vöhringer 15mm plywood faced on both sides was used extensively. For example, it was used to frame

A panel of Vöhringer 15mm plywood was fitted with an edging strip and mounted on a Zwaardvis base to make a table.

Some manufacturers use Vöhringer 15mm plywood for locker doors; there are plenty of available colours. Flexible edging trims are sold by specialists like Woolies.

the opened rear panel of the cab as shown in the previous chapter. It was used to form a structural support for the high-level double bed and for the table tops mounted on Zwaardvis support pillars.

Many converters also fit plastic edging surround supplied by specialists like Woolies so that the ply can be used to make locker doors. This is certainly a product to keep in mind.

Web-based suppliers

Not surprisingly, some suppliers of appliances and parts are now operating as web-based companies. This method of purchasing components will undoubtedly grow at a considerable pace. Two specialists often quoted are:

www.caravanparts.net
www.worldofmotorhomes.com

Noteworthy catalogues

To complete this summary of contacts, the following suppliers publish informative catalogues and operate a mail order service. (Addresses in the Appendix; they also have web sites.)

■ **ALBERT JAGGER LTD** supplies products to commercial vehicle converters and the catalogue lists thousands of items including rugged road-light assemblies, truck-grade mud flaps, heavy-grade hinges and virtually every component used on commercial vehicles. It is also a supplier of Centaflex nylon flexible hinges which are drilled and mounted along the top-hung external locker lids fitted on many buses and coaches. Centaflex was used to suspend the GRP locker door built for the Mystique and Albert Jagger supplied handles, locks and stainless steel hinges for the hatchback door.

■ **CARAVAN ACCESSORIES KENILWORTH (CAK)** manufactures a huge range of water tanks which are used throughout the

motorhome industry, with 174 different-shaped tanks listed in the latest catalogue. Two of these were purchased for the Mystique and connections were specially mounted on the bespoke tanks. The company used to be known mainly for its water supply products but now the annual catalogue includes most items used in caravans and motorhomes – from air conditioners to ventilators. The company attends just one show a year, namely the National Boat, Caravan and Leisure Show held in February at the National Exhibition Centre near Birmingham.

■ **EUROPA SPECIALIST SPARES** is well-known by classic and kit car enthusiasts. Again, there's an extraordinary and colourful catalogue, most of which includes items like seat belts, rally seats, fascia instruments as opposed to motorhome components. However, the quality door catches, locks, road lights, battery cut-off switches and other electrical goods should be noted. The paddle-type latch on the Mystique entrance door was purchased from Europa.

■ **HÄFELE** publishes the biggest catalogue of all. The *Complete Häfele of Furniture and Hardware Fittings* (2001/02 edition) contained 1,150 pages, weighed 3kg and was 50mm thick – and that is only one of several Häfele publications! These catalogues are still being published although the incredible stock lists are also presented on a CD. This is a trade only supplier and you need to find your nearest retailer by phoning the headquarters. Moreover, many of the small-scale motorhome converters hold an account with Häfele and can order the products you want. The push-button catches you've seen on motorhome lockers, drawer units, wire blanket boxes and cabinet hinges of any type can normally be obtained from a Häfele dealer.

Tracing unusual fittings

■ **JUST CAMPERS** runs a mail order supply of camping and leisure accessories, but the

Above: Centaflex nylon flexible hinge supplied by Albert Jagger Ltd was used for a top-hung external locker lid – just like it is on coaches.

Right: When attending the exhibition at the NEC each year, CAK displays dozens of components on presentation boards.

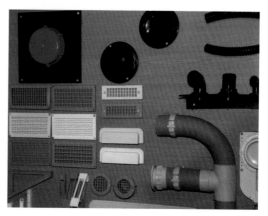

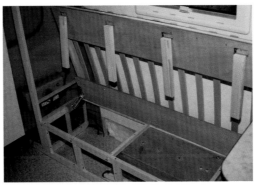

Far left: Furniture components like this spring-loaded hinge can usually be ordered through a Häfele supplier.

Left: This Häfele hinge allowed a single-bed in the Mystique project to be held open while items were stowed in the locker below.

company's particular strength is the supply of parts and accessories for 1968–2003 VW Campers and Transporters. Body panels, brake components, exchange engines, piston sets, and badges are just a few of the items in this impressive line-up of products. It's an essential sourcebook for anyone renovating a VW campervan.

■ **REIMO** is a German company whose products can be ordered through two UK specialists. Apart from Reimo's larger publication which lists an extensive range of camping/accessories, a smaller Reimo catalogue gives details of pre-assembled furniture kits to suit a wide range of vans. Seat assemblies, floor coverings, high-top roofs, elevating roofs, insulation materials and furniture components are all included here. Using the appropriate kit for a particular van should be a great help for anyone wanting a modular approach to conversion work. Detailed line drawings show each of the layouts.

■ **RoadPro** is an electrical accessory supplier which sources appliances from many countries and from the automotive, marine, motorhome and narrow boat industries. Sophisticated battery chargers, power inverters, satellite TV products and many other items fill an interesting catalogue. There are also explanatory articles about how to choose the products you need.

■ **WOODFIT** has operated a mail order supply service of DIY furniture components for several decades. There's a showroom at the headquarters near Chorley and the annual catalogue is well-illustrated. Kitchen products are especially prominent although the company also supplies items like bed slat suspension products.

All the drawer runners in the Mystique were purchased from Woodfit and these act like the systems on filing cabinets. So, too, was a self-assembly steel-sided drawer which supports the waste bin shown in Chapter 15. The drawers fitted to carry tinned food and drinks

can be disconnected from the runners and carried into the house for loading/unloading.

■ **WOOLIES** supplies trim and upholstery to classic, kit, and vintage car enthusiasts. The illustrated catalogue includes things like snap-on edge trims to protect sharp steel edges, draught excluders for doors, wing piping, headlining, vinyls and leather cloth. Also supplied are rubber surrounds of the type shown in Chapter 9 which was used for mounting a safety glass window in a GRP bodyshell. The company has been running for over 25 years and attends many vehicle shows – although most people make purchases using the mail order service.

This list does not claim to be complete although every company with the exception of Reimo has supplied the author with products for various car and motorhome building projects. Using the companies' addresses in the Appendix, it is suggested you get copies of the catalogues as a useful starting point. Alternatively, visit their web sites.

Some items supplied by Woodfit

In the kitchen section of the Woodfit catalogue you will find moulded cutlery trays that are designed to drop into drawers.

Offering comfort and ventilation, cambered hardwood bed slats are obtainable using the Woodfit mail order service.

EXTERNAL WORK ON THE BODY

Installing ventilators, fitting a roof window, adding a locker door, and the application of graphic embellishments are tasks that you may want to tackle yourself.

Reference has been made in earlier chapters to different types of body structures. In Chapter 1, a series of illustrations showed a coachbuilt model under construction using prefabricated, sandwich-bonded sides and roof sections. Chapter 8 focussed on panel van conversions and Chapter 9 showed a GRP monocoque shell being mounted on a chassis.

Whatever body type is preferred, holes will have to be cut in the sides and the roof. In the previous two chapters, for example, photo sequences showed windows being fitted. During those operations, sealants were used to ensure the installations were weathertight.

The aim here is to look at sealants in more detail. Having done that, photographic sequences show further components being mounted on the walls and roof.

Finally, attention turns to external embellishments. Nowadays, the term graphics is used for cosmetic additions like stripes, decals and badges; these add an attractive finish to a bare and featureless body.

Sealants

When any kind of fitment is mounted on a motorcaravan's body, the installation has got to be rainproof. That's where sealants play an important part. Unfortunately, the term sealant is imprecise. For example, a product used to seal around a wash basin is unlikely to be much use on external fittings exposed to the wind and the rain. Hence, there are different sealants for different jobs and the list opposite shows some of the products used by motorhome builders.

NOTES:

■ This isn't a comprehensive list by any means and it only refers to products that the author has used for repairs and conversions. Most of these manufacturers sell many other products, too. Sika, for example, manufactures a wide range of sealants for different applications. Carafax also supplies ribbon-type sealants in various colours and widths, but unlike the company's cartridge products, these are normally only sold to caravan and motorhome manufacturers.

■ To be effective, a sealant is dependent on the joining surfaces being clean and you will find that specially formulated cleaners are usually sold for that purpose. Similarly there may be hand cleaners and safety warnings about contact with human tissue.

■ Products from different manufacturers will often have different working characteristics.

Technical Note

SETTING TIMES
Whereas mastic-type sealants are described as non-setting products, sealants such as Sikaflex-512 Caravan and Sikaflex-252 have adhesive properties and have to be left to cure for several hours.

The setting period might hold up production, and that is why some builders apply Sikaflex-512 Caravan but cover a small part of the bonding surfaces with adhesive delivered from a hot-melt glue gun. This dries very quickly and although it doesn't achieve a notable bond, it usually holds an item in place while the Sikaflex is setting.

Other constructers use temporary screws or duct tape to hold Sikaflex-coated components in register. That's a common strategy, especially when an awning rail or trim strip is being reinstated using adhesive sealant instead of mastic and screws.

■ SILICONE SEALANT

Example: Dow Corning 785 Sanitary Acetoxy mildew-resistant silicone sealant.

Purpose: Sealing sanitary wear like shower trays, wash basins and non-porous surfaces.

Form: Cartridge (310ml) to fit standard DIY dispenser gun.

Available from: Builders' merchants.

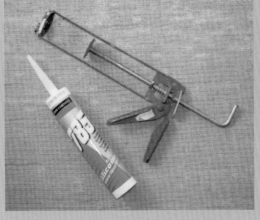

Sold in several colours, silicone sealant is mainly used for sealing around sanitary ware like shower trays or wash basins.

■ BEDDING SEALANT

Example: Carafax Caraseal IDL 99 non-drying bedding sealant.

Purpose: To provide a flexible bedding layer on which to mount external fittings like ventilators, awning rails, and trim strips.

Form: Cartridge to fit standard DIY dispenser gun.

Available from: Caravan accessory shops.

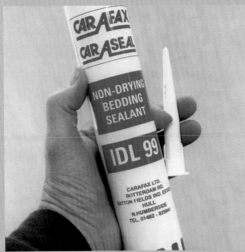

A non-drying bedding sealant is used to weatherproof components which might need to be removed from the body at some future point.

■ ADHESIVE SEALANT

Example: Sikaflex-512 Caravan, Technique adhesive sealant systems.

Purpose: For creating permanent bonds between dissimilar materials which attain a high level of adhesion and a barrier to the passage of moisture.

Form: Cartridge to fit standard DIY dispenser guns.

Available from: Automotive specialists and selected caravan accessory suppliers – addresses from Sika Ltd.

Sikaflex-512 Caravan sealant is used here to seal a lamp fitting, but its adhesive properties also commend it for bonding body panels.

■ RIBBON-TYPE BEDDING SEALANT

Example: W4 mastic sealing strip.

Purpose: For the sealing and re-bedding of caravan and motorhome fittings.

Form: Sold in 5m (approx.) rolls with a non-stick backing paper.

Available from: Caravan and motorhome accessory shops.

A non-setting sealant sold in ribbon form is sometimes easier to position than a similar product applied from a cartridge gun.

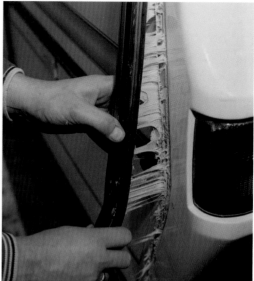

Above: Ribbon sealants are produced in various colours, widths and thicknesses but these are usually only sold direct to manufacturers.

Above right: Cartridge-applied non-setting bedding sealants often have good 'grab' characteristics – but they allow a component to be removed.

For example, some of the ribbon sealants from Carafax have impressive 'grab characteristics' and adhere well to adjoining contact surfaces. That's fine, except when you need to make a slight adjustment when positioning a new component. The same thing happens with many cartridge-dispensed sealants. In contrast, the Mastic Sealing Strip from W4 has much less 'grab' – which is useful if you want to remove a component or readjust its position.

■ The matter of removal is also important when considering an adhesive sealant such as Sikaflex-512 Caravan. Once this has been applied, a component derives some bonding with a surface after three or four hours. However, it takes at least 24 hours to accomplish full strength. Thereafter, the removal of a product can be extremely difficult. Some people use a special cutting wire, but breaking a join is seldom easy – and it shouldn't be. Adhesive sealant is used for jobs like bonding a high-top GRP roof moulding to a

metal panelled van; you wouldn't want the roof becoming detached without a fight.

■ An adhesive sealant will create a bond without any need for mechanical fixings like screws or bolts. That's noteworthy because anything held in place with a screw is going to offer a potential leak point in the future. Even though a mastic product used for bedding the awning rail shown above has good grab characteristics, screws are also required. What is more, mastic like this eventually start to dry, then the material cracks, and eventually it falls away. That's when rain finds a way into the structure, tracking a course through the numerous screw holes.

Polyester-based repair pastes

When a component has to be fitted quickly, you can use a product such as Upol B (also marketed by the same manufacturer as Davids Isopon P40). This is used in car repair work and consists of a polyester paste which contains glass strands to afford improved bonding strength.

As long as the joining surfaces are suitably roughened, this car repair product will bond a variety of materials. It was used, for example, to bond a hardwood block to the roughened side of the Mystique door when a security bolt was fitted. This is shown in Chapter 10.

The accompanying panel shows the product in use.

Davids Isopon P40 consists of a polyester paste reinforced with glass strands and a catalyst or hardener.

Making an aperture in a sandwich-bonded panel

In this project, a Thetford Cassette toilet door was being fitted into a caravan that had been built in a conventional manner using sandwich bonded walls. First, the hole was cut with an electric jigsaw. (Templates are supplied with the product.)

When the panel had been removed, an old chisel was used to chip away polystyrene insulation all around the aperture. You only need to remove it to a depth of 25mm because the small recess you're creating will be filled with four softwood battens of appropriate size. These will be inserted around the aperture

a) To add strength, and
b) to provide something for the screws to grip when securing the frame.

The timber inserts were liberally coated with woodworking adhesive to bond against the inner lining ply. Small G-cramps held them in place while the adhesive was setting. Of course, the aluminium outer skin gets fastened to the battens when the door frame is screwed into place.

This opening was cut in a sandwich-construction bonded wall to accept a cassette toilet door; a wood frame was fitted next.

Woodworking adhesive was used to bond wooden frame members to the interior facing plywood; G-cramps held it in place.

Installing a Remis roof window

Many professionally built motorcaravans are fitted with a large roof light and Heki rectangular models are especially popular. Heki roof lights are manufactured by Seitz whose framed windows are featured in the installation photographs shown in Chapter 9.

Like S4 Seitz windows, the outer framework containing the acrylic window is firmly coupled to the inner frame using purpose-made screws. Their clamping action achieves a firm grasp on both sides of the roof panel. However, this installation demands that the roof construction has a consistent thickness.

When the Mystique was built, it was acknowledged that it would be impracticable to replicate the curvaceous and shapely roof when constructing the ceiling inside. A similar challenge faced builders of the Sydney opera house where a false ceiling was duly built instead.

Of course, the ceiling boards in the Mystique still follow the main angle of the roof line but not its curvaceous form. Moreover, the void between the outer roof and the inner ceiling varies in depth and that's why a Heki roof window wasn't suitable.

Fortunately there are roof lights manufactured by Remis in which the outer and inner units can be fitted independently. Moreover, the prototype Mystique moulding featured a flat mounting area on the roof intended to accept a square-shaped roof light – and some of the Remi tops are square.

So a Remi top was fitted as shown in the photographs here.

Note: There are several types of Remis roof windows available including electrically operated units. The one fitted here had manual operation and its square dimension was better-suited to the roof of the Mystique.

To cover the gap created by the irregular void above the ceiling, some white plastic trim was used. This was found discarded in a skip after PVCu windows had been installed in a nearby house. It was cut to length, trimmed, bonded to both frames using white Sikaflex adhesive sealant and the result is most pleasing.

Several types of white, plastic boards are now on sale at builders' merchants. But be careful; some of the plastics don't bond with Sikaflex sealant, in which case, you might trim the sides using 3mm ceiling plywood instead.

1 Using the window frame as a template, a cutting line was marked; then the corners were drilled through the ceiling board.

2 The aperture location was confirmed inside, the sole of the jigsaw was covered with tape, and then the cutting commenced.

3 As long as a jigsaw is running at a slow speed and the correct blade has been fitted, an aperture like this is easily formed in GRP.

4 With its protective covering still in place, the outer frame of the Remi top roof window was offered-up to check that it fitted.

5 Ribbon sealant is preferred here. When placed on the frame's flange and around the aperture, you get consistent thickness.

6 Clips are provided to anchor the outer window framework to the roof. Tightening them pulls the frame deep into the bed of sealant.

7 To be certain of a weather-tight installation, masking tape was applied and adhesive sealant was added round the edges.

8 From inside you will note the changing depth of the void over the ceiling. This was covered using 100mm wide plastic boarding from a double glazing job.

9 The inner frame is wired-up for low-wattage ceiling lights and supply cables had previously been laid in the ceiling void.

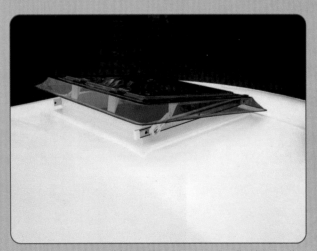

10 From the outside the Remi top can be tilted as well as slid fully open; the sliding mechanism forms part of the outer frame.

Hatchback opening

Few builders are likely to want to create a large hatchback door like the one built on the author's motorhome so the details which follow are brief. Forming a large door like this is challenging, especially in a GRP moulding. For example, if you were to cut a large opening, then line the inside of the cut-out section, create flanges around its perimeter, and then offer it up again, you could find it no longer fits because the aperture has distorted.

Knowing about this problem, cutting lines were marked in pencil on the outside and 2mm holes were then drilled at 150mm (6in) intervals along the proposed cutting line. This meant that the proposed cutting line could be identified from the inside as well.

Four stainless-steel heavy-duty hinges were also fitted to the top even though the cutting wouldn't be undertaken until several weeks later. The attention then moved inside – adding insulation, installing a Seitz window, constructing support frameworks on the intended door *and* around the intended aperture. Bonding a framework inside, adding a 3mm ply skin, and building GRP door surrounds had the effect of 'locking' the entire rear wall into a shape that wouldn't distort when the cutting commenced.

To brace its shape the framework and side flanges of this hatchback door were constructed internally before cutting the body.

Fitting a Dometic fridge vent in a GRP bodyshell

If you decide to install a Dometic or Thetford absorption refrigerator, external ventilators will have to be fitted.

On the Mystique project the upper vent had been sprayed silver using cellulose automotive paint. The vent's plastic surface was roughened, the paint was applied, and several seasons later, its appearance is still very pleasing.

Creating an aperture for this type of ventilator is much the same on a panel van as it is when working on a GRP body. In both instances, make sure there are no obstructions inside. Although a jigsaw forming a cut-out in a steel panel would be fitted with a fine-toothed blade, cutting work in GRP calls for a purpose-designed blade with slightly coarser teeth.

As always, safety procedures must be followed and approved eye protection should be worn. The job is shown with stage-by-stage photographs.

NOTES:

If fitting a vent like this in a panel van, the four lengths of softwood forming a frame around the aperture would be bonded inside using an adhesive sealant such as Sikaflex-512 Caravan.

When fitting small ventilators in prefabricated bonded sandwich panels, many manufacturers don't bother with a frame. Arguably, you hardly need to strengthen an aperture intended to house a vent the size of a pack of playing cards. On the other hand, wooden battens afford better anchorage when a ventilator's held in place with screws.

1 Having checked the interior for obstructions and with the fridge location finalised, the vent is used to mark the cutting line.

2 The sole plate of a jig saw can often leave marks on a painted surface, so layers of masking tape were applied with care.

3 After removing the GRP panel, the polystyrene insulation below the skin and the 3mm ply inside were both cut away.

4 Softwood battens coated with Davids Isopon P40 were inserted around the cut-out and held in place with G-cramps.

5 To ensure the timber frame around the aperture was totally secure, several wood screws were driven home as well.

6 Any high spots around the opening were removed using a barbed wood rasp; this trims both the GRP panel and the ply inside.

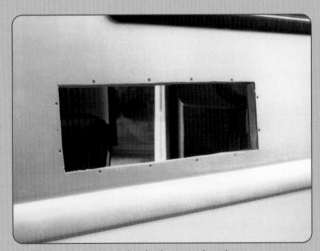

7 The aperture was checked to see that the corners were squared off and the ventilator was offered-up to confirm it fitted.

8 Before making the final installation, each flange around the ventilator's frame was covered with black ribbon sealant.

Silver panels here were being sprayed by a paint specialist. When using modern paints, protective breathing equipment is essential.

When a jigsaw was finally brought into use, both the door and its aperture remained rigid. All that remained was to fit security catches, add some gas struts and mount an aluminium rain-diffusing gutter above the opening. This hatchback has proved to be extremely useful, although it construction extended over three months.

Painting bodywork

The graphics fitted on many professionally manufactured UK motorhomes are initially created on this computer at Graphicraft.

If you have painted kit cars with GRP bodies, you will know it takes ages to get a dry, wind-free day. Accordingly the silver panels on the Mystique were finished indoors by a specialist. Moreover, many modern automotive paints contain quantities of cyanide and having the correct breathing apparatus is critically important.

Thus, I merely painted all the satin black sections using aerosol cans: a professional car repairer did the rest.

Applying graphics

Many towns have sign-writing specialists who create bespoke graphics which are supplied on adhesive-backed vinyl. Ideas are created on a computer and subsequently transferred electronically to machines which cut the vinyl to size.

On the earlier Starcraft campervan, I purchased pre-printed stripes from a car accessory shop and applied them with reasonable success. However, on the Mystique something more elaborate seemed justified. So I drew up a design, took photographs of the vehicle, added detailed dimensions and sought the help of a graphics specialist.

When the designs reached the vinyl stage, their application was carried out in a couple of hours. The installer had spent the morning applying orange graphics on an EasyJet airliner at Luton Airport so a motorhome must have seemed quite easy.

These are the techniques involved:
- The vehicle has to be scrupulously clean.
- All the larger stripes and fade-in relief patterns were temporarily positioned using masking tape.
- The graphics where studied by eye and their effect was checked from all angles.
- When everything seemed right, small tags of masking tape were placed along the edges and at corners to confirm the final location.
- When a backing sheet was removed, the vehicle body and the sticky side of the graphic were sprayed with a mist of water from an atomising bottle used for house plants. Water retards adhesion and allows you to shift a graphic around.
- Later, you go over the surface with a squeegee tool to force out the water and that's when adhesion takes place.
- Air bubbles are forced out with the squeegee, too, and you only prick them with a pin as a last resort.
- The face-covering paper is then removed to reveal an emergent graphic.
- Lastly, any special nameplates are located and fixed. Many kinds of lettering, size and colours are on offer and the names shown here are raised slightly proud of the surface.

Far left: A mist of water applied from an atomiser normally used for watering house plants allows a graphic to be slid into place.

Left: When the position of a design is exactly right, a squeegee tool is used to expel all the water, whereupon the adhesive takes its grip.

Far left: Throughout the handling and positioning stages, a graphic has protective face paper as well as an adhesive backing paper.

Left: Name plates can be created in all types of lettering and colours. This one had a raised finish and was created on a computer.

Technical Note

APPLYING LONG STRIPS OF VINYL

On long graphics such as wide stripe designs, a technique is adopted in which the product is applied in two stages. First, the strip is temporarily taped in place adding tags to confirm its location; then a vertical strip of masking tape is applied on the face paper across the middle of the whole section. This vertical piece of masking tape acts like a hinge so that either the front or rear section of the long graphic can be hinged away from the body.

Now the operative tackles each section separately. One section is lifted forward on the paper hinge, the body panel is sprayed with water, the backing paper is removed as far as the hinge, then it is torn off at that point, and the vinyl is sprayed as well. This prepared section is then fixed into place on the body.

The paper hinge is then slightly repositioned so that the procedure can be repeated on the remaining half of the graphic.

At the mid point of a long graphic, a vertical piece of masking tape allows it to hinge away from the body so it can be applied in two stages.

Bespoke graphic designing is not a cheap service. On the other hand, it's like the icing on a cake; the results can be really stunning.

12 INSULATING A MOTORCARAVAN

Whatever type of motorcaravan you decide to build, installing thermal insulation is a job which has to be done.

This chapter is concerned with thermal insulation, which has three functions:

1. It helps to reduce heat loss from the interior during cold weather, thereby enhancing the fuel efficiency of space heating appliances.
2. It helps reduce the likelihood of an interior getting unbearably hot when a vehicle is parked in sunshine.
3. It plays an important part in reducing the amount of condensation forming inside.

Not surprisingly, most thermal insulants are not the same as acoustic insulation products. On the other hand, they usually play *some* part in reducing the noise of passing traffic, a neighbour's petrol generator or a noisy nightclub on a holiday site.

However, noise reduction is certainly a feature of a product called Thinsulant™ acoustic insulation from 3M which is now being used by several campervan manufacturers. It is more expensive than the thermal insulation products traditionally used by van converters but its ability to reduce the passage of both heat *and* sound is certainly a bonus. It is also more pleasant to handle than many other synthetic wool products. Converters now using Thinsulant™ include Auto-Sleepers, Devon Conversions, and Middlesex Motorcaravans.

It is also interesting to note that the thermal benefits of Thinsulant™ have been recognised in the outdoor clothing industry. For instance, it has been used for a number of years in the manufacture of skiing gloves and winter mountaineering jackets.

In contrast, most flexible and rigid insulating materials are from the building industry and can be purchased from builders' merchants and DIY stores. If you want to use Thinsulant™, you can purchase the product from van converters such as Middlesex Motorcaravans.

Either way, fitting an insulation layer is important – as anyone who has slept in the back of an unconverted van would confirm. It doesn't take long before condensation starts streaming down the inside of the bare-metal vehicle.

Condensation

To understand the subject of condensation, it is necessary to be aware of the creation of vapour.

In the living area of a motorcaravan, exposed gas flames on a hob, a steaming kettle, hot water in a sink, and humans doing what humans do – breathing – all lead to vapour creation. Furthermore, the warmer the air, the more vapour it is able to hold.

In a motorcaravan, as soon as vapour-laden air comes into contact with a cold surface, e.g. windscreen glass, its temperature falls, its vapour condenses and water droplets then start to form.

To clear a windscreen when driving, we switch on the vehicle's demister which sends warm air across the glass. This passage of air soon clears a misting window – at least while the blower is running.

Of course, when a motorcaravan is parked and its screen demister isn't operating, single-glazed cab windows soon become coated in condensation when it's cold. That's why a lot of owners fit insulated covers, some of which fit inside or outside the cab windows. The range of insulated silver covers from Silverscreens is particularly well-known and much-liked.

In the living area, however, double-glazed plastic windows are less likely to get misted up because the inner pane of a double-glazed plastic window isn't in direct contact with colder air outside. That is why wall and roof panels need insulating to achieve a similar effect.

Not surprisingly, the bonded sandwich panels of a coachbuilt are very unlikely to present a cold surface inside a living area. That's not the case in models constructed using a moulded GRP shell. A GRP panel certainly does get cold inside and that is why *all* its internal surfaces have to be insulated. One of the ways to do this, using expanded polystyrene boards, was shown in Chapter 9.

A bigger challenge faces van converters because metal panels conduct hot or cold outside temperatures with great efficiency. Flat panels are easy to cover but it is harder to insulate a van's structural frame members. These create what is known in the building industry as a 'cold bridge'.

Cold bridges and condensation

Any metal structure which has an unbroken structure between the outside air and the inside living space produces a cold bridge. For example, the aluminium-frames of patio doors fitted in houses twenty or so years ago stream with condensation on the inside during cold weather. Aluminium-framed caravan and motorhome doors are built in the same way and condensation similarly forms inside.

On account of this, regulations applicable in the building industry now require what is known as a thermal break or barrier. This necessitates fitting an insulation material within the structure of a metal door or window frame so that its external sections don't have direct contact with sections on the inside. In new houses, there's even a thermal break constructed around window openings so that bricks on the outside wall are not directly connected to those forming the inner walls.

The provision of a thermal break prevents damp patches appearing inside a building and also helps to reduce heat loss. At the time of writing, these requirements do not apply to motorhome builders or the manufacturers of components like external doors. Nor, for that matter, is it current practice to augment an insulation envelope by the addition of a vapour barrier.

Vapour barriers

Unfortunately, vapour-laden air is able to seep through gaps in a lining board, thereby reaching cold surfaces where condensation starts to form undetected. To prevent this, a vapour barrier is sometimes installed. In the construction industry, a continuous sheet of heavy duty polythene or a special plasterboard backed with a foil is often used.

Some DIY motorhome builders have written to magazines to enquire if a vapour barrier needs to be fitted before lining ply is installed on the walls and ceiling of a motorhome. Without

doubt a barrier helps reduce the formation of condensation on unseen surfaces and the development of what is known as interstitial condensation. This develops deep in the fibres of timber and hastens their demise. But the fact of the matter is that in motorcaravan construction, vapour barriers are omitted. Perhaps they will appear in the future.

For the present, you are faced with two issues:
1. Choosing insulation materials.
2. Installing the chosen products.

INSULATION MATERIALS COMPARED
Three main types of insulation are used in motorcaravan construction:
1. **Rigid panels such as expanded polystyrene (EPS) and Styrafoam**
The former is available from builders' merchants; the latter can sometimes be supplied by motorhome service and repair centres.
2. **Flexible synthetic wool**
There's both the type of flexible quilt typically used for loft insulation, and Thinsulant™ which is a polyester and polypropylene 'blown microfibre' that doesn't absorb water.
3. **Semi-flexible panels**
These products are often used to insulate cavities in brickwork.

NOTES:
■ Granular insulation like Vermiculite used in loft insulation and the insulation of household flues seems not to be used in motorhomes
■ It is believed that some German manufacturers inject foam into wall voids but their procedures and products are seldom revealed.
■ Spray-on foam used to insulate the underside of roof tiles and slates can also be used in van conversions. However, only one DIY van converter known to the author has adopted this approach – albeit to the builder's satisfaction.

The cab windows can be insulated using Silver Screens and several variations are available, including products for different vehicles.

Rigid panels

It is most unlikely that a self-builder would be able to purchase bonded composite panels with insulation in the core. These are normally manufactured by professional caravan and motorhome builders solely for their own use. Accordingly, rigid panel insulation has to be laid 'loose' rather than bonded, but not in such a way that it can move about. Expanded polystyrene tends to make squeaking noises when it chafes; abrading Styrafoam tends to grind into dust.

On flat surfaces these are both good products as long as they aren't subjected to flexion. Bend a panel and it snaps like a cheese biscuit. However, cutting is easy – just use an old hand saw.

Styrafoam has a tight closed cell structure and boards 35mm thick are commonly used for insulating floors. For walls, most manufacturers use 25mm expanded polystyrene although Auto-Trail is an exception. This company's models have a higher level of insulation which appeals to winter users and polystyrene in Auto-Trail's wall panels is 35mm thick.

Semi-flexible insulation panels are sold in packs rather than rolls; used in cavity walls, these are sold by builders' merchants.

The use of Styrafoam to insulate a floor is shown in the panel alongside.

Flexible and semi-flexible quilts

Where you have to insulate zones of irregular shape, varying thickness and with curving profiles, a flexible product has to be used. Before the advent of bonded construction, 'Fibre Glass' roof insulation was used in motorcaravan wall voids but it tends to slump down over time. If you're renovating an older model, the upper section of the walls may have lost some of the cavity fill through slumping and that leaves cold spots.

Flexible quilt insulation is sold in rolls and is often laid between the ceiling joists in a loft. However, a variation on this type of product is now made for filling cavity walls and that has greater rigidity to overcome the slumping problem. This is usually sold in packs at builders' merchants as shown alongside.

Since there are few flat walls in a panel van, flexible or semi-flexible quilt material is the obvious choice. The accompanying photo sequence shows Thinsulant™ being installed in a van conversion being carried out by Middlesex Motorcaravans. These photographs were kindly loaned by *Motor Caravan Magazine* (IPC Media).

In the Mystique project, flexible loft insulation purchased from a DIY store was also used for the entrance door; that's because it has variable depths and a curving profile. The building stages are shown in the panel alongside.

Flexible insulation was also used in the roof of the Mystique project. The accompanying sequence shows how a false ceiling was created in order to smooth out the pronounced curves of the roof. That's because the later application of 3mm ceiling ply would be exceedingly difficult if it had to be bent in two planes. Accordingly, struts were created with a gentle curvature in *one* plane as the sequence photographs show. Of course, cable runs for roof lights were installed before fitting the ceiling ply.

Note: Ceiling boards could be held in place using a woodworking adhesive like Evo-Stik Resin W but again, props would be needed. An early attempt using a fixing adhesive that is meant to take the place of nails was not successful. Although they have different working characteristics, Sikaflex-512 Caravan, Sikaflex 252 and Sikaflex 221 all proved to be effective and were preferred here.

Insulating a van using Thinsulant™

1 One of the features of Thinsulant™ is the ease at which it can be cut to size; the product is also surprisingly pleasant to handle.

2 As soon as a section has been cut to shape, each panel is laid out and coated using a spray-on adhesive.

3 The prepared section is now offered up to its intended location and pressed firmly on to the metal panel.

4 There are generally pillars and recesses in a panel van and all of these need to be filled with insulating material.

Insulating a door

1 The curving and profiled door was hinged, fitted with a catch, and bolt blocks. Flexible insulation was obviously needed here.

2 To create a flat base on which to mount 3mm lining ply, a framework was constructed using struts of 22mm x 22mm softwood.

3 A flexible quilt was laid between the strutting and its thickness was varied to suit the changing depth of the door moulding.

4 Having made a framework to go around the catch assembly, 3mm decorative faced wall ply was fixed to the frame using Sikaflex.

Insulating the ceiling

1 Wood blocks bonded to the GRP moulding with Sikaflex supported copper pipe spacers and a framework of 6mm ply strips.

2 Across the entire ceiling, a framework of 6mm ply mounted on wood blocks created a flatter base than that of the moulded roof.

3 Flexible insulation was laid across all the 6mm ply battens of the suspended ceiling and cable runs were laid for halogen lights.

4 The ceiling ply was stuck in place with Sikaflex 512; struts held it in place for 24 hours. This ceiling is in the over-cab area.

LAYOUTS, STORAGE AND WEIGHT DISTRIBUTION

Compliance with a base vehicle's weight limits is closely linked to the conversion itself. Some components are surprisingly heavy.

There's a growing concern that many motorcaravans are driven in an overladen state. This was discussed in Chapter 6 and the point was made that a base vehicle's maximum permitted weight (MTPLM – maximum technically permitted laden mass) is only one of several issues to consider.

Individual axles have maximum weight limits, too. Moreover, road-side checks have found that the load being carried by the *rear* axle of many motorcaravans is often in excess of the stated limit. This is not only dangerous; it is also an offence.

It doesn't help, of course, when bicycles or motorscooters are carried on the back of vehicles. Loads like this are significant contributors to an overladen rear axle.

The matter is made even worse when a motorcaravan is built with an overhang extending a considerable distance rearwards of the back axle. A fundamental understanding of leverage reveals that when there's a prominent overhang, the weight of a rack and a motorscooter exerts considerably *greater* down force on a rear axle. Of course, motorscooters are not the only contributors to an overladen axle; battery-driven mobility vehicles are also heavy products to carry.

In practice, a lot of motorcaravanners fit racks on the back of their vehicles at some stage during ownership. Accordingly, that is something a builder needs to keep in mind when planning locations for permanent fixtures, too.

To give an example, kitchen appliances such as a full-size cooker and a refrigerator are usually the heaviest domestic products of all. In contrast, a shower tray, wash basin and cassette toilet, are considerably lighter. A double bed will be even lighter still – even though it might occupy a greater amount of floor space.

As the following section reveals, these weight differences need to be borne in mind if you are building or refurbishing a coachbuilt motorcaravan.

Left: When a motorscooter is carried on a rack fitted to a motorhome, there's a risk that the back axle might exceed its permitted limit.

Below: The transportation of this mobility vehicle on a rack extending a long way behind the back axle could possibly be breaking the law.

Above: It's popular to build a kitchen right at the back as can be seen on this Autocruise CH Starquest.

Right: Like many van conversions, this 1999 Swift Mondial has a minimal rear overhang behind the back axle.

Layouts and coachbuilt models

Some people like a layout in which the kitchen is right at the back. It's not an uncommon arrangement although in the case of a coachbuilt model, the appliances place considerable weight on the rear axle – especially if there's a pronounced rear overhang and a scooter rack on the back as well.

If the motorhome you want to build is likely to be carrying heavy items on a rack, constructing a fully-fitted kitchen at the back might not be advisable especially if the chassis has a large rear overhang. Using this part of the living area for seating with bed conversion possibilities might be a more sensible strategy.

Layouts and van conversions

Generally, problems like this are less acute with van conversions. That's because many of the latest panel vans have their rear axle mounted so close to the back of the vehicle that the overhang is almost negligible. Of course, there are *still* weight limits that have to be observed and many owners of campervans similarly want to carry bikes or other heavy items on racks fixed at the back.

The weight of accessories

An interior layout isn't the only thing that needs to be designed in recognition of a vehicle's weight restrictions. You also need to give careful thought to where you're going to fit heavy items of fixed equipment. For example:

■ A 95Ah battery might easily tip the scales at 25kg (55lb).
■ Once you've decided on the types of gas cylinders that you want to use, put a full one on the bathroom scales to establish its weight.
■ Fresh and waste water tanks are heavy when filled to the brim.
■ You might want to carry a leisure generator and these are heavier than you might expect. Even the compact Honda EU10i is listed at 13kg (29lb) in its dry state; add fuel and it weighs even more.

It's worth putting a topped-up gas cylinder on some bathroom scales to establish what it actually weighs.

Locating accessories

The water tank installed within the long rear overhang on this 2006 Orian Aquilas can certainly impose a significant downforce on the back axle.

When you've carried out some weight checking it is immediately clear why you need to give careful consideration to the location of accessories. Strangely enough, some professional manufacturers still make ill-judged decisions. If you compare different models,

don't be surprised to find motorcaravans where a leisure battery is fitted right at the back. You will also find models which have a water tank at the back, as well.

Not that weight is the only issue dictating the position of components. In Chapter 16, you will read about several other technical matters that influence the preferred locations for a leisure battery.

When it comes to water tanks, it would be logical to mount them indoors so that their contents are less likely to freeze in sub-zero conditions. The trouble is that you also need space inside for your personal possessions and that's why tanks are often installed under the floor instead. If there *is* room inside, it is normally only the fresh water supply tank which gets mounted in a locker box or purpose-made enclosure.

With regard to the Mystique self-build project, chassis alterations described in Chapter 6 made sure that the rear overhang was unusually short. Having made that modification, all heavy items were also installed *between* the front and rear axles so that both would carry some of the load. Accordingly, twin 95Ah leisure batteries were mounted in a cupboard constructed just behind the passenger seat. On the other side of the vehicle behind the driver's seat, an upright 59-litre (13-gallon) fresh water tank was mounted in a similar enclosure.

Towards the rear of the living space, but still situated in front of the back axle on the off-side, a compartment was made to accommodate one 4.5kg butane Calor Gas cylinder and one 2.72kg butane Campingaz cylinder. On the nearside in a compartment of similar size, a 9.09-litre (2-gallon) copper cylinder for hot water was installed. This forms part of an Eberspächer Hydronic water and space heating system.

The result of careful planning meant that a balanced distribution of components was achieved, *none* of which was located rearwards of the back axle. To support this further, the kitchen was constructed at the mid-point on the offside which was balanced by a shower/toilet room in a GRP moulded pod on the nearside.

Not surprisingly, there's less scope to achieve such a distributed arrangement in a panel van, especially when the base vehicle has

a large sliding door along its nearside wall. However, you still need to consider weight when deciding where to fit all these items.

Maximising space

Irrespective of the size of a motorcaravan, there are always unavoidable compromises – not to mention national preferences. In Germany, the designers usually create very small kitchens because their clients often take major meals in restaurants and bars. A modest kitchen is often unacceptable to a British owner, although we marvel at German motorcaravanners' opulent, spacious, and brightly illuminated shower and

Fitting cab seat swivels

1 A turntable swivel, sold by many accessory specialists, has been bolted between a Fiat seat and its original sliding mechanism.

2 The addition of a swivel raises the seat height and so many people therefore remove the four bolts securing the original base and dispose of it.

3 A replacement Fiat base sold by TEK Seating is sufficiently low to make certain that a passenger's feet will reach the floor in comfort.

4 On this 1999 Fiat, a removable steering wheel allows the driver's seat to revolve as well; the cab now forms part of the living area.

washroom facilities. However, you can't have everything and as a self-builder, you have to establish your own priorities backed by strategies that achieve the best use of space.

One way to do this is to integrate the cab into the living space and for which seat swivels are sold by many suppliers. Unfortunately, these swivels add unacceptable height for many people, so reduced-height seat plinths are needed to replace the original ones.

Moreover, in older Fiat and Peugeot models, the only way to achieve sufficient space to swivel a driver's seat is to fit a removable steering wheel, but this also acts as a security device. Regrettably, 'clip-on' steering wheels cannot be fitted on the more recent models because factory-fitted wheels contain an airbag. On the other hand, there seems to be more room to rotate the driver's seat in later cabs.

Storage strategies

To yield more floor space, there's certainly good logic in bringing the cab space into play, although this doesn't provide any more room for storing your clothes.

In an original VW T2 campervan, you have to exercise great constraint when selecting your holiday clothing. Some owners of van conversions therefore fit roof boxes to gain space; others have all kinds of ingenious expanding pockets and storage features in order to squeeze a quart into their pint pot.

Another limiting factor is the reduced amount of wall space as a result of the sliding side door. However, you don't have to leave the entire width of the door open to the world outside and a number of manufacturers install furniture across part of the opening.

Creating storage opportunities is certainly easier on coachbuilt models. For example, under-floor drawers can be tailor-made to fit between chassis obstructions. Products like Beeny Boxes are excellent for providing useful storage. These are fitted low down which helps driving stability and these bespoke sliding drawers are ideal for carrying items including levelling blocks, a jack, warning triangle, jump leads and so on. The supplying company doesn't market a DIY product because each Beeny Box has to be specially crafted to suit you particular coachbuilt. This necessitates a trip to the headquarters in Cornwall although

Some plastic roof boxes lack aerodynamic lines but this one certainly increases storage in a Manhattan Tardis van conversion.

Like several van converters, IH Campers often fits furniture within the aperture that's revealed when a sliding door is fully open.

many owners combine this with a recreational break.

As regards roof boxes, these can take a surprising amount of gear, but the weight is just where it shouldn't be – high above a vehicle's centre of gravity. What is more, many boxes are as streamlined as a household brick.

Long, cigar-like, ski boxes are much more aerodynamic although they generally offer a smaller carrying capacity. Either way, you need access to a roof box for loading and unloading which raises another issue as some

motorcaravan roofs are not strong enough to walk on. It has even been reported that a marketing specialist for Arto A-class models stated that '… the roof is not actually designed to be walked on.' That's a surprising admission when the 2004 Arto 69 GL Lux was sold with a ladder on the back and roof rack side members.

All-in-all, the quest for space always poses a challenge, but challenges are part of the self-builder's experience and where there's a will there's a way.

Many owners of coachbuilt models have specially made Beeny Box storage drawers fitted below the floor.

Like all Beeny Boxes, the product made for this Ace Novella Capri is able to carry a load up to 45kg (99lb), even when the drawer is open.

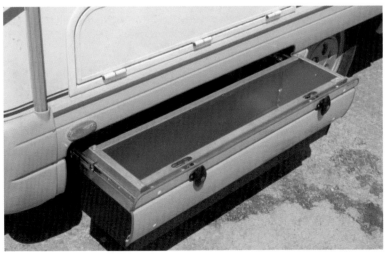

WORKING WITH PLASTICS

Both ABS and GRP mouldings are used extensively by motorcaravan builders. Whether renovating an older model or building from scratch you will come across both types of plastic.

The term 'fibre glass' is often used inaccurately to describe moulded products made from glass-reinforced plastic' – or GRP for short. Making GRP panels is a messy process and in many motorhomes acrylic-capped ABS plastic is often used instead. Check the fittings in any shower room and you'll see ABS products.

For the record, 'ABS' stands for acrylonitrile-butadiene-styrene. When finished with a textured matt surface, ABS plastic is used for the bumpers fitted on many motorcaravan base vehicles. However, a layer of acrylic adds shine and acrylic-capped ABS is used for shower trays, washbasins, external mouldings – and also for the body panels on many modern cars.

Here's a material ideal for large-volume production runs although expensive equipment is needed. In contrast, the manufacture of a GRP moulding requires very little equipment. In fact, you can even construct panels for yourself in a work-shed at home.

Both *The Caravan Manual* and *The Motorcaravan Manual* contain sections on repairing these materials. This manual is more about 'making things' and GRP panels had to be created during the Mystique motorhome project. These included:

- A large locker lid as the original one had been destroyed
- An embellishing cover to fit over alloy rainwater channelling

- Flanges around the door and the aperture of the large hatch-back.

So how would you go about making similar items, and who supplies the materials?

Obtaining materials

Searching the Internet reveals a number of UK suppliers of polyester resin, glass reinforcement mat, and associated products needed to create a GRP mould or its final product referred to as the 'moulding'. In this chapter, reference is made to a long-established supplier called Trylon which has served the needs of DIY enthusiasts for nearly fifty years.

This workers' cooperative company doesn't just supply materials; Trylon also distributes free instruction sheets which describe safety precautions, storage information, guidance about using materials and so on. When I first used the company's products to build canoes in the 1960s, long distances had to be driven to the Northamptonshire base. Today, Trylon produces an informative catalogue, runs a website, and operates a mail order and carrier service.

Some GRP chemicals are pretty unpleasant and whatever supplier you choose, advice notes on safety and storage must be read with great care. What follows is only a broad overview.

Right: A cover to hide an aluminium drainage channel was made in black GRP to match the window frame.

Far right: Having prepared a ply former and transferred the shape to white-faced chipboard, a mould was created for the sides and reveals of a hatchback door.

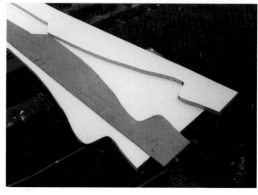

Tools required

Some of the tools you will require are shown in the following panel. A set of old kitchen scales is adequate for weighing resin and tools like a Surform and wood rasp are sold by good tool suppliers. Brushes, rollers and a catalyst dispenser are available from most resin suppliers.

You'll need a plastic mixing container and a set of scales. Since resin is mixed by weight, the container is placed on the scales and its pointer should be set to zero before adding the resin.

Resin is applied to the mould using brushes which are also used to stipple the impregnated glass mat. A roller is later used to draw the resin through the mat so the glass strands start to curl.

Scissors are used to cut large, irregular sections of chopped strand mat. This glass-fibre material is unpleasant to handle and may cause an itching feeling – hence the need to wear gloves.

Many operatives also use gloves when applying resin and handling resin-impregnated mat. Others prefer to protect their hands using a barrier cream, followed later by a purpose-made cleaner.

When a moulding has been laminated, surplus material extending beyond the mould can be cut with a sharp knife before it gets too hard (called the 'green stage'). If left, you'll then need a saw.

After a moulded panel has set completely, you can trim any surplus using a Surform. When you want to release it, prise it away gently but never introduce metal wedges between the two sections.

An alternative approach is to remove a product from a mould by easing on its surplus flanges. These can then be trimmed afterwards using a hacksaw and a barbed rasp as shown here.

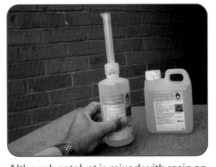

Although catalyst is mixed with resin on a weight basis, it is easier to measure this out using a special container with a built-in graduated measure and the supplier's guidelines.

Eye protection is essential when handling or measuring catalyst. This container is held at arm's length; when squeezed, the catalyst flows up a tube and pours into the graduated cylinder.

Safety in use

Laminating resin, gel coat resin, acetone cleaner and catalyst all have to be handled according to the safety advice instructions issued by the supplier. One of the worst accidents of all is to get catalyst splashed into your eyes; that's why safety goggles should be worn whenever it is being measured-out and added to the resin.

Even the smallest amount of catalyst can threaten your sight and in the event of it getting splashed into your face, flood the eyes with copious quantities of clean water for at least 15 minutes and seek immediate help from a doctor or an eye specialist.

In car repair work, the catalyst (often referred to here as hardener) is supplied as a coloured paste so that it cannot splash on to human tissue. However, when creating a body panel from a mould, catalyst in liquid form has to be measured out and mixed with the resin – hence the possible danger.

When working with all resin-based products, protect your hands either by wearing gloves or by coating them liberally with a barrier cream sold by GRP specialists.

Safety in storage

Advice leaflets from suppliers draw attention to the flammable nature of materials, especially acetone cleaner. All the products need storing in a 'No Smoking' environment and away from naked flames.

Also ensure that the catalyst is kept in the type of container used by the supplier. If it is transferred to anything other than a plastic container with a screw cap you are really asking for trouble. For instance, were you to transfer catalyst into a tin with a push fit lid, a change of temperature may create a pressure build-up

inside. This can cause the lid to be forced off unexpectedly along with a mist of vaporised catalyst. I'm ashamed to confess that I learnt that lesson many years ago so please ensure that you heed all advice in the safety leaflets.

Accelerator

Nowadays a polyester resin is described as 'pre-accelerated' and it sometimes bears the 'PA' letters against its name. However, at one time the resin didn't contain an accelerator and this was duly supplied as a third chemical which had to be added to the resin prior to its use. When you were about to embark on a job, catalyst was then added to the pre-accelerated resin to activate the chemical reaction.

Clear warnings stated that if you accidentally mixed the purple-coloured accelerator directly with catalyst, there would be an explosion. In spite of this warning, accidents happened. So nowadays, the accelerator is already pre-mixed into both a gel coat and lay-up resin, which often gives it a slightly pinkish or bluish hue.

This strategy makes sense but it also means that pre-accelerated resin has a reduced shelf life. If stored in the recommended conditions, it should last for several months but when it acquires a thick, treacle-like consistency, it needs to be disposed of. To maximise shelf life, both resins and catalyst should be stored at temperatures no higher than 20°C (68°F), preferably in the dark.

Resins

In most projects, two types of resin are needed to make a GRP panel using a mould. The first layer of resin is called the gel coat and that eventually represents the finished surface of the panel you're making. Gel coat adheres closely to the shape of a mould and produces a resistant surface finish.

To give the moulding colour, a pigment paste is added to a gel coat on a weight basis of 6–10%. Sometimes, you can buy pre-coloured gel coat in white and a few other colours. When adding your own pigment, some colours are more prone to create a patchy finish so I use a 10% addition – except with black paste which is much more dense.

After mixing-in the pigment, you then add the catalyst to start the chemical action. That's when you have to work with purposeful speed, but don't neglect stirring the resin thoroughly; catalyst must be totally distributed and not just swirled around the edges of the mixing container.

Gel coat is brushed thickly into a pre-polished

Technical Note

CLEANING BRUSHES AND ROLLERS

When resin starts to cure, it sets rock hard on the bristles of a brush or the sections of a roller. Quite quickly they'll be ruined, so they have to be cleaned at intervals using acetone poured into a container wide enough to accommodate the tools. When working on a large mould, this needs to be done frequently and it helps to have a throw-away towel to dry off excess acetone before bringing tools back into use. When the lamination work is completed, follow up the acetone bath cleaning by washing the equipment with warm water and generous amounts of washing-up liquid.

Creating a mould

Normally a mould is made in GRP – just like the moulding, albeit considerably thicker and braced to prevent distortion.

However, a flat GRP panel can be created using a thick sheet of glass; this acts as a rudimentary mould and gives the plastic a notable shine. You can create a similarly basic mould using plastic-laminated chipboard and that's what was done when constructing a locker door for the Mystique.

In a similar manner, plastic containers can often be used to create a copy in GRP. A plastic bucket, a pudding basin, and a plastic tea tray are just a few examples, bearing in mind that you need to decide on which side needs to have the finished shiny surface.

To create a more complex mould from scratch is more difficult and falls beyond the scope of this book. However, there are specialists who can do this and a caravan repairer at Whittlesey near Peterborough has gained a national reputation for recreating replicas of unobtainable mouldings. The company, V&G Caravans, has staff who can take a cracked shower tray, wash basin, wheel cover or whatever and make a copy mould in order to create a GRP replica.

This service is worth noting if you're renovating an old motorhome whose ABS or GRP panels are damaged and irreplaceable. Many manufacturers of motorhomes are no longer in business but V&G can often help. The accompanying photographs show a selection of typical projects.

Note: Bear in mind that there are often copyright issues involved in this kind of work. Court cases have arisen when entrepreneurs have made illegal copies of exotic sports car bodies and then offered them for sale in a kit-build package. However, the replication of an obsolete shower tray needed in a motorcaravan whose manufacturer is no longer in business is less likely to infringe a copyright.

Moulds for large body panels take up a lot of space, but V&G has a huge collection, many of which have been passed on by their manufacturers.

A complex mould created from sections from a badly damaged ABS locker lid is nearing completion. The surface is being polished in readiness to make a replica lid.

A customer presented a badly cracked ABS corner wash basin which was no longer obtainable. This is the new copy mould that can now produce replicas.

This bespoke wheel box was designed and laminated at V&G Caravans for a DIY coachbuilt motorcaravan. Before being removed from the wooden mould, its fixing flanges are trimmed.

mould and you don't brush it out as you would a normal paint. Every part of the mould must be coated and if your timing is bad and the gel starts to convert into solid lumps in the container, stop, take a fresh container and promptly prepare a further mix.

Once the mould is fully coated, the gel coat is left to cure but that doesn't mean to dry completely. Initial curing may take an hour or considerably longer; this depends on the temperature and the amount of catalyst used. The test is to touch the surface with your finger. A print should be left on the tacky gel, but nothing should come away on your finger. If it does, continue to wait longer.

The next operation involves the application of 'lay-up' PA resin, suitably coloured with pigment paste (but only 2.5%) and then activated using catalyst at 2% on a weight basis. Thorough stirring is needed again.

Lay-up resin is brushed on top of the gel coat and a pre-cut piece of chopped strand mat or glass cloth is added. Sometimes a piece of mat is laid on newspaper and 'wetted-out' with resin – hastily transferring it to the mould before it shreds into pieces. Occasionally, resin is sparingly added on top of the mat once it's in the mould but either way, the next objective is to use the brush and roller to force resin right into the heart of the matting. The roller also helps to break down a binding agent in the mat so that its straight strands of fibre start to curl.

Reinforcing materials

Since motorcaravan components normally need rigidity, a chopped strand mat is used – often described as CSM. Alternatively, if flexible strength is needed rather than rigidity, a woven cloth is used instead.

When making a panel using GRP, the glass reinforcing layer is usually visible on the reverse face. Admittedly, a final layer of special tissue can be used to reduce the roughness but it still doesn't achieve the smooth reverse face found on ABS components.

Bear in mind when cutting the CSM that the number of layers used determines the moulding's final strength and weight. CSM is sold in different thicknesses, too. Popular versions are 300g and 450g, both of which relate to its weight per square metre. Some people still use imperial measures and call the former 1oz and the latter 1.5oz (ounces per square foot).

As regards working characteristics, 300g CSM is more likely to settle into the tight recesses and curves of an intricate mould. A failure to do this leaves small air bubbles between the gel coat and the glass-reinforced resin layer. The bubbles are not always apparent when a moulding is first sprung out of its mould. Later, however, the thin gel coat cracks and unpleasant pitted areas appear on the surface. Where a mould has very sharp edges, I often apply several initial layers of finishing tissue around these zones because it folds easily round prominent profiles.

Catalyst

This is sold in various quantities to suit your needs and catalyst is usually added to PA gelcoat and PA lay-up resin at a 2% quantity on the basis of weight. Don't forget that one gram of catalyst (which is very hard to weigh) is the same as one ml (which is easier to measure). So in practical terms, if you weigh out 100g of resin it will need 2ml of catalyst to activate the chemical action. Similarly, 250g of resin needs 5ml, and so on.

Of course, the reaction speeds up in hot weather and you are also advised not to use resins in cold conditions. Suffice it to say, it's often necessary to make adjustments to the percentage mix to suit the temperature of the work place.

Ancillary products

Mould release wax, liquid release agent, colour paste pigments, mixing cups, glass woven ribbons, acetone cleaner, barrier creams and hand wipes are all sold by GRP product specialists. You can also buy inert fillers as described in the accompanying Tip box.

Technical Note

CAR REPAIR PRODUCTS

In car repair work, body filler is used in the repair of steel panels and this is often polyester resin which contains an inert compound such as calcium carbonate. If you need a small amount you can always mix up some PA resin with talcum powder, but it's an expensive option as it takes a surprising volume of powder to convert liquid resin into a paste.

Alternatively, the type of reinforced repair paste mentioned in Chapter 11 can be made using a mixture of PA lay-up resin and chopped strands. Both calcium carbonate and chopped strands are sold by specialists including Trylon.

Note: An 'inert' additive doesn't play a part in the chemical activity.

Case histories

MAKING A GRP COVER TO HIDE AN ALUMINIUM DRAINAGE CHANNEL

This was a cosmetic addition rather than anything else. The 'U'-shaped aluminium channel had been purchased from a DIY superstore and mounted across the head of the hatchback to divert rain away from the opening. Covering the channel with a satin black GRP cover improved its appearance and matched the frame of the Seitz S4 window as shown on page 126.

1 Black pigment paste was purchased and mixed into the gel coat. Be careful! This can leave marks everywhere and you only need a 6% mix of paste – it's one of the densest colours of all.

2 The simple mould was made using a narrow length of plastic-faced chipboard. Stuck along the edge was a length of white plastic angle-moulding purchased from a DIY superstore.

3 When taken from the mould, a lot of edge-trimming, shaping and rubbing down was needed on the face of the moulding. In particular a ridge left by the plastic angle had to be removed.

4 The face was smoothed with mild wet-and-dry paper and finally, toothpaste created a matt finish. The facing was bonded on using Sikaflex-512 Caravan adhesive sealant and a screw at either end.

CREATING A MOULDED GRP LOCKER LID

When a large locker lid with edge flanges was needed for the Mystique self-build motorhome, a simple mould was created using plastic laminated chipboard purchased from a DIY superstore.

Note: Ample space had to be left around the bottom part of the lid so that it could be opened without the flange fouling the aperture.

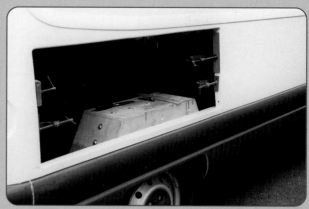

1 The fact that the face of the locker lid had to be flat meant that it could be created using a shiny-faced board. Measurements were taken to give good clearance gaps around the completed lid.

2 A mould has to be made 'in reverse' and flanges were screwed into place. Corners were checked with a try-square and newspaper patterns were prepared to cut the CSM accurately.

3 It pays to cut all the CSM before starting and strips needed for the flanges were prepared using a woodworking knife. The lid was made using three layers of 300g CSM.

4 Although the surface of plastic laminated chipboard is fairly shiny, it needed several coatings of mould release wax. This ensures that a moulding won't be irretrievably stuck in its mould.

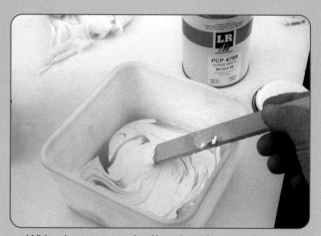

5 White pigment was mixed into the gel coat, and as experience has shown, this colour can sometime look patchy. Accordingly, it was added to the gel coat on a 10% weight basis.

6 Once catalyst had been added to the mix on a 2% basis (on weight) the gel coat was thoroughly stirred. It was then brushed without delay to achieve a thick coating all over the mould.

7 Mixes of lay-up resin required to complete the job all used a 2% addition of white pigment and 2% catalyst. To avoid creating air bubbles, care was taken to bed the CSM tightly into the edges.

8 The roller plays an important part and was used on all three layers of CSM. Rolling helps impregnate the resin within the mat and it ensures that the straight glass strands achieve a curled shape.

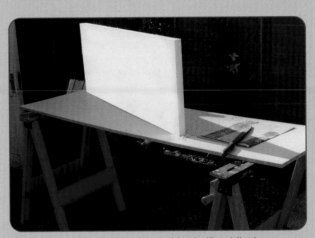

9 Having trimmed the edges with a knife while the lamination was still green (see text) the moulding was left curing for around 36 hours. It was eased clear of the mould using small wooden wedges.

10 Sharp edges were rounded off and then the lid was located in the aperture using temporary spacers. The Centaflex continuous top hinge purchased from Albert Jagger was shown on page 100.

WORKING WITH WOOD

Fitting out an interior involves techniques which you might not have used in previous projects.

Constructional work in a road-going vehicle is different from work in your home. On one hand a motorcaravan's furniture needs to be light, but on the other, it needs to be strong.

In Chapter 10 it was stated that whereas products like veneered chipboard are frequently used in our homes, it's too heavy to use in motorcaravans. Alternative materials include 3mm plywood which is faced with a decorative surface and is also remarkably light. For structural work, reference was also made to Vöhringer 15mm plywood. Boards are faced on both sides – with several choices of finish – and it is significantly lighter than chipboard. But is this quest to save weight so critical that specialist products are needed?

To be honest, it certainly is. For instance, in Chapter 6 it was pointed out that all vehicles have a maximum technically permitted laden mass (MTPLM). The stated figure marked on a plate in the vehicle must *not* be exceeded and this affects what possessions can be carried; it also limits the number of accessories that you might want to fit. With this MTPLM restriction in mind, the lighter you can build the furniture, the more payload that's left for your travelling gear.

That's the rationale behind the recommendations which follow. Here are a variety of strategies which will make your fitted furniture look smart without imposing needless weight.

Tools

A question that many self-builders ask is: 'What tools will be needed?' There's no answer to that and I question the merits of preceding a DIY project with a 'must-have' tool list. This anecdote proves the point.

When tackling a self-build house I decided to complete all the jobs involving wood. A reasonable array of hand tools was available but on the power tool front, I only possessed one electric drill and three add-on accessory items. Working to a tight budget and with a lack of sophisticated power tools all the joinery and cabinet-making work was duly accomplished, albeit at a slow pace.

After two years of hard effort, the completion was celebrated by the purchase of a compact circular saw table. When fitted with a TCT tipped blade the Coronet Consort saw cuts both hardwoods and softwoods, leaving a very smooth finish. I still use it and delight at being able to create veneer; it can even produce slender edging strips of plastic laminate by paring away the wood from narrow lengths of Vöhringer 15mm plywood.

A good saw bench will also square-off the ends of timber with extraordinary precision and wood can be cut to exact dimensions. It forms grooves, cuts rebates and creates intricate joints. From that point onwards my output of DIY projects increased in quantity and improved

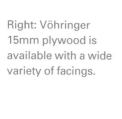

Right: Vöhringer 15mm plywood is available with a wide variety of facings.

Far right: The Coronet Consort circular saw table gives a precision finish and second-hand models are often on sale.

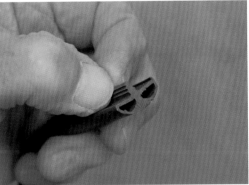

Far left: Many DIY enthusiasts own power tools like jig saws, sanders, or the type of stapler shown here.

Left: Some edging trim has a barbed tongue which has to be fitted tightly into a narrow groove.

in quality, too. Clearly it was rather foolish not to have bought this machine *before* building a house, and it continues giving good service.

The message here is clear. It *is* possible to accomplish major projects with hand tools as the Pyramid builders have shown. On the other hand, if you purchase power tools and learn how to use them safely, your work rate can then increase.

Also apparent is the fact that nowadays, no-one adds accessories to fit on a power drill. Prices have tumbled on stand-alone jigsaws, planers, circular saws, and staplers and many readers will own them already.

Of course, other woodworkers might extol the merits of buying a portable bandsaw; I cut curving shapes with a jig saw. Then there's the router. As a self-taught woodworker, this was always a mystery machine which certainly wasn't needed when fitting-out a Starcraft campervan.

The situation changed, though, when the Mystique was subsequently started because there were occasions when flexible plastic trims had to be fitted to the edges of panels. These trims have a barbed section which is pressed tightly into a narrow groove and this kind of edging is often used on drawer fronts.

Grooves cut on a circular saw are usually too wide for this and you can't use a saw to create a narrow slot in the kind of concave curve shown in the project on page 143. Similarly, when a groove had to be cut in the curving corner of a table top the router came out of its box.

In spite of that, you don't necessarily have to go out and purchase a router. There are several other ways to create a finish without resorting to trim strips of the kind described. To prove the point, there's a set of sequence photographs on page 142 showing how doors were built for cupboards, whose edges were finished with paint.

So don't postpone plans to fit-out a motorhome because you've only got a modicum

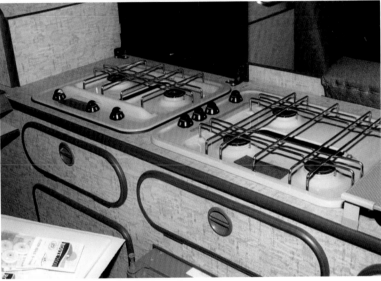

Above: On this dealer display, flexible plastic edging trims were fitted on work tops and drawer fronts.

Left: Cutting a groove in curving surfaces is usually done with a router.

of tools. When you're determined to accomplish a task, you can 'make do' with surprisingly little – you can even build a house.

Working with thin, faced plywood

Perhaps the most important feature of 3mm plywood is its negligible weight. Versions are made with imitation wood effects, various types of textured finishes and white ceiling

Preparing a small shelf using thin plywood

1 Not only is the facing-ply used in motorhome interiors extremely light, it is only 3mm thick.

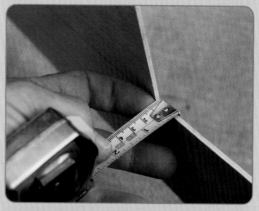

2 Making straight cuts is best achieved using a woodworking knife and a metal scale.

3 To prevent the material flexing, a length of mahogany lipping was prepared with a 3mm groove.

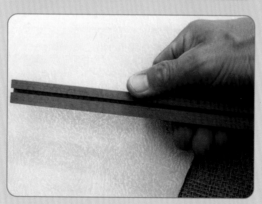

4 The grooved lipping was glued along the front of the shelf to stop it sagging; at the back the shelf was screwed to a wall-mounted batten.

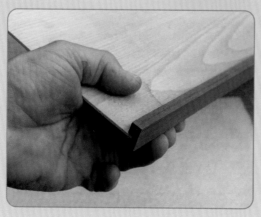

NOTES:
- This technique enables you to make small shelves for cupboards.
- If you cut wider lipping so that it projects well above the ply, the upstand helps to prevent items slipping off the shelf when you're driving on the road.
- If you need far larger shelves with sufficient rigidity to carry items like books, you can create a double plywood structure. Small pieces of wood will act as spacers between the 3mm ply sheets and the void in between is useful if you need to hide runs of electricity cables.

This shallow bookshelf was constructed over a bench seat; two layers of 3mm ply were used and strength was provided by using Vöhringer 15mm plywood prepared with two 3mm grooves to offer support across the front.

Two pairs of directional reading lamps like this unit were mounted under the shelf and the void between the two sheets of ply was wide enough to house the light fittings and hide the cables.

board facing. The fact that it flexes easily is a benefit if it has to be mounted on a curving surface but that's a weakness when it's needed for shelving. It bends with the lightest of loads.

There's a remedy, however, and all you need is a strengthening strip referred to as 'lipping'. A typical piece of lipping would measure 25mm x 6mm (1in x $^1/_4$in) and it is prepared and finished with a 3mm groove. This can be formed using a circular saw, a router or a grooving plane.

Making curved cuts in 3mm ply is often done using a jigsaw. However, to make straight cuts it's better to carry this out using a woodworking knife fitted with a sharp blade and a metal scale. This produces a pleasingly accurate edge.

Lightweight doors and drawer fronts

To achieve further weight-saving, many cupboard and drawer fronts are hollow. In fact, surplus hollow doors were purchased from Magnum Mobiles for the Starcraft campervan project. Of course, some of these had to be reduced in size but they were easily modified without compromising their lightweight construction. A project in progress is shown in the following sequence and you will deduce from this that it is equally feasible to build-up hollow doors in this way using two panels of ply and softwood spacers. All that's needed to prevent a long door – hollow *or* solid – from distorting is to add a long bracing batten.

A bracing batten helps prevent a long door from bending; this one was screwed from the front of the door before its plastic laminate facing was added.

Altering hollow drawer fronts

1 This drawer front was cut to size by passing it across the circular saw, thereby revealing its hollow interior.

2 A 19mm (3/4in) insert was cut to the exact thickness to fit within the hollow core; it was glued and held in place using G-cramps.

3 You can then tidy-up edges using a veneer strip, but for a tougher edging, thin hardwood lipping was cut on a saw table.

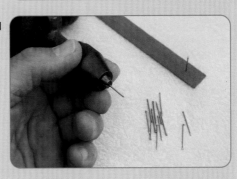

4 A veneer pin was used in a hand drill to prepare holes in the lipping; these pins are later used to support the glued edging.

NOTES:

- Veneer pins are much more slender than panel pins and bend annoyingly easily when they're hammered home. Their heads, however, are barely visible.
- Both types of pin are inclined to split thin lipping like this so it pays to drill small pilot holes.
- It is hard to find a sufficiently slender drill bit and these can all-too-easily get broken.
- That's why it's useful to use a veneer pin itself as a make-shift drill – nipping off its head with pliers so that it seats well in the chuck. The pin inevitably gets hot as you form the hole but keep the hand drill turning fast and don't push too hard.

Building a high-level cupboard

In the Mystique a fuse box had been built at head height near the entrance door and while it was usefully accessible, it seemed logical to build a cupboard around it to provide additional storage.

It was evident that the cupboard would need a curving side to prevent people cracking their heads when climbing aboard. It would also need some sliding doors.

It couldn't be fitted with a conventional top-hinged cupboard door because that would bump into an adjacent top-hung door serving the over-cab locker. Adjacent doors often bump into each other on motorhomes, so sliding doors were the answer here.

This new cupboard was constructed in situ using techniques already described.

NOTES:
- Building in situ like this is time-consuming and boxing round the fuse box, building a cupboard around it, fitting it with a shelf and laminating the two doors took the best part of a week.
- When bending 3mm ply, check which way it prefers to flex. The piece here had to go around a tight curve but the support frame helped and taking it around in stages over three days eliminated the need to dampen the ply or apply any steam.

1 The first task was to screw a batten to the walls to support the base. To save weight, the base was made using 3mm ceiling ply.

2 It was stated earlier that 3mm ply can be bent to create a curved finish. So a frame was built to support the flexed panel.

3 The top of the curving frame was screwed to ceiling struts; this framework thus helped to support the plywood base as well.

4 The front of the cupboard was now constructed using Vöhringer 15mm ply with plastic edging round the aperture.

5 Bending the ply round the frame was done in stages over 3 days. It was fixed to the wall and the frame using Sikaflex-512.

6 The bottom channelling for the doors was prepared on a circular saw using faced Vöhringer 15mm plywood.

7 Two sliding doors were made from 6mm ply and Warerite plastic laminates were bonded on both faces.

8 Push-fit catches were fitted to complete the job. Note the curving side near the main entrance and the effect of sliding doors.

Building furniture frameworks

There are two completely different ways to construct large items of furniture. The first approach shown here is often used by van converters and the units can be built in a workshop and installed in the vehicle later.

Junctions

The point where panels meet always poses a challenge. If you offer-up adjoining boards dozens of times and keep trimming the edges here and there, you eventually get an impressive fit. Then you drive down the road and a bumpy ride opens the tight-fitting joints you proudly created.

In the Starcraft project, points where panels met were often covered with carefully trimmed fillets of hardwood. These suited the 'woody' look inside the campervan but something different was needed in the Mystique. Three different techniques were employed.

On the ceiling, long joins between adjacent panels of white plywood were covered by plastic trims as used in the caravan industry. Small-volume manufacturers often sell these interlocking mouldings to DIY builders and they are in two parts. The first plastic length covers the junction and is held in place with screws. Then its cover piece is merely clipped on top to hide the heads of the screws.

That's fine for a ceiling but these strips wouldn't look right on a wall. So let's take an actual example and describe how the curved side of a high-level cupboard (see previous sequence) was finished-off at the point where it abutted against the wall.

First, a reasonable fit was achieved but to disguise imperfections, white adhesive sealant was put to use.

A preliminary task is to fix 25mm masking tape to those edges of a panel which are going to make contact with an adjacent surface. In the case of the cupboard panel described above, this was going to make contact with the upper part of a wall along one edge and the ceiling board on the other. It helps to fix masking tape before starting an installation though it can always be added later.

Once the side panel had been installed, it was time to disguise the gaps. This entailed fitting a further strip of masking tape along the wall as well, but leaving a narrow space

Contrasting types of furniture assembly

A quick way to assemble a unit is to use Vöhringer 15mm ply; the carcass will be pleasingly strong – but fairly heavy.

Assembly fittings are available from DIY shops; manufacturers often used these inserts which have a cover cap to hide the screws.

To reduce even more weight, an alternative approach is to build a light framework of struts in situ and to clad it later with 3mm ply.

This is the upper section of a compact, space-saving wardrobe. First, a light, but strong framework was built in situ.

The unit was finally clad with 3mm plywood, and a door was made using a pre-made frame from Magnum Surplus and an infill of ply.

between the two lengths of tape to expose the place where the panels meet.

A narrow bead of Sikaflex-512 Caravan was then injected along the gap between the masking tape. What follows should be done wearing thin

If you intend adding a line of sealant along a join it helps to apply masking tape to a board before it is finally installed.

The fact that adjoining panels don't align closely can be cleverly disguised with piping.

rubber gloves, but I prefer to use a finger coated with spittle. With as much force as I could muster, the thin bead of sealant was pressed deeply into the scarcely discernible crack between the boards. This takes several passes of the finger, additional spittle and a 'throw-away' towel for wiping the hands. The majority of sealant ends up on the masking tape but that's unavoidable, and before the sealant starts to set, the tape is peeled off and dropped in a bin.

The results are certainly pleasing. However, there's a third strategy which was preferred in several other places and it involves the use of plastic piping. This type of product can be purchased from suppliers like Woolies, and I purchased both white piping and a grey version to match other fittings inside the vehicle.

To make a neat junction between adjoining panels, you have to stick the flange of the piping to the edge of one panel and wait until it sets. When you subsequently offer-up a further board against the piped edge, they might not sit together in close register, but this is disguised by the piping itself. The photograph shows the result.

Plastic channelling sold in DIY stores can also be used where panels abut each other.

A skilled craftsman would say that this is cheating, and of course it is. Another way to cheat is to cover a join using thin plastic edging strips sold in DIY superstores. However, I don't like this strategy quite as much and if you rely too often on plastic mouldings, the results look rather amateurish.

Self-assembly drawers

Continuing on the cheating theme, Woodfit sells rugged self-assembly steel drawers. Arguably they're a bit heavy, but the fact that they have the roller runners used on office filing cabinets means that the drawers can be easily removed. As it happened, only one pre-fabricated drawer was fitted in the Mystique, while other drawers were self-made but equipped with similar roller runners supplied separately by Woodfit.

Being able to remove drawers was important in the Mystique because I wanted access to all fresh water pipe couplings, the waste water runs and every electrical component. Equally, one of the best ways to fill a motorcaravan's kitchen with food is to install easily removable drawers that can be carried into your house.

Then there's the waste bin. It's peculiar that most kitchens in British-built caravans and motorhomes are not equipped with a small waste bin. In consequence, owners dangle a plastic bag on the handle of an oven which is hardly state-of-the-art kitchen design.

In a well-designed kitchen, all that's needed is a compact bin with sufficient capacity to hold a few spent tea bags and an empty baked bean can or two. Not a tall order but one which defeats most British designers. It's standard practice in Germany, of course, where some motorhome designers go 'over the top' and fit three different-coloured bins in response to recycling strategies.

The Mystique has just one bin which is housed in a Woodfit drawer as shown alongside.

Custom-made cupboard doors

Whereas the Starcraft had a 'woody' look inside, a lighter ambiance was required in the Mystique, but not too clinically white. A subtle colour was chosen for the cupboard doors and drawer fronts – so these had to be purpose-made.

In a way, that was a silly idea because it took

Self-assembly steel drawers

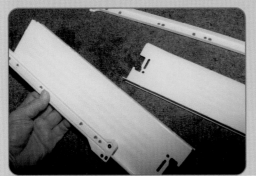

Self assembly drawers in the Woodfit catalogue are made in various materials, colours and sizes.

This unit was made in painted steel and includes sides with built-in runners. You contribute the front, back and base panels.

Below the removable drawer is storage for a dustpan and brush. At the back is access to all the pipes serving the kitchen sink.

A removable plastic waste bin was fitted in the front part of the drawer. It took time to track down a rectangular product but it does what the builder intended.

a whole day to complete just a single door. A further day was spent fitting the catches, hinges and locking stays. Still, if you insist on fitting drawers with a soft mint-green hue, that's what you have to do.

These were duly made using panels of medium density fibre board, or MDF for short. It has been suggested that the dust from MDF is carcinogenic, i.e. encouraging the growth of cancer. This was the first time I had used this popular product and I duly purchased new safety masks and carried out the cutting and planing preparation outdoors so that dust would be swiftly dispersed.

Bearing in mind the need for weight-saving, MDF is not the best choice of material although it *has* been used for cupboard fronts fitted in several British and German models. Mindful of the weight issue, I opted for thin 9mm board but this necessitated using packing pieces for catches and hinges. The catches are really made to fit thicker panels.

If you like the idea of making panels using your choice of coloured plastic laminate, make sure that you fit a balancing piece of laminate on the reverse face. Like most domestic kitchen cabinet manufacturers, I used a white laminate on the backs.

The reason for fitting a laminate on *both* faces is to achieve stability in the panel. If a laminate is only applied to one face, a board usually starts to bend on account of the differential expansion of the fibrous wood and the facing plastic. The photos alongside show how these sections were made.

NOTES:

- The doors and drawer fronts were face-mounted rather than cut to fit tightly within an aperture. Any movements are then much less apparent because they overlap all around the opening.
- Impact adhesive was purchased from a kitchen specialist who also supplied the

1 The MDF was cut outdoors on a pair of trestles. This door was needed for the storage cupboard over the cab.

2 One face was covered with impact adhesive as was the laminate. When it was fixed, surplus laminate was cut away.

3 When both sides were covered with laminate and trimmed to size, the board was masked ready for spraying the edges.

4 Note the bracing bars on the rear face. These were screwed from the front side *before* its face plastic was added.

5 A hole-saw was purchased to suit the size of the catch. The door was cramped firmly to some scrap and drilled right through.

6 The catch kit was purchased from a low volume van converter; fitting items like these is a time-consuming operation.

7 A folding strut was mounted on the back of the door using a packing piece so that longer screws could be used in the panel.

8 Similar panels were made for the kitchen unit's drawers, the control panel for the hob and the door covering the cooker grill.

Warerite plastic laminate. The adhesive is applied with a brush and left until the surfaces are touch-dry.

- Passing a woodworking knife with a sharp blade several times around the MDF panel will cut through the excess plastic; a cork block covered with abrasive paper was used to tidy-up the edges.
- Cut edges of the MDF were very absorbent. It was found best to apply three coats of car priming paint followed by four coats of Halfords Car Spray. Rover Hurricane Grey perfectly matched the plastic catches and other grey fittings.
- When a hole-saw penetrates through wood it rips part of the rear surface badly. To avoid this, the fronts were cramped firmly to some old scrap backing board so that the penetrating drill damages that instead.
- Support stays are always hard to fit in the right place and it is easy to locate them wrongly. Think about their intended operating movements before you start drilling holes.
- On the main kitchen unit, push-fit button catches were fitted which are popular at present. However, it took a long time to find a supplier who stocked these in dark grey.

Open-access storage

In many motorcaravans there's a need for a storage facility in which items are deposited with ease and retained without needing a door. Something along these lines was required on top of the GRP moulded toilet compartment in the Mystique project; however, its construction had to be light in weight.

The completed structure is pleasingly rigid although it doesn't look as if it has been built mostly using 3mm ply.

NOTES:

- If you can't get hold of a router, there's nothing wrong in creating apertures squared at the corners. Lipping can then be used to cap the exposed edges.
- In this project, it was important to work out the exact thickness of the softwood frame. When added to the depth of the ply (3mm), the total thickness of the cut-out had to match the covering capacity of the plastic edging strip which was 17mm. Accordingly the thickness of the softwood frame was a fraction under 14mm – taking into account the width of the glued join.

Building an open access storage facility

1 This is the finished product. Since the base of the shelf is well below the level of both openings, nothing falls out on a trip.

2 The panel is 3mm ply but a softwood frame was added round the proposed aperture using Evo-Stik Resin W woodworking adhesive.

3 A cutter was purchased for a router to create grooves narrow enough to grip the barbed attachment of an edging strip like the one on page 135.

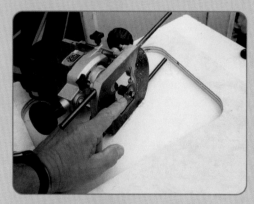

4 Negotiating concave curves clearly needed a router; when the groove was finished the edging strip was simply pushed into the slot.

During the day, the bed is lifted to provide headroom in the lounge.

At night, it takes less than ten seconds to lower the bed; its occupants sleep in line with the vehicle rather than across its width. This means that neither person has to climb across the other in order to leave via the ladder.

Constructing a master bed

The requirements for the main bed in the Mystique were particularly demanding. This had to be:

- A double-bed with a single-piece mattress. Many motorhome beds are assembled each evening using a jigsaw of oddly shaped foam pieces. Sometimes there are as many as six or seven and that leaves a lot of gaps between the pieces.
- A permanently made-up bed – but without resorting to the creation of a fixed type which takes up a large part of the living space needed during the day.
- A bed offering exceptional comfort which can be set up in seconds and without a major upheaval in the living area.

The resulting design was a hinged, drop-down bed above the lounge. The lounge, incidentally, doubles up as a potential transporting area for a

1 The cambered beech slats are laminated for strength and assembled in pairs; on this project each slat had to be shortened.

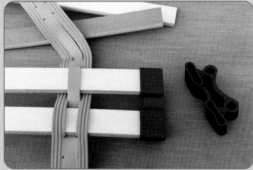

2 Each pair of slats is retained in two full-length rubber straps; these ensure the units remain the same distance apart.

3 A clever feature of the system is the fact that it is not just the slats which provide springing; the end caps contribute as well.

4 Two sets of slats are used for a double-bed but when a mattress is added, there's no evidence of a junction down the centre.

The box frame is a simple construction made using Vöhringer 15mm plywood, a central spine of aluminium 'U'-section, and grey edging trim around the perimeter panels. Robust hinges purchased from Albert Jagger were fitted to the long side panel on the hinging side of the frame, at the commencement of the construction. To facilitate the lifting action, a pair of gas struts was purchased from Metrol Springs.

Plans to construct a safety rail were not followed-up. It was found that if an occupant strays near to the edge, the prominent sides of the box frame exert an appropriate warning even when the person's asleep.

The dimensions of a 'bed box' were intentionally made to suit the owner. These are:
Depth of box section sides: 185mm (7$\frac{1}{2}$in) excluding the edging trims
Width (outside measurement): 1,320mm (52in)
Length (outside measurement): 1,730mm (68in)
Extension on length to increase pillow area: 100mm (4in)
Overall length of the bed: 1,830mm (72in)

Far left: Headroom in the lounge is lost when the bed is lowered but the bench seat below can also be converted to create two-adult length singles for occasional visitors.

micro car or two motorscooters on account of its large hatchback door.

The slatted system on the double-bed used components purchased from the Natural Mat Company.

1 Having bolted the four main sides together using steel brackets in each corner, cross members of ply braced it together.

2 The central spine consisted of an inverted 'U' tube in aluminium, enclosing a pine batten bonded with adhesive sealant.

3 Fitments were designed to support the bed when lowered. This support block was later clad in plastic laminate and painted grey.

4 When the beech slats were added, this was the view from underneath before the addition of headlining carpet.

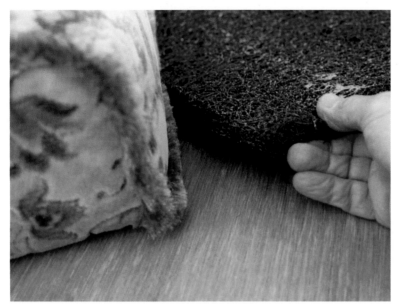

A rubberised coir matting is used under mattresses to prevent the tendency for condensation to form at night.

Several products are available from boat suppliers but fewer motorhome accessory shops stock underlays. The product illustrated here is made from coir which has been coated with a rubberising treatment. It can be purchased from the Natural Mat Company.

Bed support systems

The problem of damp forming on the underside of a mattress doesn't arise if a bed is constructed using one of the following systems:

- The Froli system involves mounting flexible plastic lozenge units on a solid base. The coloured inserts can be changed to harden or soften the supports and if necessary specific areas of a bed can be altered to suit an owner's needs. Air is able to move freely underneath to prevent the formation of damp.
- The CarWinx system from Lattoflex is made using plastic flexible cross rails which carry mattress support discs. Like the Froli system, you'll see this product fitted in several German motorhomes including La Strada models.
- In Britain, cambered wood systems are more readily available and examples are sold by Woodfit. For the main bed in the Mystique project, laminated beech slats were purchased from the Natural Mat Company and a bed framework was made to accommodate them.

Bed wetting

Not a medical condition here, but a problem well-known to those caravan and motorhome users whose bed mattress rests on a ply sheet base or a table top. In all but hot summer conditions, there's a tendency for damp to form overnight on the underside of the mattress.

During an extended holiday, the increasing problem of under-mattress-damp can lead to mould formation and discoloration of the lining on the underside of cushions. It's certainly a nuisance.

Incidence of damp is usually eliminated by rolling out an underlay to permit air circulation.

Left: The Froli mattress system offers adjustable comfort by changing the centre inserts in the plastic supports.

Below: The CarWinx bed support system is fitted in a number of German-built motorcaravans like this model from La Strada.

In the author's Starcraft Campervan, a crockery racking arrangement was designed so that none of the plates, cups or saucers could strike each other in transit.

Other projects

Items like crockery cupboards present two options. You either purchase the plastic-coated wire racks that manufacturers use or you design your own storage arrangement.

Regarding cutlery, a shallow drawer was designed to occupy the small gap above the refrigerator. A pre-made tray was purchased complete with cutlery and this was accommodated in the drawer.

The trouble with cutlery drawers is that sometimes you pull them too far and the contents fall on the floor. However, this one has long slider arms fitted so the problem doesn't occur.

NOTES:

■ The old trick of rubbing a candle along the wood runner made the unit slide well.

■ The drawer had to be kept independent from the refrigerator because this has to be removed for servicing. It was therefore decided to assemble the purpose-made drawer (other than the drawer front) to ensure that the rails and wooden supports were parallel to each and in accurate register. Sikaflex-512 Caravan was then applied to the wooden sliders from which the drawer is suspended and the whole assembly was wedged up so that it bonded to the underside of the GRP draining board. Twenty-four hours later the bond was complete so the drawer front was squared-up and added as well. The push-fit catch was the final addition, and the system has worked really well.

Above: Obstructions prevented this cutlery drawer from being fitted centrally but it filled a narrow gap above the fridge.

Left: Runners slid well using candle grease and were lengthened so the short drawer wouldn't fall out unexpectedly.

16

CONTENTS

The systems

Products and user procedures

Installing a mains supply system

Installing a 12V dc supply system

Installation details in the Mystique project

Other installation details

ELECTRICAL SYSTEMS

Unlike the supply system in our homes, an electricity supply in a motorcaravan is drawn from either a mains 'hook-up' or a battery.

It is important to start this chapter with some safety advice. An accident involving a 230V ac mains supply can lead to fatality. In contrast, a 12V dc supply doesn't have the power to electrocute a human, but if there's a short circuit, it can soon lead to a fire. These are indisputable facts.

It is therefore important that any self-builder unfamiliar with electrical theory and practice should entrust this part of a project to suitably qualified persons. Wiring a motorcaravan can become surprisingly involved and many auto-electricians are sufficiently experienced to install a 12V system on your behalf. Equally, an electrician qualified to wire your house could also wire-up your motorhome.

Having said that, the person installing a 230V supply would need to understand that the practices followed when wiring a house are different from those adopted when wiring-up a motorcaravan. For example, in caravans and motorhomes, it's important to use *flexible* three-core mains cable; that's a product in which the live, neutral and earth cables are made up from a large number of copper strands. In contrast, the supply circuit in a house uses flat three-core cable in which the conductors are solid strands

Wiring a motorcaravan can be complicated and many self-builders entrust this task to qualified electricians.

of copper wire. That type of cable should not be used in a motorcaravan.

The systems

Wiring in a motorcaravan is quite complicated because there are different systems. For the most part these remain separate although there are *some* interrelationships. The systems include:

A MAINS 230V AC SYSTEM

This is fitted so that mains hook-ups can be used on a camping site. A 230V supply will run a mains-operated battery charger, mains lighting and most refrigerators can be run on a 230V setting, too. In addition, nearly all air conditioning appliances require a 230V supply.

THE BASE VEHICLE'S 12V DC SUPPLY

This will already be in place but it usually supports part of the 12V system in the living area. For example,
- an absorption fridge can operate on a 12V supply drawn from the base vehicle with alternator assistance – as shown in the wiring diagram on page 155.

Technical Note

WHY USE FLEXIBLE CABLE?

Flexible cable made from a number of copper filaments is used in motorcaravans because it achieves a more positive fixing in screw-in connectors. The connectors in items like power sockets are an example. If flat PVC-sheathed cable with its thick, single strands of copper were used, the inevitable movements experienced when driving along ordinary roads are more likely to shake loose a screw-type connection.

- an alternator can charge the leisure battery that runs 12V accessories in the living area – as well as the vehicle's starter battery. See wiring diagram.
- if a leisure battery becomes totally discharged, the vehicle's battery can usually be switched to supply 12V appliances in the living space as a temporary measure.

THE LEISURE BATTERY'S 12V DC SUPPLY
The supply normally employs automotive cable and its power is principally drawn from a leisure battery. However, there is also:
- A link with the 230V ac supply which runs a fixed battery charger for replenishing the leisure battery. This charger also acts like a transformer/rectifier because it not, only charges the leisure battery, it can also supply 12V accessories at the same time. However, there *must* always be a leisure battery coupled within the circuit.

Products and user procedures

To find out more about electricity in motorhomes, please refer to Chapter 5 in *The Motorcaravan Manual* (2nd Edition). This 16-page chapter covers both mains and 12V systems and gives advice about different products, basic theoretical issues, and the safe use of electricity on a site. The function of the chapter here is to look more closely at constructional matters.

Installing a mains supply system

To ensure that the correct components are purchased, it is strongly recommended that you purchase a mains installation kit. These are available from motorcaravan accessory shops and kits from Powerpart and W4 Accessories are well-known.

However, some kits leave you to purchase an external coupling socket to fit on the outside of the vehicle and several types are available. Similarly, you are usually left to purchase an approved hook-up cable which creates the link between a site's distribution pillar and the coupling socket on the motorcaravan. Remember that you **must** buy products designed for use with motorcaravans which are compliant with British Standards/European Norms.

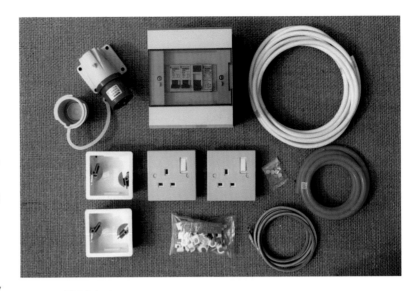

Above: To fit a mains system, it is best to buy a kit like this one from W4 Accessories. Follow all the instructions in the kit with great care.

Left: An approved input socket will need to be fitted to accept a mains supply for your motorhome.

ITEMS THAT YOU'LL NEED
Starting at the site's hook-up pillar, you will need these items:
- An approved cable, no longer than 25m, to connect to the hook-up. This should comply with BS EN 60309-2 and will comprise three flexible cores with a cross section area of 2.5mm². The connections are live (positive: brown insulation), neutral (negative: blue insulation) and earth (yellow and green insulation).
- An input socket for the external wall of your motorcaravan which complies with BS EN 60309-2.

Technical Note

TESTING PROCEDURE
Before being put into commission, an owner-built 230V ac installation must be tested by a qualified electrician who should provide a signed and dated certificate confirming that it complies with the latest IEE regulations. Contact the NICEIC or ECA for contact addresses of your nearest approved inspectors.

Above: This mains consumer unit has three MCBs on the left. The switch for the RCD is on the right and a yellow test button is directly above it.

■ A short length of 2.5mm² flexible three-core cable to take the power from the input socket to the mains consumer unit. Its specification is the same as that of the hook-up cable described above.

■ A mains consumer unit fitted with a double-pole switching residual current device (RCD), miniature circuit breakers (MCBs) and a test button. Typically, one MCB is allocated for the refrigerator; a second MCB protects the other 13-amp sockets. On larger motorcaravans with more elaborate systems, three MCBs are sometimes fitted in a consumer unit.

■ An earth wire covered with green and yellow sheathing which must be connected to the earth bar in the consumer unit and bolted to the chassis together with a warning plate.

■ A length of 1.5mm² flexible cable which will run from the mains consumer unit to the 13-amp sockets.

■ Switched 13-amp sockets. Double-pole switched sockets are preferred but are not always easy to obtain. Sockets in the Concept Range from W4 Accessories are double-pole switched.

■ A polarity tester for inserting into one of the sockets to check the site's supply. Information on the coupling-up procedure at

Technical Note

COMPONENTS IN A CONSUMER UNIT
A consumer unit should include:

1. A miniature circuit breaker (MCB) which is a trip-switch providing over-current protection. It is the modern equivalent of an old-fashioned re-wirable fuse.
2. A residual current device (RCD) which used to be called an earth leakage circuit breaker or a residual current circuit breaker. The latest RCDs incorporate double-pole switching which means they control current flow on both live *and* neutral connections. The device protects the user and if you were to accidentally touch a live wire, the RCD immediately cuts off the supply. Bear in mind, however, that the RCD only affords protection on cables that come *out* of the consumer unit and *not* those which bring power *into* the unit. In other words it offers no protection from an accident involving the hook-up lead, the coupling socket on the wall of a motorcaravan, or the short length of cable between the coupling socket and the consumer unit.

To check the operation of an RCD, use the test button every time you couple up to a supply; if the RCD 'trips' – as it should – then re-set its switch in the knowledge that the device is working correctly.

a camping site is given in *The Motorcaravan Manual* (2nd Edition).

■ A supply of cable clips. If cable is surface mounted, clips should be fitted at intervals no greater than 250mm (10in) on horizontal runs, and at intervals no greater than 400mm (16in) on vertical runs.

Right: The earth cable from the mains consumer unit has to be fixed to the chassis and the connection has to be marked with a warning label.

Far right: A polarity and fault tester should be purchased from an electrical suppliers.

INSTALLATION

By using a kit, all you have to do is to fit the input socket, mount the consumer unit and 13-amp sockets, clip the cables in discreet locations and make the final connections. If you purchase a Powerpart kit, the input, output and earth cables are already pre-connected in the consumer unit as shown alongside. Admittedly, you will have to detach its lid in order to screw the base to a board but the only electrical tasks you'll have to carry out are connecting the orange cable to the inlet socket on the external wall and connecting-up each of the 13-amp sockets using the white cable.

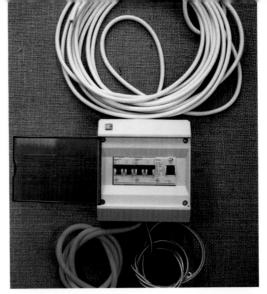

The mains consumer unit in a Powerpart kit is pre-wired: the white cable connects to the 13-amp sockets, the yellow and green cable is connected to the vehicle's body or chassis, and the orange cable is connected to the mains input socket.

Although a Powerpart mains consumer unit is pre-wired, you have to remove its lid in order to screw down the base plate.

In this VW campervan the furniture was solid enough for mounting face-fitted sockets. Where 3mm ply panel has been used, this will need boosting up with additional ply to create a sturdier base.

Technical Note

INSTALLATION TIPS

■ You won't achieve a strong enough mounting for 13-amp sockets or a consumer unit on 3mm plywood. However, you can strengthen thin ply by bonding on a piece of 9mm ply (or thicker) using an impact adhesive like Evo-Stik. If mounting items on a thin panel of a cupboard, bond the extra ply on the inside. Alternatively, cut it to the exact dimension of the consumer unit so that it is barely conspicuous. Screws holding a unit in place then achieve better purchase in the thickened panel.

Installing a 12V dc supply system

There are many products that run on a 12V supply and here is a list of items needed when assembling a typical supply system.

■ A digital multimeter is strongly recommended although a simple test device is also useful.

■ Leisure battery
■ Master switch
■ Battery source switch with condition gauge
■ Battery charger
■ Relays
■ Fused distribution panel
■ Cables, clips and connectors
■ In-line fuse holders and fuses.

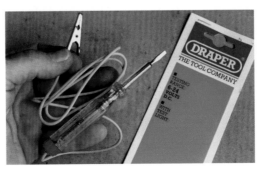

You will need a multimeter when installing a 12V system although simple testers are often useful as well.

THE FUNCTION OF PRODUCTS

If you merely wanted to fit a 12V fluorescent light, you could fit a leisure battery, place an in-line 5-amp fuse fairly close to its live terminal, and run two 1.0mm² automotive cables to the lamp unit. If a fault subsequently developed in the lamp or if a short circuit occurred in the cable, the fuse would 'blow'; simple, but safe. This provides a starting point before looking at more sophisticated systems.

■ Leisure battery

Even to run a simple light, it's wisest to fit an extra, leisure battery rather than discharging the vehicle's starter battery. Leisure batteries are different from starter batteries and are built to cope with a life of heavy discharging and regular re-charging. Further information is given in *The Motorcaravan Manual* (2nd Edition).

Installation details in the Mystique project

The electrical controls, batteries and a drum-mounted mains cable were installed in a specially-designed enclosure at floor level.

The fuse box, a remote control box for an awning light and a battery selector switch were installed at head height above the battery enclosure.

A master control for the 12V supply was fitted close to the batteries so that power could be disconnected instantly.

The mains consumer unit is mounted on the right; a white-cased motorcaravan battery charger from Powerpart Accessories is to its left.

■ The leisure battery fuse

In the event of a short circuit a fuse sometimes sparks when it fails, and that is why it should never be *too* close to a battery. When receiving a high rate of charge (14.4V or more), a battery gives off an explosive, lighter-than-air gas and if there's a spark from a failing fuse, ignited gas can blast a battery casing apart.

Therefore it is best to fit a battery in a separate enclosure with ventilation to release the gas; the fuse should be fitted close to the live terminal, but *outside* the enclosure.

■ Locating the controls

In practice, 12V circuits have to operate more than just a lighting system. So you need to list all the 12V dc powered accessories you intend installing and to draw up a plan. It is also advisable to establish a location so that the leisure battery, the fixed charger, the mains consumer unit and all the 12V controls are installed in close proximity. In addition, a 12V master switch on the cable coming from a battery's live terminal is strongly recommended. (These are sold by automotive factors and firms such as Europa.)

■ Fixed battery charger

You will also need to install a battery charger (see wiring diagram) and the ones designed for motorcaravans normally have a maximum output of 13.8V. This means that the battery doesn't start 'gassing' and you can also run your 12V accessories while the charger is in operation, without damaging them. It's true that a discharged leisure battery is better served by a charger whose output starts as high as 14.8V and the circuitry of which creates a progressive drop as it recovers. With this charging regime, gassing occurs in the early stages, but that's good for a battery because it prevents the formation of sulphate on the plates. However, 14.8V is *not* good for your accessories which will often be running at the same time as the charging is taking place; 12V light bulbs and other items are likely to fail. That's why standard motorcaravan chargers have their maximum output limited to 13.8V.

■ Battery selector switch

You will also need a switching device that lets you choose whether to draw the 12V supply from the leisure battery, the vehicle battery, or to switch it off completely. You can purchase a panel which performs this function and the connections should be clearly marked on the back.

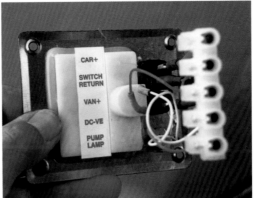

Far left: A battery source-selector switch panel together with a battery condition meter are available as independent units. Alternatively these devices are sometimes built within fused distribution panels.

Left: The terminals on this battery source selector panel are clearly marked so it is easy to connect it up correctly.

■ Fused distribution unit

Presuming that you will want to run a variety of 12V accessories, a fused distribution unit is needed, too. These products take the power supplied by a battery and then send it along separate branches, each of which has its own specific fuse. This arrangement makes fault-finding much easier.

Units sold by a dealer to the public will have all the connections clearly marked on a coupling block on the back. However, if you buy one from a caravan breaker, it's likely to have a pre-connected plug instead that coupled-up to the original caravan/motorcaravan wiring harness. There won't be any markings and that leaves you to discover which cable is which.

■ Cable

It is important that everything is wired-up using cable with the correct gauge of copper

Technical Note

TYPICAL FUSE RATINGS
Fuses typically used by manufacturers for 12V dc accessories are:

Fridge ignition – 5 amps
Fridge supply – 15 amps
Gas water heater ignition – 5 amps
Gas space heater ignition – 5 amps
Radio cassette – 5 amps
Omnivent roof vent fan – 10 amps
Water pump – 10 amps
Security alarm – 5 amps
Lighting – 10 amps
Other auxiliaries – 10 amps
Leisure battery live terminal – 15 amps
Starter battery live terminal – 15 amps

Far left: Fused distribution panels come in many different designs. This one is more simple to operate than some of the electronic versions.

Left: The connection block on the rear of this fused distribution panel is clearly marked.

It's very important to wire an appliance using cable of the correct gauge. You can check its rating by counting its copper filaments.

Table A –
CONFIRMING CABLE RATING

No of strands	Cross sectional area in mm²	Current rating in amps	Application in motorcaravans
14	1.00	8.75	Interior lights.
21	1.50	12.75	Wire to extractor fans, but check the model.
28	2.00	17.50	Feed to fridge (minimum) See note.
36	2.50	21.75	Feed to battery from a charger. Feed to a diaphragm water pump e.g. Whale Evenflow.

Note: *For a number of years, Electrolux installation manuals stated that if 2.0mm² cable is fitted, the cable run mustn't exceed 8m. Longer cable runs – between 8 to 10.5m – need 2.5mm² cable to avoid an unacceptable drop in voltage. More recently, however, Electrolux is strongly recommending 2.5mm² cable as a minimum in order to be certain of good refrigerator performance. Moreover, on the latest Dometic (formerly Electrolux) automatic energy selector (AES) fridges, the supply cable should be 6.0mm².*

Table B –
MAXIMUM CURRENT (AMPS) PERMITTED FOR CABLE OF DIFFERENT CROSS SECTIONAL AREAS ON THE BASIS OF LENGTH

Cable size	Maximum cable lengths (supply and return)		
	4 metres	8 metres	12 metres
1.00 mm²	9.4A	4.7A	3.1A
1.5 mm²	14.1A	7.0A	4.7A
2.0 mm²	18.8A	9.3A	6.3A
2.5 mm²	23.5A	11.7A	7.8A

conductor (i.e. 'wire thickness') to suit the appliances being served. If you use cable that's too thin for a high-consumption appliance, it creates a resistance, the cable gets warm and in a severe case the insulation starts to melt. If several supply cables are bunched together, this can lead to a short circuit and serious problems. So check the accompanying tables and note that if a cable isn't supplied on a drum with a label showing its rating, you can work this out by carefully counting its filaments.

The hardest part when wiring a motorcaravan is running cables where they can take the shortest route but without being visible. To achieve this, most of an installation has to be carried out at an early stage in construction. It is often difficult running a cable discreetly at a later stage in a build project although there *are* ways to achieve this as shown when a shelf was constructed with reading lamps on page 136.

■ Wiring harness
If your planning is particularly good and you know where everything is to be fitted, you can get a specialist to make up a wiring harness (or loom). Advertisements for this service sometimes appear in kit car magazines and a professionally built harness was specially made for the Mystique project.

■ Circuit isolation
Since the publication of *BS EN 1648-2: 12V Direct Current Extra Low Voltage Electrical Installations* it has become the practice to fit an isolating relay which terminates all but two 12V supplies to the living area when the engine is running. An isolating relay is shown in the accompanying wiring diagram.

Exceptions that by-pass the isolating relay include the supply to run a refrigerator on its 12V setting, and a charge current from the alternator which serves the leisure battery.

The reason for having an isolating system is explained in *The Motorcaravan Manual* under 'Electromagnetic compatibility'. However, an isolating facility is not often fitted in older vehicles. It tends to be confined to vehicles with electronic controls whose operation on the road might be affected if too many 12V accessories were being used simultaneously in the living area.

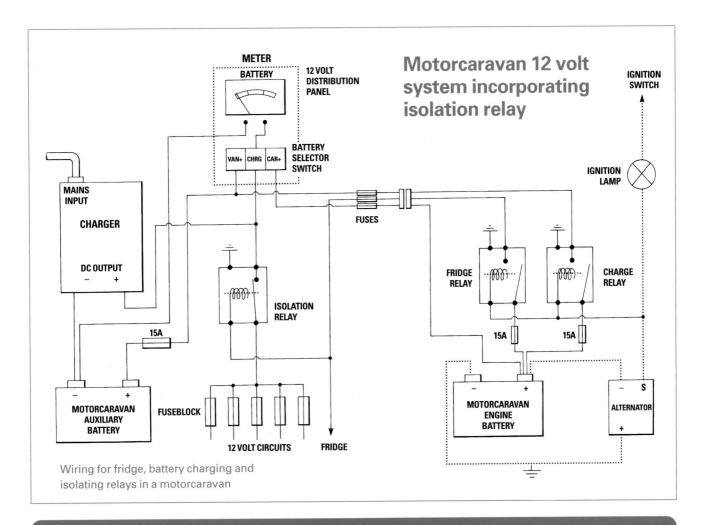

MOTORCARAVAN 12 VOLT SYSTEM INCORPORATING ISOLATION RELAY

Motorcaravan 12 volt system incorporating isolation relay

Wiring for fridge, battery charging and isolating relays in a motorcaravan

Technical Note

RELAYS

A relay is a switch, except that it isn't operated manually. Instead, it is activated by an electric current and since it operates automatically a relay is used to control refrigerator operation.

A motorcaravan absorption refrigerator running on 12V draws a considerable amount of current although that isn't a problem when the engine's running on account of the alternator. However, difficulties arise when the engine is switched off because the supplying battery would soon discharge completely. To prevent this, a relay is fitted to ensure that a fridge is *only* capable of operating on 12V when the engine is running. Conversely, the relay automatically terminates the supply as soon as the ignition is switched off. (See wiring diagram.)

Traditional relays employ an electromagnetic switch although many modern relays operate electronically.

Some relays switch *on* an accessory when the engine is running – like the one operating a refrigerator or the one which sends a charging current to a leisure

battery. Others switch *off* accessories when the engine is running – like the one which cuts off the 12V supply to accessories in the living area.

Relays are sold by automotive suppliers. Hella also sells a kit for fridge and charging control in caravan tow cars and for installation in motorcaravans.

A relay is essentially a switch which is operated electrically rather than by hand. This one is sold with a mounting socket, too.

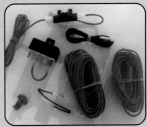

The relays needed in an engine compartment to control fridge operation and charging are sold in a kit by Hella.

Other installation details

■ Battery location

A leisure battery is heavy and earlier chapters suggested that its location needs to consider the overall weight distribution in a motorcaravan. There are electrical issues as well. For example, to receive a good charge from an alternator, the closer together they are the better. This is because there's a significant voltage loss in long cable runs. This would suggest that one of the best places for a leisure battery is in the engine compartment. That's true, but you don't often find sufficient room under the bonnet in present-day light commercial vehicles.

A battery should also be located where the cells can be inspected easily and topped-up periodically. That dismisses the wisdom of hiding it under the driver's seat and there are even current models whose seats have to be completely removed to gain access to the leisure battery.

Maybe it could be fitted in a retractable drawer like a Beeny Box which slides beneath the floor. Some people have found that this arrangement works well but it poses a problem in winter. The operating period of a battery before it needs a recharge (described as its amp hour capacity) is considerably reduced in low temperatures. So it is obviously better to find a place in the warmth of the interior.

That's what was done in the Mystique project. Twin batteries were fitted between the axles, low down and just to the rear of the passenger seat. They were vented through the floor in the approved way using a gas relief tube. However, a panel that keeps them well away from fuses can be slid forwards, thereby ensuring that inspecting and topping-up the cells is easy. Equally, the indoor location of the batteries allows them to benefit from the warmth of the interior.

■ Connections

When creating a 12V supply circuit, good connections must be made in cables, and some methods are better than others.

Except in a few cases, the use of snap locks is not recommended by electricians, partly because they cut through an insulation sleeve.

CABLE CONNECTORS COMPARED AND IN USE

Miniature connecting blocks are useful in some situations as long as the screws are tightened securely.

Auto electricians prefer to use crimp connectors and when you're tackling an ambitious self-build project, it's worth buying one of the better quality crimping tools.

The accompanying sequence shows halogen lights being installed in a ceiling with crimp-spade connectors being used.

Right: Snap locks, sometimes called Scotchlocks, allow a cable to couple up to an adjacent one by cutting through its insulation sleeve.

Far right: Sometimes a connection block is useful and in this instance it's used to couple a feed to a fluorescent light on the ceiling.

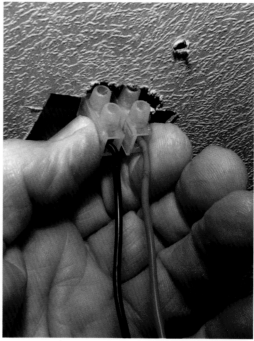

1 To prepare this halogen light for installation in a ceiling panel, crimp-fit spade terminals are fitted to its cables.

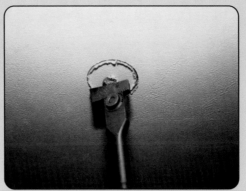

2 In order to cut a precise, tight-fitting hole to accept the halogen light, an expansive drill bit was used in a hand brace.

3 As shown in Chapter 12, cables for ceiling lights in the Mystique project were installed before the panels were fixed into place.

4 Once the connections were made, the lamp units were pushed into the apertures and held in place with two screws.

Technical Note

Lastly, before putting your 230V ac and 12V dc systems into commission, make sure that you get the work checked by a qualified electricians. If you decide to sell the vehicle at a later date it is wise to supply dated certificates attesting to the safety of both electrical installations.

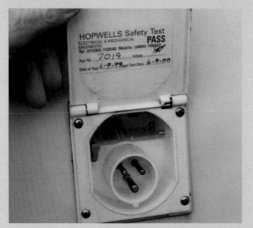

Electrical appliances for installation in motorcaravans are often supplied with safety labels that should be affixed on or close to the appliances. Some include a date panel which shows when the next recommended inspection is needed.

When systems are checked by electrical contractors, the dated certificates are sometimes supported by additional labels that are affixed to key items.

FRESH AND WASTE WATER SYSTEMS

This is one of the easier supply systems to install in a motorcaravan although some professionally-built water systems are not as good as they ought to be.

Although a water system shouldn't be difficult to design, the plumbing in professionally built models is sometimes disappointing. Waste water often drains sluggishly out of sinks and many owners report intolerable smells reaching the living area from their waste tanks.

Another reported disappointment occurs when underfloor waste tanks are installed just rearwards of a shower. When the driver brakes sharply, remnants of dirty water from the waste tank surge forwards and discharge into the shower tray.

Needless-to-say, problems like this shouldn't occur. However, before discussing practical issues, the question is: 'What kind of system will you want?'

Decisions

As regards fresh water provision, some motorcaravans used to be only equipped with a cold water supply comprising a faucet (i.e. an open pipe rather than a tap) and a manually

TYPICAL HOT AND COLD WATER SUPPLY SYSTEM

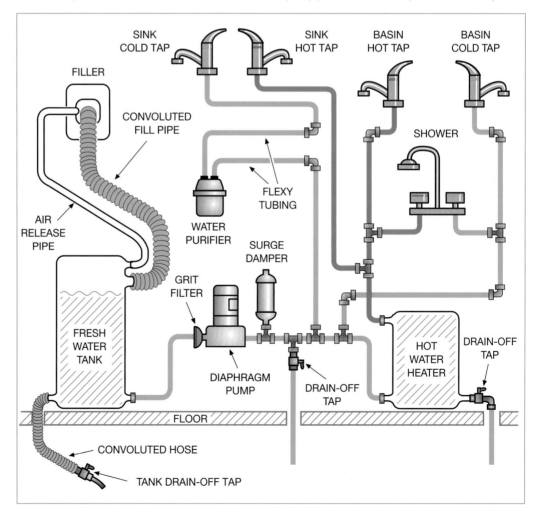

SINK COLD TAP · SINK HOT TAP · BASIN HOT TAP · BASIN COLD TAP

FILLER

CONVOLUTED FILL PIPE

SHOWER

FLEXY TUBING

AIR RELEASE PIPE

WATER PURIFIER

SURGE DAMPER

GRIT FILTER

FRESH WATER TANK

DIAPHRAGM PUMP

DRAIN-OFF TAP

HOT WATER HEATER

DRAIN-OFF TAP

FLOOR

CONVOLUTED HOSE

TANK DRAIN-OFF TAP

operated pump. It's a simple arrangement with little to go wrong. If you want hot water for personal washing or for washing-up, you merely boil a kettle on the hob. In a small campervan this arrangement is fine and both foot-operated and hand-operated pumps from Whale's range of water accessories are fitted in small boats and older caravans.

Today, most motorcaravanners now expect to have a water heater, a shower and hot water on tap; in fact, few people would purchase a new motorcaravan which didn't have these 'luxuries'. However, the installation of a facility like this needs a heating unit, an electric water pump, a switch to activate its motor, a 12V supply and an elaborate pipe system as shown alongside.

Decisions relate to the choice of pipes, whether you intend having fixed tanks (as opposed to portable water containers), choosing taps and picking the right type of pump.

To find out more about such products, see the detailed descriptions given in Chapter 7 of *The Motorcaravan Manual* (2nd Edition) which also includes guidance on:

- avoiding frost damage,
- fully serviced pitches (which offer permanent stand pipe connections),
- characteristics of different pumps,
- replacing micro-switches in taps,
- pressure-sensitive switching, and so on.

The objective in this chapter is to single out some recommended components and to explain how to fit them. Let's start with the fresh water system.

Fresh water

SOURCES
There are four alternative supply sources:

- A direct coupling to a stand-pipe using a pressure-reducing product e.g. the Whale Aquasource. This arrangement is commonplace at camping grounds in the USA but not many sites in Europe offer 'fully serviced pitches'.
- There's the arrangement used in the UK by touring caravanners which requires two external portable containers – one for fresh water, and another taking waste water from a sink or shower.

- A tank system in which a waste water tank is installed under the floor and a fresh water tank is mounted either nearby or indoors where it cannot freeze-up in cold weather.
- A system (seldom used by manufacturers) employing a submersible pump and portable water containers stored indoors in a purpose-made enclosure. This means that the containers can be carried to a service point instead of the owner having to drive the vehicle there.

PORTABLE EXTERNAL CONTAINERS
In my Starcraft campervan project, the provision included a 22.7-litre (5-gallon) plastic water container, a connecting hose, a caravan-type coupling, and an electric diaphragm pump fitted on the floor inside. In winter, the water container was brought indoors at night. It was simple, effective, and a water heater was added at a later date.

An alternative is to fit an electric submersible pump, products being available from both Whale and Truma. Wall couplings are supplied which couple-up the water pipe feed and

Caravanners normally use portable containers to deal with both the fresh and waste water.

This campervan is equipped with portable fresh water containers instead of a fixed tank.

On this Starcraft motorcaravan, water is supplied 'caravan style' and the container can be stowed indoors at night if it's frosty.

Installing a freshwater tank

1 A base was made to enclose the vertical tank. An indentation in its side is a surge baffle to restrain excessive water movement.

2 A wood block and battens prevent the tank from moving. The left outlet is for draining down; the one on the right feeds the supply system.

3 An enclosing framework was constructed and cables on the side are coupled to stainless steel water-level studs. Connections at the top are for the feed pipe and an air release pipe.

4 To achieve a watertight connection with ribbed hose, bathroom silicone sealant was applied round the nozzle, the pipe coupled at once and its hose clip tightened before the sealant set.

5 A drain-down outlet was fitted below the floor using convoluted, lined pipe. This was supplied by CAK and the provision allows the tank to be emptied when severe frost is likely.

6 A water-level gauge was connected-up to the studs on the tank and a display panel was mounted in the kitchen. This product is supplied with coloured cables and connecting instructions.

Note: The narrow breather pipe at the top is connected to a coupling on the filler inlet.

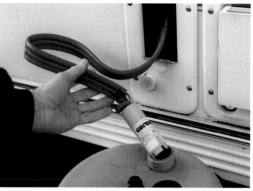

Many caravans have an electric submersible water pump which is lowered into a portable water container.

provide an electrical connection to drive the pump.

FITTING A FRESH WATER TANK
Provision in the Mystique project was more elaborate. A tank from CAK was installed inside and to minimise loss of floor space this was mounted in an upright position.

A water-level indicator was also needed. There's a popular Plug-in-Systems product which has stainless-steel probes that are fitted through an aperture in the top of a tank. However, for the Mystique, CAK supplied a tank fitted with stainless steel studs along the side. These detect the water level and convey an electrical signal to an LED panel which is fitted in a convenient location.

With a capacity of around 55 litres (12 gallons) a full tank would weigh around 55kg (120lb) so a robust structure was needed. For fuel economy and to keep the payload as low as possible you should always empty water tanks before taking to the road; in practice, many motorcaravanners carry *some* fresh water for use en route. To achieve good weight distribution a location was chosen between the front and rear axles and to the rear of the driver's seat.

Note: There are over 170 shapes and sizes of polyethylene tanks in CAK's current catalogue and the company can add connections to suit your installation. Advice on tank position and related advice is freely given by CAK's managing director. Moreover, the catalogues from CAK and Munster Simms Engineering (Whale products) are recommended reading.

Far left: The trouble with flexible hose is that it can easily kink when there's an acute bend.

SUPPLY PIPES

Plumbing which uses plastic hose and clips seems rather primitive. Admittedly, when good-quality worm drive ('Jubilee') clips are used, a system can operate faultlessly for many years, but not all owners are so lucky and cheap quality clip joints often fail.

Moreover, flexible hose can develop kinks and once these appear, it's difficult to remove the deformation. In addition, there are situations where an assembly of couplings needs a mass of clips and it hardly looks like state-of-the-art plumbing.

An alternative is to use semi-rigid pipe and push-fit couplings. These products have been used in the building industry for over thirty years and joints can be made with ease; it is also fairly easy to disconnect a coupling. Incidentally if you're renovating an older motorcaravan and want to fit new appliances using semi-rigid pipe, adaptors are obtainable which connect old hose to new pipe.

Left: When several connections are in close proximity, an array of hose clips hardly looks like state-of-the-art plumbing.

Adaptor couplings are available so that water hose can be coupled up to semi-rigid pipe.

Using semi-rigid pipe

1 To create good joins, a pipe must be cut squarely; an inexpensive tool for the job is sold by Whale.

2 The pipe is pushed hard into a coupling. There may be initial movement, but keep pushing until the pipe is fully home.

3 To detach a pipe, push the small connector (called a collet) inwards at the same time as you pull the pipe out from the coupling.

4 To prevent pipe deforming when negotiating a sharp bend, 'cold forming bend' channelling is available to provide support.

Note: Quick Connect push-fit semi-rigid piping is sold under the Whale brand name by Munster Simms Engineering. The pipe – which Whale refers to as tubing - is sold in 12mm, 15mm and 22mm external diameters. The 12mm product is normally fitted in motorcaravans.

John Guest Speedfit is used in the building industry and this range includes 'cold forming' channelling which supports pipe that needs to negotiate a tight bend.

Be warned: more-recently manufactured semi-rigid pipe can jam when used on older push-fit couplings.

Mounting the fresh water supply on a plywood board in the Mystique makes everything tidy and accessible.

Water drawn from the internal tank is first taken through a grit filter. These filters must be easily accessible for cleaning.

The outflow from the Whale Universal diaphragm pump travels to the smaller white vessel on the extreme right, which is a surge control device. The larger white component is a Nature-Pure Ultrafine water purifier.

After the surge control, a T piece provides a drain down facility; the Whale release tap is near the bottom of the draining pipe.

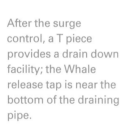

OTHER COMPONENTS

The remaining items needed include a pump, grit filter, surge control and tap. You might also require shower controls and a water purifier.

As mentioned earlier, products are compared in *The Motorcaravan Manual* (2nd Edition). Diaphragm pumps are usually more robust than submersible units although they normally need to be fitted in conjunction with a surge control unit. This helps to smooth out flow irregularities and suppresses pulsing actions which can be evident when a diaphragm pump is installed. Incidentally, a diaphragm pump with a powerful output is needed if a water purifier (as opposed to a taste filter) is required.

Another feature of a diaphragm pump is the pressure-sensitive switching device that's fitted within its casing. This is how it operates: when you operate a tap, the 'opening-up' of a pipe leads to a drop in pressure which immediately activates the switch that controls the pump's motor. It is a reliable system except when there's a small air leak in a pipe connection. This can activate the pump making it pulse a few times – and that's disturbing at night. So it is normal to fit a cut-off switch although you will often find that 12V control panels have a switch to isolate a water pump.

The alternative is to fit taps which incorporate tiny mechanical micro-switches to activate an electric pump. Unfortunately, these fail if damp gets onto the contacts; replacement procedures are shown in Chapter 7 of *The Motorcaravan Manual.*

FRESH WATER SUPPLY

When designing a water system for the Mystique, it was decided to mount components on 6mm plywood. Board of this thickness is light, although strengthening layers were added on the reverse side where the main components were fitted.

The board was wall mounted below the sink and when drawers and shelves are removed from the kitchen unit, there's full access to all components and pipe couplings; easy access is important when repairs are needed.

Looking at the layout more closely, water from the supply tank is drawn through a grit filter by a Whale diaphragm pump. A grit interception filter is essential to prevent damage to the piston mechanism so a filter is always supplied with a diaphragm pump.

The outflow from the pump then progresses towards a surge damper and subsequently reaches a 'T' coupling. This is the lowest point and a drain-down tap is fitted so that residual water can be emptied efficiently from the system. When a 'van is stored during cold conditions, all taps must be left open and the system should be drained completely.

If the drain tap is *closed*, pumped water is fed into two separate routeways: a) the cold feed for the sink tap, and b) the feed supplying a wash basin, shower and water heater.

When the Mystique was first put into service, the supply to the sink was directed through an in-line Whale Aqua Source Clear taste filter to improve water palatability.

This kind of filter is fine but it doesn't purify water so it was later replaced by a Nature-Pure Ultrafine water purifier from General Ecology (shown on previous page).

As long as a diaphragm pump achieves the required pressure, this type of purifier not only improves palatability; it also ensures that water is totally safe to drink. Hence you can obtain drinking water directly from a tank without any concerns about its quality. Some motorcaravanners purchase bottled water, but that's unnecessary when one of these products is fitted.

Finally, an adaptor connection was fitted to the semi-rigid pipe, thereby providing a threaded coupling for the flexible braided tail that connects to a Whale marine-style stainless steel mixer tap.

The tap was mounted on the GRP draining board which was 'thickened-up' with 9mm ply below the prepared hole to prevent the plastic from flexing.

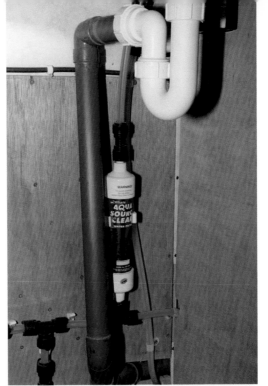

This shows Whale's compact Aqua Source Clear taste filter which has been fitted in-line near the tap that is mounted on the sink above.

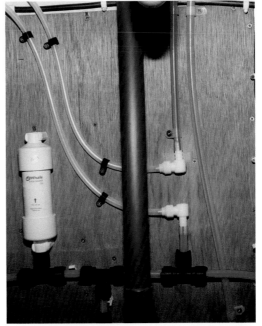

Later, the Aqua Source Clear was replaced by two 90 deg couplings, flexible connecting pipes and a Nature-Pure Ultrafine water purifier.

Far left: Adaptors are available which are fitted in the end of a fresh water supply pipe to accept the flexible 'tails' that connect with taps.

Left: This high-quality mixer tap in a brushed stainless-steel finish was first seen in Whale's marine range of water accessories.

This type of convoluted waste hose may have prominent ridges on the outside, but the inside has a smooth lining sleeve.

The compact water trap from CAK is made to couple up with a waste water system that has been assembled using flexible hose.

A water trap from DLS Plastics is designed for installation in motorcaravans and the interceptor bowl can be removed for cleaning.

Domestic PVCu waste pipe can be assembled using various couplings and a solvent weld adhesive such as that supplied by Osma.

Waste water

WASTE PIPE

When buying waste pipe don't use convoluted pipe which has ridges on the *inside* as well as the outside. Manufacturers often fit this type but it slows the flow rate and food particles easily get caught. More-discerning manufacturers fit a flexible hose which has reinforcing ridges on the outside, but a smooth lining on the *inside*. Check this when making a purchase.

This type of hose is rather narrow, although it is needed if an outlet fitted to a sink or basin has a similarly narrow coupling nozzle.

Mention was made earlier that many motorhome owners report smells rising up from the water tank and these can be dreadful in hot weather. This is aggravated if the positioning of the tank's outlet doesn't allow it to drain out *all* water and floating food particles. A cure is to employ the system as used in our homes in which every sink and toilet basin has a deep water trap to prevent smells rising from the public sewer.

Curiously, few manufacturers ever bother to fit a trap, but two products have recently been introduced which couple-up with flexible hose. Occasionally, the all-important barrier of water might shake out when you're driving, but a turn of a tap soon reinstates this water on arrival.

Notwithstanding the launch of these miniature traps, experiments with caravans twenty years ago led me to install rigid domestic waste pipe instead. Both of my self-built motorhomes have this system fitted.

DOMESTIC WASTE PIPE

In the Mystique project it was decided to employ PVCu domestic, rigid waste pipe and couplings which are sold by builders' merchants. Toilet cistern 25mm overflow pipe can be used, but 30mm pipe creates a much faster flow rate.

Accordingly, domestic traps were fitted under the sink and wash basin although the trap under the shower tray was purpose-made using several 25mm, 90° bend couplings.

As regards the sinks, their apertures had to be enlarged to take a domestic outlet. If you don't like that prospect, you can fit a narrow-bore motorhome outlet coupled-up to a short tail of flexible hose under the sink. The hose is draped *inside* a length of 30mm rigid PVCu pipe – just like the flexible emptying hose from a washing machine is draped inside a rigid waste pipe. With this arrangement, the domestic trap is then fitted lower down.

Of course, your choice of pipe dictates the size of the inlet nozzles needed on your waste tank – bearing in mind that CAK welds the couplings to meet customers' requirements.

Note that it usually pays to fit an underfloor tank *first,* fine-tuning the position of pipe runs *later*, rather than the other way round. Also pay heed to a mistake that had to be corrected on the Mystique. If you don't fit lengths of dense-foam padding to protect a tank where it comes into contact with the underside of the floor, it may creak whenever you walk in that area.

Note: On a small campervan, the use of a portable waste container may be preferred. Even if you do have a waste tank fitted, its contents could freeze in winter, whereupon you

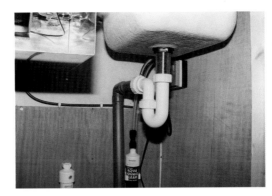

Under both the sink and wash basin in the Mystique, a domestic water trap was fitted to prevent odours rising up from the tank.

can't drain water from your sink. That's why winter motorhome users run waste water directly through a tank and straight into a portable container.

Fitting an under-floor tank

1 It is best to purchase a tank which has a cleaning port and screw cap. Products from CAK can be supplied with steel support brackets and flexible straps.

2 Manoeuvring a tank into position can be difficult and there might not be as much space underneath as you imagined. That's why it is better to mount the tank *before* installing the feed pipes.

3 Float devices which show when a tank needs emptying can fail if food remnants jam-up the hinging mechanism. Stainless-steel studs were fitted here, and wired to a warning light system.

4 Tanks supplied by CAK can be supplied with welded outlets in the locations needed by a customer. After roughening them up, the surfaces were coated with Osma Weld adhesive.

5 Although Osma adhesive is sold for PCVu rainwater pipes, it also bonded the couplings to the tank. Outlet key – top left: from shower tray; top right: water from sink and basin; bottom right: drain down outlet.

Note: *Before fitting the waste pipes, park the motorcaravan completely level.* This means that if you use a spirit level and the pipes are installed with a fall (i.e. a slope) throughout their entire run, you'll always have an efficient system whenever you're parked level.

GAS SUPPLY SYSTEMS

18

In spite of the increasing use of electricity and diesel fuel for cooking and heating in motorcaravans, liquefied petroleum gas remains a dominant force.

Liquefied Petroleum Gas (LPG) is a 'clean fuel', a good heat producer and its explosive qualities make it sufficiently powerful to propel a vehicle. Herein lies a problem. On one hand it is an extremely convenient fuel to use in a motorcaravan; on the other, its misuse can lead to fatalities.

Safety first

Service engineers who work on gas installations and appliances fitted in a motorcaravan that is hired to the public must be Gas Safe™ registered. (Gas Safe™ replaced the CORGI scheme on 1st April 2009.)

Curiously, this requirement doesn't apply to privately owned motorcaravans. Instead, it is stated in *The Gas Safety (Installation and Use) Regulations 1998* that: 'No person shall carry out any work in relation to a gas fitting unless he is competent to do so.' From a safety point of view, that makes good sense, except that the word 'competent' is not defined.

Whether an experienced DIY enthusiast can be deemed sufficiently competent to connect a gas supply to a new appliance depends on his or her background. If a motorcaravan self-builder has attended a wide range of practical and theoretical training courses which focus on the installation and servicing of gas appliances, they would probably regard themselves as 'competent'.

There's no doubt that connecting up copper gas pipe is not a complex operation, especially for a DIY plumber who has frequently used compression joints when coupling water pipe.

On the other hand, copper gas pipe is different from domestic copper water pipe. For example, if you *over-tighten* a gas compression joint, it distorts and gas will leak from the coupling. Conversely, if you *under-tighten* a gas compression coupling, again you get a leak. Needless-to-say, whenever there's a leak there's an ever-present possibility of an explosion.

With that in mind, a person who has never attended training courses relating to LPG installations will have neither the knowledge nor the practical experience to construct gas supply systems. Similarly they should never attempt to service or repair gas appliances. Work on gas connections, flues and the final testing of an appliance should be entrusted to a competent gas engineer. This advice is not just for the benefit of self-builders but also for anyone who subsequently purchases a motorcaravan from a DIY enthusiast.

Safety tip

SAFETY STANDARDS
For further information on gas installation matters refer to the *European Standard EN 1949: 2002* which is concerned with installations and the *European Standard EN 12864: 2001* which is concerned with regulators. Both European Standards have the status of a British Standard and their full titles are given later in the chapter.

The self-builder's involvement

Don't be too disappointed by the fact that you will need to get gas couplings carried out by a trained specialist in LPG work. If you analyse the work involved when installing a gas appliance, you will notice that making a gas coupling represents a very small part of the job as a whole.

For instance, a confident woodworker is likely to be able to fit appliances like an absorption refrigerator, a hob, or a gas heater. Most of the installation work is structural and the fitting instructions supplied with new

Far left: Copper gas pipe can be covered with a protective sleeve to avoid abrasion damage.

Left: A pipe-bending tool allows sharp bends to be formed without kinking the pipe.

appliances are usually comprehensive. For example, photographs of the Mazda project in Chapter 8 show typical structural work when a fridge was being installed. Similarly, in Chapter 11, photographs trace the stages when a ventilator was fitted. Ventilators are needed to control temperature around a cooling unit on absorption refrigerators manufactured by Dometic, Electrolux and Thetford.

In the same way, if the installation instructions state that a refrigerator needs a 6mm gas feed pipe, a competent DIY enthusiast should be able to run a continuous length of copper pipe along an unobstructed pathway inside the living space in accordance with specifications laid down in *BS EN 1949: 2002.*

For instance, the pipe should be fully supported with clips no greater than 500mm apart. A pipe run should also be kept separate from other services with at least 30mm minimum clearance in a parallel path and 10mm at a crossover point. Where a chosen route might cause a length of pipe to receive mechanical damage it has to be protected. Some manufacturers protect copper pipe using a sleeve of rubber hose or ribbed plastic pipe.

Gentle bends can be formed by hand but a pipe-bending tool is needed to prevent a pipe kinking when creating small radius curves.

Safety tip

GAS PIPE

Whereas steel pipe is sometimes found in appliances, the supply pipe normally used in motorcaravans is made of copper complying with EN 1057. The outside diameters of pipes typically used are:

5mm ($^3/_{16}$in) used in historic models for gas lamps.

6mm ($^1/_4$in) used for many appliances including most refrigerators.

8mm ($^5/_{16}$in) used for some space heating appliances and typically used for the main trunkway in a supply system.

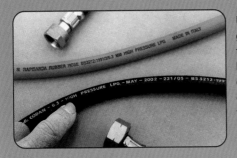

Under the latest gas standards, the flexible hose connecting a cylinder to a fixed regulator has to be 'High-pressure' rated.

Notes:
- Some fittings designed for metric pipes will not fit imperial pipes.
- Gas pipes must be bonded to an earth conductor which is normally connected to a steel body panel or part of the chassis.
- Only one length of flexible hose is normally permitted and that's used to couple a cylinder to the fixed supply system.
- In vehicles constructed prior to the implementation of *BS EN 1949: 2002,* where the gas regulator is mounted directly on a cylinder, approved *low-pressure* flexible hose is used and an owner can install this using suitable clips. However, where a 30mbar regulator (described later) is wall-mounted, *high-pressure* hose is needed complete with factory-fitted couplings. This must not exceed 450mm in length unless the gas supply cylinders are mounted on a slide-out tray, in which case the maximum permitted length is 750mm.
- Further information on installation requirements is set out in *BS EN 1949: 2002.*

An untrained self-builder must not create gas connections but pipe can be installed using procedures laid down in *BS EN 1942: 2002*.

The kind of preparatory work involved when a Dometic AES refrigerator was being installed is shown in the accompanying photograph. The gas pipes are in place and ready for a gas specialist to connect-up the appliance later.

When preparations are made to run a length of gas pipe to an appliance, bear in mind that pipes serving appliances are connected to a bank of readily accessible gas shut-off valves.

The installation should comply with *BS EN 1949: 2002 Sections 7.5 and 8.8* and ensure the valves allow individual branches to be isolated if required. The DIY builder can mount the shut-off valves to a suitable base although the job of making the final gas couplings will be undertaken by an appropriately qualified LPG specialist.

Clearly marked gas isolation valves should be fitted on the branches servicing separate appliances.

As a general precaution, you should also construct a drop-out hole under this assembly of isolation valves just in case a leak were to occur. Furthermore, the 'Off–On' positions should be clearly marked together with identification to show which appliances they serve.

Drop-out holes

A series of gas drop-out holes are needed in case a gas leak develops.

In the event of a gas coupling failing, leaking LPG drops downwards and starts accumulating at the lowest point it reaches. Potentially this is very dangerous and that is why 'drop-out holes' have to be constructed to provide a safe escape for leaking gas.

If you check the installation instructions supplied with gas appliances, you will often see reference to drop-out holes and their required dimensions. These are critically important. An escape vent is also required in a gas cylinder locker as well as defined in *BS EN 1949: 2002 Section 5*.

When planning locations for drop-out holes in a system, it often helps to imagine that it is water trickling out of a faulty connection and predict where it would accumulate. LPG isn't visible like water, but it's likely to get trapped in the same places – hence the need for escape outlets.

To keep out vermin, a gas drop-out hole will need some form of mesh or moulded grill.

On the underside of the floor, thoughtfully formed shielding can prevent draughts from blowing into gas drop-out holes.

It also needs a deflector mounted on the underside of the floor so that draughts and water don't get forced into the living space when you're driving in heavy rain. You can form a deflector yourself using some spare aluminium sheet or by using flexible plastic.

Guidance on LPG

Anyone using LPG in a leisure vehicle needs to know how to use it safely. A helpful reference is Chapter 6 in *The Motorcaravan Manual* (2nd Edition) which covers topics including the characteristics of LPG, different types of cylinders, storage of cylinders, pressure regulation, pipework installation, leak detection and an appraisal of gas-operated appliances.

Some of these topics are mentioned briefly in the section which follows and it is especially important to check the later section on gas pressure regulation. This relates to all self-build projects.

GENERAL FACTS

Liquefied petroleum gas is:

- Odourless and its distinctive smell is added before it is sold to the public.
- Not a poisonous gas, but it is highly flammable.
- Heavier than air and if it escapes from a faulty coupling, it sinks to the lowest point available. That is why a cylinder should *never* be stored in a cellar and why motorcaravans have low-level drop-out holes.
- Available in two distinctive forms – butane and propane. Their characteristics are quite different, as listed in *The Motorcaravan Manual* (2nd Edition) on page 75.
- Only capable of changing from a liquefied state into a gas when the temperature is right. For instance butane doesn't vaporise at temperatures lower than 0°C (32°F) at atmospheric pressure. Propane, however, is able to vaporise at temperatures as low as −40°C (−44°F), so it is the preferred fuel in winter.

- Readily available in both butane and propane portable cylinders in the UK. In mainland Europe, propane is used in many commercial situations but in a number of countries it is not sold to the public in portable cylinders.

Pressures and performance

The fact that propane has a vapour pressure between three and four times that of butane (at 15°C) has implications for the choice of regulator.

The function of a regulator is to ensure that gas is delivered from a cylinder at a stable and constant pressure to suit the appliances it's required to run. Using a regulator also means that gas coming from a new cylinder will reach appliances at the same pressure as it does from one that's approaching exhaustion.

Also important is the fact that appliances fitted in European leisure vehicles have sometimes been built to work at different pressures. For example, it has been the practice in Britain to install appliances which run on gas supplied at a pressure of 28–37mbars. In Germany, appliances have been fitted to run on gas supplied at a pressure of 50mbars.

As soon as motorcaravans were being exported and imported in greater numbers, it was clear that standardisation was needed. Even the gas cylinders have different couplings from country to country. Moreover in the UK, appliances are built to run on either butane *or* propane, but in the past you had to purchase a gas-specific regulator to suit your preferred gas. Typically, the butane regulator sold in Britain is blue while propane regulators are red, and their respective couplings only fit on cylinders filled with the right type of gas.

Below left: Cylinder-mounted 28mbar regulators for use with butane are usually painted blue.

Below: The cylinder-mounted 37mbar regulators intended for use with propane are usually painted red.

Right: The 30mbar regulators introduced since the publication of *BS EN 1949: 2002* and *BS EN 12864: 2001* accept both butane and propane.

Far right: As a result of the most recent gas standards, regulators are usually wall-mounted and form part of the fixed supply system.

A standardised system had to be introduced and this prompted the publication of two British Standards/European norms, namely:

BS EN 12864: 2001 Low-pressure, non-adjustable regulators having a maximum outlet pressure of less than or equal to 200mbar, with a capacity of less than or equal to 4kg/h, and their associated safety devices for butane, propane or their mixtures.

BS EN 1949: 2002 Specification for the installation of LPG systems for habitation purposes in leisure accommodation vehicles and other road vehicles.

In Britain, the manufacturers of caravans and motorhomes who were members of the National Caravan Council (NCC) implemented the new BS EN standards in vehicles built from 1 September 2003. Even though the new system was a 'standard' as opposed to a regulation, other non-NCC manufacturers have voluntarily chosen to adopt the new practices as well.

This major change has particular importance for self-builders and those DIY enthusiasts who decide to renovate an older vehicle. A fuller description appears in *The Motorcaravan Manual* (2nd Edition) and the following summary only covers the points which have relevance to self-builders.

Below: If a fixed 30mbar regulator is used, the owner merely has to buy a coupling hose to suit the type of cylinders chosen for use.

Practical implications of the revised gas standards

Since 2003, a standardised gas pressure of 30mbar has been adopted for motorcaravans throughout member countries of the European Union. Therefore, all current gas appliances are built to run at a pressure of 30mbar and are labelled accordingly. This necessitated the

development of new regulators which deliver gas at a pressure of 30mbar, but the change doesn't end there.

The 30mbar regulator is also designed so that it can accept both butane *and* propane. The manufacturers in most countries have also mounted the 30mbar regulator permanently on a bulkhead panel near the gas cylinders thereby forming an integral part of the fixed pipework.

(Note: Some German caravans have been manufactured with 30mbar *cylinder-mounted* regulators and flexible hose, which is perhaps rather surprising.)

When a regulator forms part of the fixed supply system, all that is needed to couple up to a gas cylinder is a *high-pressure* flexible hose bearing factory-fitted couplings. Versions are sold to suit different cylinder connections, thereby enabling you to couple-up to a cylinder purchased elsewhere in Europe, as well as those used in the UK.

The versatility afforded by the new system is useful but there's a warning footnote. If you own a pre-September 2003 motorcaravan fitted with appliances labelled at 28–37mbar, you must NOT replace your cylinder-mounted butane and propane regulators with one of the bulkhead-mounted universal regulators rated at 30mbar. The Calor Gas leaflet *New Requirements for LPG in Caravans,* distributed in 2003, states: 'The gas pressures of the new regulator and your existing installation are *not* compatible. You should continue to use the appropriate cylinder-mounted regulator…' This advice has been endorsed by the National Caravan Council.

Gas pressures and the self-builder

If you have purchased new gas appliances labelled at 30mbar to install in your project van, you need to have a 30mbar regulator installed. On the other hand, if you have purchased pre-owned appliances, perhaps from a breakers' yard, and which are labelled to operate at 28-37mbar, you will have to fit one of the older type of butane or propane, cylinder-mounted regulators. Obviously, pre-owned appliances would have to be checked thoroughly by a gas engineer to verify that they are safe and fit for purpose.

In use, both systems are fine, but as gas specialists point out, they must not be mixed and matched. Some amateur installers think otherwise, but gas specialists are quite adamant; you must *not* fit a 30mbar regulator in a motorcaravan whose appliances are labelled to run on supplies of 28–37mbar.

Examples of projects

CYLINDER COMPARTMENT

The requirements for compartments for carrying gas cylinders are specified in *BS EN 1949: 2002 Section 5*. This publication covers examples of compartments *with* internal access from the living space and those *without*. In both types,

strict minimum distances from heat sources are laid down and in a diagram relating to motorhomes this refers to 'exhausters'. It transpires that this oddly chosen term refers to silencers and (presumably) exhaust pipes.

Other requirements include:
- A facility which permits a cylinder to be secured in an upright position with its valve uppermost.
- A security system which allows a cylinder to be retrieved without need of tools.
- Fixed low-level ventilation at least 2% of the compartment's floor area and 10,000mm² minimum, fitted in such a manner that it cannot be obstructed by a cylinder. (See *BS EN 1949: 2002* for permitted variations.)
- An absence of any items in the compartment which might ignite leaking gas – no locker lights, battery, or uninsulated electrical connections, etc.
- A self-builder must consult *BS EN 1949: 2002* for fuller descriptions of approved LPG installations.

Constructing a gas cylinder compartment with internal access

1 The system here is for a pre-2003 installation with a cylinder-mounted butane 28–37mbar regulator. A gas drop-out vent was fitted in the floor panel, situated 1.6m from the silencer.

2 A steel panel bought from an auto supplier was cut, bent and riveted to create a non-flammable box to house one Calor Gas 4.5kg butane cylinder and one Campingaz 2.72kg Type 907 cylinder.

3 A jigsaw was used to cut the gas drop-out aperture in the base of the compartment and an aluminium vent was purchased from an accessory shop to ensure vermin cannot force an entry.

4 The compartment was fitted so that the gas controls were not obscured. Retention bases were mounted on the floor and these locate the cylinders so that they don't obscure the drop-out.

5 Section 5.7a) of *BS EN 1949: 2002* requires high-level supports to prevent cylinders from toppling over. Rather than relying on a strap arrangement, a collar was cut for the Calor Gas cylinder.

6 A further collar was cut for the Campingaz cylinder. All that remained to be done was to construct an attached and sealed metal lid, the lowest portion of which is well over the required 50mm minimum height from the floor.

When a kitchen is being fitted with a hob, the minimum proximity of combustible surfaces to the sides and above the burners is specified in the installation instructions.

INSTALLING A CRAMER HOB AND GRILL

A four-burner hob was purchased which includes a pre-installed grill compartment and a safety-glass lid. The intention was to install this in a fitted GRP worktop and sink unit. Care was taken to follow the manufacturer's specified distances from combustible surfaces, the height above the burners being an especially critical dimension. When a burner is alight but its kettle has been removed to prepare coffee, the heat from an uncovered burner will rise with surprising intensity.

Like all modern hobs the burners are fitted with flame failure devices. This means that if one of the burners were to blow out, the gas supply is automatically terminated. Notwithstanding this provision, the structure

below the hob features discreet drop-out holes. In consequence, if gas were to escape from a hob burner, the grill or the supply coupling, there are routes for gas to disperse down to a floor vent below.

Completion

When an installation is complete, do *not* put it into commission until the system has been checked by a Gas Safe™ registered specialist. (The Gas Safe Register™ has replaced CORGI registration). Having confirmed that it is safe to use, a dated and signed certificate should be issued. LPG is a fuel which has to be treated with the greatest of care.

Installing a Cramer hob and grill

1 The position of the appliance's coupling was noted so that a feed gas pipe could be installed later in the appropriate place.

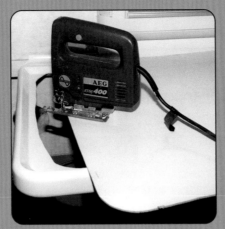

2 A cut-out was formed in the work top using a jigsaw. A slow speed was selected and a blade for cutting GRP was fitted.

3 Strengthening ply was bonded around the cut-out to accept fixing screws and to give support near the hinges of the glass lid.

4 Pilot holes for the fixing screws were prepared in the GRP at each corner and 9mm ply was bonded on the underside.

5 The kitchen unit was assembled around the grill compartment with generous clearances and gas escape routes.

6 A paper pattern was made and transferred to a plastic laminated fascia; holes were then drilled for the control knobs.

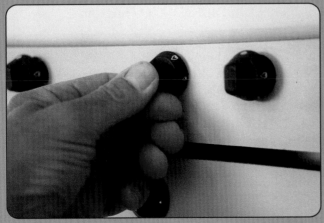

7 It is important that the control knobs can be held fully depressed when lighting burners, to heat the flame-failure probes.

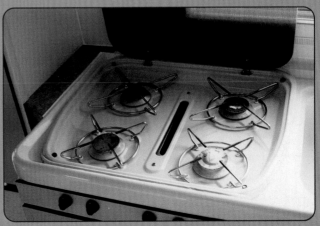

8 Gradually, the kitchen unit was created around the location of the hob and a drop-down front was fitted to cover the grill.

APPLIANCES AND ACCESSORIES

Kitchen appliances, heating systems, washroom products and other fixtures need to be selected and installed with care.

The preceding chapters have already made reference to a selection of products fitted in motorcaravans. Case histories have shown typical installations in progress and step-by-step photographs have highlighted some of the tasks involved. The purpose of this chapter is to look further into the subject of appliances, systems and accessories.

Whatever products you decide to purchase, it is important to follow the installation instructions with great care, especially when they relate to safety issues. It's true that fitting instructions are sometimes disappointing, but I've always been impressed by the guidance supplied by manufacturers such as Truma (heating/air conditioning/water appliances) and Thetford (toilets).

When commissioned to write installation manuals to accompany Electrolux refrigerators, I prepared the content on the presumption that the reader had no prior knowledge about the products. Any technical terms relating were fully explained and my personal involvement of installing refrigerators in caravans helped to make the text more informative. First-hand experience had provided a clear insight into the

work required and one of the early Electrolux electronic-ignition models was fitted in my Starcraft campervan.

Since those instructional leaflets were published, Dometic (which inherited several of the products from Electrolux Leisure) continues to provide comprehensive installation literature. In fact the Dometic instructions proved helpful when I fitted an Automatic Energy Selector (AES) absorption fridge in the Mystique motorhome. This model draws 12V power in a slightly different manner to usual and its electronic brain has to be 'fed' from the leisure battery. However, this was fully explained in the fitting instructions.

Since many product installation manuals are comprehensive, this chapter doesn't replicate information which is already supplied when you buy an appliance. However, a pictorial case history shows the installation of a Thetford swivel-bowl toilet. In addition, there are illustrations relating to the installing of a washbasin and shower tray. These last-mentioned items are seldom supplied with instructions but if you overlook certain precautionary measures you will end-up with leaking fittings and cracked mouldings.

Decisions to make

■ TYPE OF REFRIGERATOR

When reflecting on the all-important matter of food storage, you will have to decide which type of fridge is best suited for your project 'van. Some small campervans may be better-served by a compact and portable refrigeration box as opposed to a permanently installed unit.

Then there's the contrasting merits of compressor fridges compared with three-way absorption products. These points were reported in the section 'Decisions on the type of refrigerator' in Chapter 8. Check this to confirm which type of appliance best suits your needs. It is also recommended that you consult the twelve-page chapter entitled 'Refrigerators' in

The instructions for installing an absorption refrigerator are usually very clear.

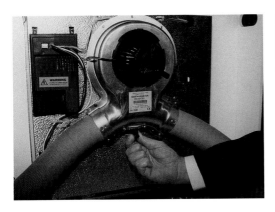

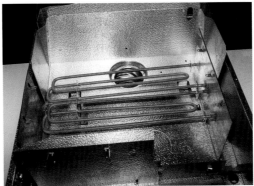

Far left: Some gas heaters, like the former Carver 2000, had a supporting mains heating element built within the fan assembly.

Left: The Carver 4000 Fanmaster was principally a gas heater but a 230V element was also fitted within the casing.

the second edition of *The Motorcaravan Manual* published by Haynes.

■ HEATING SYSTEMS

Under this broad title, you need to consider both space heaters and water heaters. It was pointed out in Chapter 8 that you will occasionally find professionally-built motorcaravans in which heating systems are sold as 'optional extras'. For summer-only users it's true that a heater might not be needed. However, most owners would expect a motorcaravan to have a fixed heater and this involves making further decisions.

Thoughts on this topic were discussed in that chapter under the section 'Space and water heating appliances' and the requirements are different in a van conversion as opposed to a coachbuilt model. In the latter example, there's not only more internal space to heat: there's also more room for the installation of an elaborate system. This raises the matter regarding your preferred choice of fuel.

Electric space-heating systems

Whereas electricity is sometimes used to augment a heating system, the current draw is too great for the 230V supplies found on the majority of sites. On some sites, a hook-up is likely to offer enough current (amps) to operate a portable domestic fan heater on its lowest 1kW (1,000-watt) setting. This typically requires a hook-up pillar which offers at least 5 amps per pitch and presumes that you won't be using other mains appliances at the same time. (See Chapter 5 in *The Motorcaravan Manual* (Second Edition) for guidance on using mains supplies.)

Some water heaters also include a built-in 230V element which can be used with higher output hook-ups; electricity is also used quite

often to run a gas heater's warm air circulation fans, some of which have a built-in auxiliary mains heating element as well.

Some Truma warm-air gas heaters and the now-obsolete Carver heaters also have a low-output heating element built within their casing. In general, however, the chief source of heat in motorcaravans is derived from either a gas or diesel/petrol appliance.

Gas-driven space and water heaters

If you are renovating an older model, you may come across a number of appliances which are no longer being manufactured. For instance, it was a big surprise when Atwood, an American manufacturer, closed its European division leaving many motorhome owners with a large 'combination heater' (air and water) for which spares were no longer available. Several manufacturers had fitted these units including Cockburn Holdsworth and Murvi.

An even greater number of owners were concerned when Carver closed its gas heating operation, too. Fortunately some Carver spares are still available from Truma (UK) although this spare-part service may not last much longer.

In the event, many of Truma's current wall-

Parts for some Carver products are still available from Truma, but the service may soon be terminated.

Right: In an upgrade operation, it may be possible to remove an older Carver heater and to modify the aperture to house a Truma product.

Far right. A Whale water heater fits into tight spaces. An adaptor plate is available if it is to replace an old Carver water heater.

A Truma water heater was neatly installed in this 2001 Auto-Trail Mohican; competent DIY enthusiasts might tackle some of this work themselves.

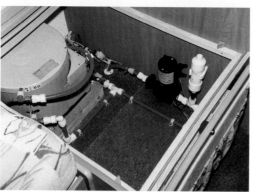

mounted heaters and the Combitronic water/space heaters can be fitted in locations originally designed to house Carver and Atwood products respectively. Since Carver Engineers of the West Midlands and Truma of Germany worked closely together in the 1980s, this isn't very surprising.

In contrast, the popular Carver Crystal water heater was unique and had a completely different fitting arrangement from Truma's present-day Ultrastore water heaters.

It is therefore pleasing that a replica of the original Carver product has since been launched and called the Henry GE. Many of its parts are interchangeable and if you are rebuilding a motorhome fitted with a moribund Carver Crystal water heater, you could now fit a complete replacement using the existing aperture in the side wall. The Henry GE is available through Johnnie Longden Ltd. whose address appears in the Appendix.

As regards wall-mounted 'instantaneous' water heaters (as opposed to storage water heaters), these are no longer fitted. In the interests of safety a water heater now has to have a room-sealed burner and a flue which vents directly to the outside. This makes good sense although the Rinnai instantaneous water heater fitted latterly in my Starcraft always produced copious supplies of really hot water.

Otherwise, there are various heating products available from small-scale manufacturers together with the Truma range which is undoubtedly the most comprehensive.

The aperture cut for a Carver Crystal water heater can now be used to fit a modern version of the product called the Henry GE.

Right: Wall-mounted instantaneous water heaters are no longer fitted in current motorhomes; storage heaters are used instead.

Far right. The combined gas/230V Whale space heater is easy to fit in tight spaces. Here it's been mounted under the floor.

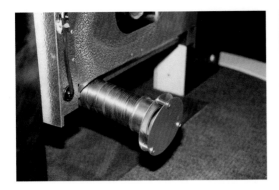

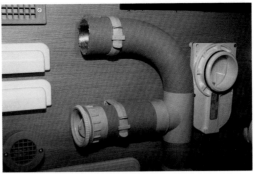

Don't forget that you must leave gas and flue connections to a qualified person as explained in Chapter 18.

The structural part of an installation, however, is well-described in Truma's instruction manuals and competent self-builders are likely to be able to carry out this part of an installation themselves. Similarly, the fitting of air distribution ducting is a straightforward operation that many DIY builders could also carry out.

Diesel and petrol-driven heaters

It was mentioned in Chapter 2 that the Mystique motorhome was the first coachbuilt model in the UK to be fitted with an Eberspächer Hydronic space and water heating system. This followed on naturally from the development and installation of Eberspächer heating systems in the van conversions manufactured by Murvi.

Not that Eberspächer's products are new by any means. These heaters have been fitted for many years in boats and in the cabs of commercial lorries.

It was hardly surprising, therefore, that the products were adapted to suit the needs of motorcaravanners and Murvi worked closely with Eberspächer to develop this application. Incidentally, although most of these systems operate on diesel fuel, the German company also manufacturers an equivalent range of heaters which run on petrol.

Several different systems have now been developed, the simplest of which is a compact, self-contained warm air heater called the Airtronic. The D2 (2.2kW) and the D4 (4kW) versions are fitted by manufacturers including Auto-Sleepers and Romahome. Typically, these Airtronic units are fitted in a bed box because they require little space.

A more complete system called the Combitronic Compact is fitted by a number of large manufacturers such as Auto-Trail; this embraces a water heating facility which incorporates a storage cylinder, too. The Combitronic Compact is now packaged in a single casing which is mounted under the floor of a vehicle, thereby freeing-up space in the living area. The product is particularly easy to install.

Finally, there's the Modular Hydronic system which combines with the vehicle's cooling system so that an owner can pre-heat the engine before setting-off in cold weather. This system includes a copper cylinder which retains a store of high-temperature water produced either by the Hydronic heater or merely as a result of driving the vehicle around. When the extremely hot water is drawn-off, a mixer valve automatically cools the out-flowing contents to a usable temperature. This means that a large quantity of usable hot water is available from the two-gallon cylinder. And to add further versatility, an Eberspächer storage cylinder is fitted with a 230V 1kW immersion heater, too.

There's also a control panel which offers a wide range of operating options. For instance, three 'On/Off' operations can be programmed in a 24-hour hour period and each day of the week can also be set to provide different 'On/Off' regimes.

As a further innovation there are remote control systems. You can purchase a battery-operated key fob for localised control, an Easy Start radio remote control device or a telephone Calltronic remote controlling facility. When you're some distance from your motorcaravan, these devices enable you:

■ to activate the heating,
■ de-frost the windscreen, and
■ pre-heat the engine

Even the key fob controller will set these systems in operation from inside your house when the vehicle's parked on the drive.

A Webasto system was fitted in this 2004 Auto-Trail Cheyenne 660SE; it featured a heat exchanger in this specially allocated compartment. The main heating unit was installed below the floor.

Components in an Eberspächer Hydronic system

The control panel is self-explanatory and easy to use. Every 24 hours, three 'On/Off' operations can be programmed. These can differ if needed on different days of the week.

When heat isn't being drawn from the engine, the compact Hydronic heater takes over. On the Mystique, a 5kW unit was mounted by the sump in order not to take up space in the living area.

The Hydronic heater is plumbed-in to the engine cooling system and takes over the task of heating the domestic water whenever the vehicle's engine is switched off.

Hot water created by either the engine or the Hydronic heater is pumped to fan-driven blower heaters fitted in the living space. Fascia heating outlets in the cab are also controlled by the system if needed.

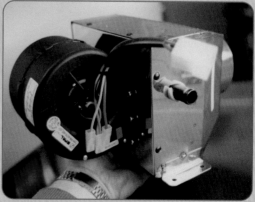

Eberspächer fan matrix units can be supplied in different sizes. This unit supplies a large air duct which splits into three smaller outlets to heat a shower room, a lounge and a high level sleeping area.

In the cylinder, hot water from the engine or heater runs down a central coil which in turn heats the domestic water around it. This system is similarly adopted in many home central-heating systems.

An upright cylinder (rather than the horizontally mounted alternative) and one of two fan units was fitted in a purpose-made compartment adjacent to the wash room in the Mystique motorhome.

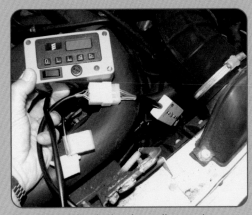

If a system fails, dealers have diagnostic meters; one of these revealed the two dates during a four-year period when the Mystique heater failed to operate. A battery discharged to 11.2V had been recorded as the cause.

Other products with similar features are manufactured by Webasto and in Autumn 2005 the company introduced a ceramic-topped two-burner hob based on similar appliances previously fitted in boats. So whereas the benefits of LPG are undeniable, there's growing competition from diesel/petrol products. This is helped by the fact that in contrast with gas-powered heaters, you are permitted to have an oil-fired heating system running while driving your motorhome on public roads.

Not surprisingly, the installation of Eberspächer and Webasto systems are not normally regarded as DIY tasks although you'd be able to carry out preparation work like that shown in Chapter 12 'Insulating a floor'. Fitting warm air ducting and installing ventilator outlets are further tasks which a practical person could undertake – just as they are when ducts are needed to distribute warm air produced by a gas heater.

■ COOKING SYSTEMS

Ovens are further items which a DIY person could install – as long as the gas connections are made by a qualified specialist.

Most of the hobs on sale are also supplied with helpful installation instructions. Photographs were presented in Chapter 18 to show the installation of a Cramer four-burner hob and grill unit.

■ BATHROOM SYSTEMS

The heating and kitchen appliances described so far are usually supplied with good fitting instructions; so, too, are the cassette toilets from Thetford. In contrast, you are unlikely to find detailed fitting instructions accompanying items such as a hand basin or shower tray for your washroom.

Having seen numerous letters of complaints sent to specialist magazines, it is evident that shower trays are sometimes installed badly by caravan and motorhome manufacturers. There is no excuse for this. If these items are made using thin ABS plastic as described in Chapter 14, the moulding must be fully supported by a timber reinforcing structure. A moulded foam support is even better. Furthermore, careful application of sealant is needed to achieve a leak-proof installation.

In view of the typical lack of instructions accompanying sanitary-ware products, the installation of both an ABS shower tray and wash basin is shown alongside.

Fitting a Thetford swivel-bowl C-200 CWE cassette toilet

There are a numerous toilets in Thetford's range. The old 'bucket and chuck it' models have long been superseded by cassette models, some of which are portable whereas others are fixed. There is also the fixed bench type as opposed to the one here which has a swivel bowl.

The swivelling system allows extra space to be created in small toilet compartments – especially if they have to double-up as a shower. Some models draw the flushing water directly from a motorcaravan's main fresh water tank: this one has a small inboard tank of its own which means that flushing additives can be used. The CW version has a hand-operated flushing
pump, but this one (the CWE model) has an electric pump.

These products are designed for mounting against a vertical rear wall and the wall in the Mystique had a curving tilt. To resolve this, narrow, wedge-shaped surrounds were cut in timber and affixed using adhesive sealant to create the verticality needed.

Note: In heavy rain, a large amount of water discharging from the roof meets up with the top of the cassette door. The Mark 3 door seems less able to cope with this than its Mark 2 predecessor and at least one caravan manufacturer continues to fit the earlier product for that reason. The problem of water seepage in severe rain was eliminated in this project by simply bonding a discreet aluminium gutter trim just above the opening. A similar lintel had previously proved to be a valuable addition over the main entrance door as well.

1 Check Thetford's catalogue carefully to make sure you select a product which is suitable for your particular motorcaravan.

2 This section, which will mount against the wall, shows the cables to the pump, the upper flush water inlet and the cassette.

3 A paper template is fixed to the wall and four 3mm holes drilled from inside reveal its precise position when viewed externally.

4 The drilled location holes pinpoint the exact register of external components with the main assembly inside.

5 On this model, the electric flushing pump is coupled-up to the leisure battery – preferably via a 12V fused distribution panel.

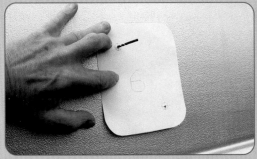

6 Two of the original four pilot holes drilled from the inside show exactly where the paper template is fitted for the filler inlet.

7 A cutting line is pencilled carefully around the paper template; the drilled holes ensure it doesn't slip out of position.

8 To protect the painted face of the external wall, masking tape was placed around the aperture to avoid damage from the saw.

9 In this project the GRP wall was cut using a jigsaw operating at slow speed and without an orbital action.

10 Thanks to accurate positioning of the templates, the external filler assembly located with the structure on the inside.

11 Masking tape allowed a neat beading of black Sikaflex-512 Caravan to be added and the white assembly was sprayed silver.

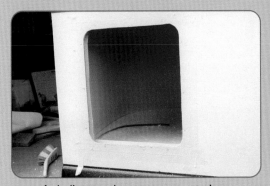

12 A similar template system created an accurate cut-out for the cassette door using a jigsaw with a blade for cutting GRP plastic.

13 This larger hole was strengthened by creating a surround frame of softwood which was secured with sealant and G-cramps.

Installing an acrylic-capped ABS hand basin in the Mystique

1 The GRP shelf in the reject prototype shower compartment was too low for the Mystique so the basin was mounted above it.

2 An outer support in mahogany was helped by vertical pieces of Vöhringer faced ply; this was also used for a lift-up flap.

3 The outlet in the hand basin was modified to take a domestic-sized chrome outlet which couples to a deep water trap.

4 In addition to mounting a Whale mixer tap, this shower control in the Elite range was mounted on the basin as well.

5 The connections for Elite taps are made to accept semi rigid push-fit pipe from Whale. Don't mix the hot and cold feeds!

6 Note the 9mm ply strength-ening plates for the tap controls. All the connections were formed *before* the basin was offered-up.

7 The basin is held with adhesive sealant and the lift-up flap at the front hides storage so that a box of toilet tissue is kept dry.

8 The toilet is on one side, the basin is on the other and the shower is in between. A shower curtain protects the window.

Creating a robust support for an ABS shower tray

1 Marine ply (9mm) was used for the support base together with a wall support batten of hardwood.

2 An expanding drill used with a brace and bit enabled the stepped shape of the outlet in the tray to be replicated.

3 Ribbon mastic sealant was used to support the surround flange of the tray and it provided a cushioning effect.

4 When fitted, the ABS tray was well-supported. A beading of white Sikaflex-510 Caravan adhesive sealant was added later.

■ OTHER ACCESSORIES.

The installation of ancillary products often form the basis of DIY articles published in specialist magazines. Several popular accessories are also described in Chapter 9 of *The Motorcaravan Manual* (Second Edition) including a section on fire extinguishers, fire blankets and smoke detectors. You are strongly advised to pay heed to the precautionary advice given in that manual.

On a different topic, the Fiat Ducato cab of the Mystique motorcaravan was used for the installation of prototype Remis concertina screen and side window blinds. The photographs of the operation are also reproduced in Chapter 9 of *The Motorcaravan Manual (Second Edition)*. So, too, are photographs showing the installation of a prototype Status 530 push-up, roof-mounted, directional TV aerial.

A further section describes: water-evaporative, and compressor refrigeration air conditioners. Lastly, the focus on Zwaardvis portable table assemblies covers a product that all motorcaravans need. Free-standing and floor mounted pillar tables are discussed and this Dutch product is currently available in the UK from IMP of Royston, which is a marine supply specialist.

Table accessories from Zwaardvis

This well-engineered assembly was mounted under some Vöhringer faced-ply to produce a table which rotates and slides.

Floor sockets are mounted inside the Mystique but this heavy-duty base allows a table to be transferred for use outdoors.

Although Zwaardvis products are quite costly, their stability is second to none. Having made the mistake of fitting a conventional steel pillar to support the dining table in the earlier Starcraft project, I went in search of something better. Experience had shown that a passing nudge of the table would set up vibration which invariably spilt the tea. Since the Mystique was built, several British manufacturers have started to fit Zwaardvis products even if they are comparatively costly. In motorcaravan building, as in other spheres of life, you 'get what you pay for'.

TAKING TO THE ROAD

After you've spent many hours building a motorcaravan, it may need to be checked by qualified engineers; it will also have to be taxed and insured before you drive on public roads.

If you have renovated a motorcaravan which had originally been built by a recognised manufacturer, its classification will already be recorded in its registration documents. Insuring it should be simple, too, although you will need to inform the insurance company of any substantial alterations that have been made.

For instance, if you have made significant changes to the base vehicle such as modifying the engine, you may subsequently find that some insurers are unwilling to offer cover.

Problems like this can occur if you build kit cars. Your completed vehicle might have a new GRP body, the engine from a Ford Cortina, the running gear from a Ford Escort Mk 2 and a modified propshaft. Kit cars are often like that: friendly Frankensteins … and many run-of-the mill companies wouldn't dream of insuring them.

Falling into this category are the Starcraft and the Rickman Rancher campervans which are essentially kit cars with accommodation facilities. At one time, only a standard MoT test was required to verify the road-going integrity of a self-built vehicle, but that has changed. Nowadays, project vehicles like these have to pass the Single Vehicle Approval (SVA) test, details of which are given in the accompanying panel.

Notwithstanding procedures that have to be followed in respect of vehicles like the Starcraft and Rickman Rancher, there is no SVA requirement regarding a professionally manufactured van that has been converted into a motorcaravan. Nor is it obligatory to submit a coachbuilt model for testing if it has been constructed using a professionally built chassis-cab vehicle. In both cases, the base vehicles will have already achieved compliance with European legislation in respect of TUV and other obligatory approvals.

Of course, the insurance issue is quite different. Furthermore, you would want to insure and register a standard base vehicle

Single Vehicle Approval (SVA) testing

The high cost of having a vehicle tested under the European-approved TUV scheme prompted the introduction of the SVA test in the United Kingdom. The scheme is used by low-volume vehicle manufacturers, self-importers who buy used vehicles from non-European countries and the builders of kit cars. This last-mentioned category is described in the literature as ' … amateur-built vehicles … using parts from a previously registered vehicle …'

Information on the SVA test is obtainable on the web site www. dft.gov.uk which in turn offers a search facility; enter SVA and the information is then brought up on screen. It is similarly retrievable using a web search engine like Google.

SOME POINTS TO NOTE:
- Detailed information about the scheme is contained in Department for Transport booklet SVA4 published 7 September 2001 and modified 23 September 2005.

- The submission of a motorcaravan for SVA testing is listed as 'optional'.
- Inspections are carried out at testing stations operated by the Vehicle & Operator Services Agency (VOSA) or at designated premises.
- A Minister's Approval Certificate (MAC) under SVA is issued when an examiner is satisfied that a vehicle complies with the regulations.
- SVA is only required for vehicles less than 10 years old which require 'first-time' licensing and registration in Great Britain.
- In 2005, the cost of an SVA test was £150. In that year, the *SVA Inspection Manual* (describing what is tested and how) was available for £37 from the Vehicle & Operator Services Agency, PO Box 12, Swansea, SA1 1BP. To apply to the agency for an SVA test or for general enquiries, see the address in the Appendix.

before adding accommodation facilities.

After completing a DIY project, you will find that some insurance companies offer cover for professionally built motorcaravans – but not for conversions undertaken by amateurs. This can be somewhat annoying, especially when the origins of several well-known manufacturers can be traced back to the efforts of an energetic DIY amateur. The Auto-Sleepers story is a case in point.

Suffice it to say, the issue of insurance is interesting to say the least.

Insurance

When comparing different schemes you will find that insurance companies react in different ways to self-build motorcaravans. Some require an engineer's report and put you in touch with specialists in your area: others do not call for independent scrutiny at all but request you to send detailed photographs of the vehicle.

You will encounter other conditions as well. For example, Shield Total Insurance (formerly Shield Direct) offers 'insurance cover for both self-build and professionally converted panel vans, provided the conversion is fully completed within 90 days of the policy inception.' (See accompanying panel.)

Shield Total Insurance requirements

When this company states that a self-build vehicle must be fully completed within 90 days of the policy inception, the term 'completed' means that the following permanent (i.e. non-removable) fixtures and fittings must be in place:

- A bed with a minimum length of six feet.
- A horizontal sliding side door or an outward hinging rear or side door.
- Seating area for diners to sit round a fixed table.
- A permanent installation to house a water container.
- Wardrobes or cupboards.
- Gas or electric hob.
- Windows on both sides.

Photographic evidence is needed to confirm that the converted vehicle meets all seven requirements. (At least four photographs are expected, two of which must be exterior shots including the registration number.) In the event of the conversion taking longer than 90 days, the cover will thereafter reduce to 'Third Party Only' and an appropriate refund is made. At present, a discount of 10% is offered to members of the Self Build Motor Caravanners Club, Tel.: 01209 821446 and website: www.sbmcc.co.uk.

For more detailed information, contact Shield Total Insurance, using the address in the Appendix.

Without doubt, you will encounter a variety of stipulations. When the author's Starcraft was first insured, the kit car insurance specialist already

The Mystique, and the support car which is sometimes trailed behind, have already provided many hours of pleasure. Insurance for the motorcaravan is arranged with Saga; the micro car is insured by Novitas Underwriting Agency.

When renewing insurance on this kit car, the author was informed by the broker, Footman James & Company Ltd., that cover can often be arranged for self-build motorcaravans as well.

knew this campervan product and offered insurance cover without needing photographic evidence. However, when the Mystique was first insured as part of a 'special vehicle' scheme operated by Norwich Union, a small portfolio of photographs had to be submitted.

It is also helpful to approach the insurers who advertise every month in kit car magazines, some of whom offer cover for self-built motorcaravans as well. When approached, Footman James & Company Ltd stated in October 2005 that: ' …our sales team are able to offer quotations for motorhome cover which also includes self-build vehicles, details of which must be submitted in order to offer cover.'

In 2005, it was also announced by a newly appointed insurance specialist serving members of the Camping and Caravanning Club that self-build motorhomes could also be insured within its scheme.

On another tack, it is also advisable to approach other owners who have completed vehicles for advice on their experiences regarding insurance. For instance, Mike Parker, Co-owner of Silver Screens, has built a number of motorcaravans including the exotic, high-quality bus conversion shown in Chapter 4. For this particular project vehicle, an insurance scheme operated by the National Farmers' Union provided the cover that Mike Parker required.

Another self-builder recently wrote to a specialist magazine to say that Cox Insurance Holdings Ltd provides cover subject to a satisfactory report from one the 30 engineers in its nationwide register. (See Appendix for address.)

So don't be put off by the suggestion that it is almost impossible to insure a self-build vehicle. This is patently not the case although you will have to spend time comparing the schemes on offer.

Gas and electricity checks

Whereas some conversions may need a report from an automotive specialist, it has also been stated in earlier chapters that gas and electrical systems should be checked by an independent, qualified person. Dated certificates confirming the integrity of these systems should be obtained and this was explained in Chapters 16 and 18. This is not a mandatory matter but it can be especially important should you decide to sell the vehicle at a later date.

Registration Certificates (V5 and V5C)

Remember that the Driver and Vehicle Licencing Agency (DVLA) must be notified of certain changes to a registered vehicle. These include a change of colour, a change of body type, and changes which create a new revenue weight as shown on the registration certificate.

DVLA, Longview Road, Swansea SA6 7JL.

Weighbridge checks

In Chapter 6, the Technical note 'Upgrading the MTPLM' highlighted several other issues of importance. A later section in this chapter also described the location and use of weighbridges. All vehicles carry a maximum weight limit and it is not only an offence to drive an overladen vehicle on the road; it could also be extremely dangerous. So re-check the points covered in that earlier chapter.

Conclusion

Thus, you have accomplished your project, bearing in mind that I never suggested that building a motorcaravan is an easy undertaking. However, when you climb aboard and embark on the very first trip, there is an

Standards and Regulations

A summary of Standards and Regulations applicable to motorcaravans is given in Appendix A of *The Motorcaravan Manual* (2nd Edition). Inevitably these are always under review so the reader will need to ensure that he or she is consulting the most recent documents.

inexplicable pleasure when you finally grasp the wheel. All those hours of hardship and the seemingly insurmountable problems are rapidly left behind. You will now feel like a king of the road ... with palatial comfort of your very own making.

When you embark on your very first trip, there's an inexplicable pleasure when you finally grasp the wheel. Hours of hardship and problems are very soon left far behind.

CONTACT ADDRESSES

Please note: This address list was correct at the time of going to press. It includes specialist suppliers and manufacturers whose products and services have been mentioned in the text. Several of the firms have web sites which are easily found using search engines.

The motorcaravan manufacturers listed here include specialists offering bespoke building services and individual fitting operations such as the installation of high top roofs. To obtain a more complete list of motorcaravan manufacturers and importers, consult the monthly Buyers' Guides published in magazines such as

1. MOTORCARAVAN, MOTORHOME MONTHLY

2. PRACTICAL MOTORHOME
and
3. WHICH MOTORHOME.

ABP Accessories,
27 Nether End,
Great Dalby,
Leicestershire,
LE14 2EY
Tel: 08700 115111
(American RV Accessories)

Adrian Bailey Classics,
Unit 1-1A Thornton Grove Works,
Thornton Grove,
Whingate, Leeds,
LS12 3JB
Tel: 0113 263 4288
(Supplier of obsolete and used spares for Bedford CF vans)

Adroit Services,
18 Monks Road,
Swineshead,
Boston, Lincolnshire, PE20 3EL
Tel: 01205 820004
(Cruise Control, Reversing Aids)

Alan H. Schofield Classic Volkswagen,
Unit 14,
Dinting Lane,
Glossop, Derbyshire,
SK13 7NU
Tel: 01457 854267
www.ahschofield.co.uk
(Fabrication and supply of VW panels and parts)

Albert Jagger Ltd,
Centaur Works,
Green Lane,
Walsall,
West Midlands,
WS2 8HG
Tel: 01922 471000
(Manufacturers/suppliers commercial vehicle fittings)

Alde International (UK) Ltd,
14 Regent Park,
Booth Drive,
Park Farm South,
Wellingborough,
Northamptonshire,
NN8 6GR
Tel: 01933 677765
(Central heating systems, SMEV cooking equipment, gas leak detector)

AL-KO Kober Ltd,
South Warwickshire Business Park,
Kineton Road,
Southam,
Warwickshire, CV47 0AL
Tel: 01926 818500
(AMC conversions)

Amber Plastics Ltd,
Broombank Road,
Chesterfield Industrial Estate,
Sheepbridge,
Chesterfield,
S41 9QJ
Tel: 01246 456525
(Rotational mouldings including inboard fixed tanks)

Anglian Developments Ltd,
The Granary,
School Road,
Neatishead,
Norfolk,
NR12 8BU
Tel: 01692 630808
(GRP specialist building monocoque commercial body shells)

Apollo Chemicals Ltd,
Sandy Way,
Amington Industrial Estate,
Tamworth,
Staffordshire,
B77 4DS
Tel: 01827 54281
(Manufacturers of adhesives for repairing delaminated composite panels)

Arc Systems,
13 Far Street,
Bradmore,
Nottingham, NG11 6PF
Tel: 0115 921 3175
(Repair/refurbishment of Carver water/space heaters)

Autocraft Motor Caravans,
Fan Road Industrial Estate,
Fan Road,
Staveley,
Chesterfield,
Derbyshire, S43 3PT
Tel: 01246 471199
(High top fitting service, accessory sales)

Autogas 2000 Ltd,
Carlton Miniott,
Thirsk,
North Yorkshire, YO7 4NJ
Tel: 01845 523213
(Caratank LPG bulk storage tanks)

Autovan Services Ltd,
32 Canford Bottom,
Wimborne,
Dorset, BH21 2HD
Tel: 01202 848414
(Major body repair and rebuilding work)

AVA Leisure,
Unit 3,
Skitts Manor Farm,
Moor Lane,
Marsh Green,
Edenbridge,
Kent, TN8 5QX
Tel: 0870 757 2277
(Roof fitting service, accessory supplier, van converter)

A. Baldassarre,
Upholsterer and Coachtrimmer,
103, Coventry Road,
Queens Park,
Bedford, MK40 4ES
Tel: 01234 359277
(Upholstery work, foam supply and soft furnishings)

Banner Batteries (GB) Ltd,
Units 5-8,
Canal View Business Park,
Wheelhouse Road,
Rugeley,
Staffordshire, WS15 1UY
Tel: 01869 571100
(Energy Bull leisure batteries. AGM batteries and light commercial vehicle batteries)

Bantam Trailers,
Units 5 and 6,
Wollaston Industrial Estate,
Raymond Close, Wollaston,
Northamptonshire, NN29 7RG
Tel: 01933 663998
(Bespoke trailers for transporting Smart Cars and other small vehicles behind motorcaravans)

BCA Leisure Ltd,
Unit H9, Premier Way,
Lowfields Business Park, Elland,
West Yorkshire, HX5 9HF
Tel: 01422-376977
(Manufacturers of Powerpart mains kits)

BeenyBox.co.uk,
Station Garage,
Trevu Road, Camborne,
Cornwall, TR14 7AE
Tel: 01209 711093
(Underfloor sliding storage locker system)

Beetles UK Ltd, - *See Danbury Motorcaravans*

Belling Appliances - *See Glen Dimplex*

Bilbo's Design,
Eastbourne Road, (A22)
South Godstone,
Surrey, RH9 8JQ
Tel: 01342 892499

Bradleys,
Old Station Yard,
Marlesford,
Suffolk, IP13 0AG
Tel: 01728 747900
(Formerly supplier of ABS repair kits; product not available at time of re-print)

Brian James Trailers, Ltd,
Sopwith Way, Drayton Fields
Industrial Estate, Daventry,
Northamptonshire, NN11 5PB
Tel: 01327 308833
(Trailers suitable for transporting large body components)

British Car Auctions Ltd,
Sales & Marketing Department,
Expedier House,
Portsmouth Road,
Hindhead,
Surrey, GU26 6TJ
Tel: 01428 607440
(Motorcaravan auctions)

British Rubber Manufacturers' Association Ltd,
6 Bath Place,
Rivington Street,
London, EC2A 3JE
Tel: 020 7457 5040
(Trade Association advising on tyres)

C.A.K. - *See Caravan Accessories*

Calor Gas Ltd,
Athena Drive, Tachbrook Park,
Warwick, CV34 6RL
Tel: 0800 626626
(Supplier of butane, propane and LPG products)

E.E. Calver Ltd,
Woodlands Park,
Bedford Road, Clapham,
Bedford, MK41 6EJ
Tel: 01234 359584
(Indoor motorcaravan storage)

The Camping & Caravanning Club,
Greenfields House,
Westwood Way,
Coventry, CV4 8JH
Tel: 024 7647 5448

Campingaz
Coleman UK Inc.,
Gordano Gate, Portishead,
Bristol, BS20 7GG
Tel: 01275 845024
(Supplier of Campingaz butane and LPG appliances)

Carafax Ltd,
Rotterdam Road,
Sutton Fields Industrial Estate,
Hull, HU7 0XD
Tel: 01482 825941
(Caraseal ribbon and cartridge sealants)

Car-A-Tow - *See Pro-Tow*

The Caravan Club
East Grinstead House,
East Grinstead,
West Sussex, RH19 1UA
Tel: 01342 326944

The Caravan Panel Shop
Unit 7, Willacy Yard,
Bay Horse Lane,
Catforth, Preston,
Lancashire, PR4 0JD
Tel: 01772 691929
(Copy GRP mouldings made from damaged body parts)

Caravan Accessories (C.A.K. Tanks) Ltd,
10 Princes Drive Industrial Estate,
Kenilworth,
Warwickshire, CV8 2FD
Tel: 0870 757 2324
(Water tanks and components, electrical products, appliances, ventilators, cabinet hardware)

The Caravan Centre,
Unit 3A,
Gilchrist Thomas Industrial Estate,
Blaenavon, NP4 9RL
Tel: 01495 792700
(Specialist breakers supplying caravan/motorhome products)

The Caravan Seat Cover Centre Ltd,
Cater Business Park,
Bishopsworth,
Bristol, BS13 7TW
Tel: 0117 941 0222
(Seat covers, new foam, new upholstery, made-to-measure curtains)

Carver products - *See Truma*

Concept Multi-Car,
Unit 4A/B,
Pennypot Industrial Estate,
Hythe, Kent, CT21 6PE
Tel: 01303 261062
(High top roof installation, Reimo products, van conversions)

The Council for Registered Gas Installers (CORGI),
1 Elmwood, Chineham Park,
Crockford Lane, Basingstoke,
Hampshire, RG24 8WG
Tel: 0870 401 2200
(Holder of gas registration scheme rights until March 2009. See Gas Safe Register for post April 2009 procedures.)

Cramer UK- *See Dometic*

Country Campers,
The Grove,
Three Gates Road,
Fawkham,
Kent, DA3 7NZ
Tel: 01474 707929
(High top roof installation, van conversions to order)

Cox Insurance Holdings Ltd,
Library House, New Road,
Brentwood, Essex,
CM14 4GD
Tel: 01277 200100
(Insurance specialist offering schemes for motorcaravans)

Crossleys,
Unit 33A, Comet Road,
Moss Side Industrial Estate,
Leyland,
Lancashire, PR26 7QN
Tel: 01772 623423
(Major body repair and rebuilding work)

Customer Enquiries (Vehicles),
DVLA,
Swansea,
SA99 1BL
Tel: 0870 2400010
(Guidance on vehicle registration)

Danbury Motorcaravans/Beetles (UK),
Unit 1, Bristol Mineral Works,
Limekiln Road, Rangeworthy,
South Gloucestershire, BS37 7QB
Tel: 0870 1202356
(VW Type 2 Campervans with modern conversions, Type 2 VW Brazilian imports, supply of retrofit interiors)

Davids Isopon – *Through auto accessory stores*
(Polyester fillers and reinforcing compounds)

Design Developments,
24 Carbis Close,
Port Solent, Portsmouth,
Hampshire, PO6 4TW
Tel: 07710 439907
(Barry Stimson design consultant and motorcaravan manufacturer)

Devon Conversions,
Mainsforth Road,
Ferryhill, Co Durham, DL17 9DE
Tel: 01740 655700
(Van conversion specialist)

DLS Plastics,
Occupation Lane,
Gonerby Moor, Grantham,
Lincolnshire, NG32 2BP
Tel: 01476 564549
(Plastic components, plumbing items for motorcaravans)

Dometic Group,
Dometic House, The Brewery,
Blandford St Mary,
Dorset, DT11 9LS
Tel: 0844 626 0133
(Formerly Electrolux Leisure; amalgamated with WAECO in 2007: Air conditioners, refrigerators, Seitz windows, Cramer cookers)

Dow Corning Ltd,
Meriden Business Park,
Copse Drive, Allesley,
Coventry,
West Midlands, CV5 9RG
Tel: 01676 528000
(Sealants used in building and allied industries)

Draper Tools, Ltd,
Hursley Road,
Chandlers Ford,
Hampshire,
S053 1YF
Tel: 023 8026 6355
(Tools of all types)

Driftgate 2000 Ltd,
27 Little End Road,
Eaton Socon, St Neots,
Cambridgeshire, PE19 8JH
Tel: 01480 470400
(Manufacturers of XCell Mains inverters; X-Calibre stage chargers)

Drinkwater Engineering -
see TVAC
(Air suspension systems, chassis work and motorhome weight upgrades)
Subsequently taken over by TVAC, Leyland which later ceased trading in January 2009. See VB Air Suspension and NE Truck & Van for air suspension product information.

Driverite Air Assistance Systems
(Available through dealers - air assistance units; NOT full air suspension)

Eberspächer (UK) Ltd,
10 Headlands Business Park,
Salisbury Road,
Ringwood,
Hampshire,
BH24 3PB
Tel: 01425 480151
(Petrol and diesel-fuelled space & water heaters)

Electrolux Leisure Appliances -
See Dometic

EMC Warehouse
1 Founder Lane,
Knottingley,
West Yorkshire,
WF11 8AU
Tel: 01977 677977
(Installation of high top & elevating roofs; suppliers of build components)

Essanjay Motohomes,
Unit 2,
Sovereign Business Park,
48 Willis Way,
Poole,
Dorset,
BH15 3TB
Tel: 01202 683608
(Motorhome servicing, components, removable steering wheels)

Europa Specialist Spares,
Fauld Industrial Estate,
Tutbury,
Burton upon Trent,
Staffordshire,
DE13 9HR
Tel: 01283 815609
(Vehicle trims, light clusters, and all specialist vehicle parts)

Exhaust Ejector Co Ltd,
Wade House Road,
Shelf,
Nr. Halifax,
West Yorkshire,
HX3 7PE
Tel: 01274 679524
(Replacement acrylic windows made to order)

Exide Leisure Batteries Ltd,
Customer Services,
6-7 Parkway Estate,
Longbridge Road,
Trafford Park,
Manchester, M17 1SN
Tel: 0161 786 3333
(Exide base vehicle and leisure
batteries)

Farécla Products Ltd,
Broadmeads, Ware,
Hertfordshire, SG12 9HS
Tel: 01920 465041
(Caravan Pride G3 acrylic
window scratch remover,
GRP surface renovator)

The Farnborough VW Centre,
10 Farnborough Road,
Farnborough,
Hampshire, GU14 6AY
Tel: 01252 521152
(High quality VW Campervan
restorations)

Fiamma accessories - *Contact
your motorcaravan dealer*

Fiat Auto (UK) Ltd,
Fiat House,
266 Bath Road,
Slough, SL1 4HJ
Tel: 01753 511431
(Book "Commercial Vehicles;
Manual for conversions/special
outfits")

Foam for Comfort Ltd,
Unit 2,
Wyther Lane Trading Estate,
Wyther Lane,
Kirkstall,
Leeds, LS5 3BT
Tel: 0113-274 8100
(Synthetic foam, latex, composite
bonded foam)

Footman James & Co Ltd,
Waterfall Lane,
Cradley Heath,
West Midlands, B64 6PU
Tel: 0845 330 1662
(Quotations on self-built
motorcaravan insurance)

**Froli Kunststoffwerk Fromme
GmbH,**
Liemker Strasse 27,
D-33758 Schloss Holte-
Stukenbrock, Germany.
Tel: 49 (0) 52 07 - 95 00 0
(Froli bed support systems)

Gaslow International,
Castle Business Park,
Pavilion Way,
Loughborough,
Leicestershire, LE11 5GW
Tel: 0845 4000 600
(Refillable gas systems, Gaslow
gauges, regulators, couplings and
components)

Gas Safe Register,
PO BOX 6804,
Basingstoke, RG24 4NB
Tel: 0800 4085 500
(Information about Gas Safety
Checks formerly conducted
by CORGI)

General Ecology Europe Ltd,
St. Andrews House,
26 Brighton Road,
Crawley, RH10 6AA
Tel: 01293 400644
(Nature Pure Ultrafine
water purifier)

GE Protimeter PLC,
Meter House,
Marlow,
Buckinghamshire, SLW 1LW
Tel: 01628 472722
(Professional moister meters)

**Glen Dimplex Home
Appliances,**
Stoney Lane, Prescot,
Merseyside, L35 2XW
Tel: 0871 22 22 503
(Belling, New World, Stoves,
Vanette appliances)

Grade UK Ltd,
3 Central Court, Finch Close,
Lenton Lane Industrial Estate,
Nottingham, NG7 2NN
Tel: 0115 986 7151
(Status TV aerials and accessories)

Häfele UK Ltd,
Swift Valley Industrial Estate,
Rugby,
Warwickshire,
CV21 1RD
Tel: 01788 542020
(Furniture components and
hardware)

HBC International A/S,
Fabriksparken 4,
DK9230 Svenstrup,
Denmark
Tel: +45 70227070
(Professional system for repairing
aluminium body panels)

Hella Ltd,
Wildmere Industrial Estate,
Banbury,
Oxfordshire,
OX16 3JU
Tel: 01295 272233
(Hella Towing electrical
Equipment)

Hodgson Sealants,
Belprin Road,
(Off Swinemoor Lane),
Beverley,
East Yorkshire,
HU17 0LN
Tel: 01482 868321
(Sealants used in the
caravan industry)

**Hornchurch Motor
Caravan Centre,**
5–7 Broadway Parade,
Elm Avenue,
Hornchurch,
Essex,
RM12 4RS
Tel: 01708 444791/443782
(Custom-made roof racks,
cycle/motorcycle racks, ladders)

IMP,
15 Jarman Way,
Royston,
Hertfordshire,
SG8 5HW
Tel: 01763 241300
(Zwaardvis high stability table
pillars and sliding mechanisms)

JC Leisure,
Strand Garage,
A259,
Winchelsea,
East Sussex,
TN36 4JT
Tel: 01797 227337
(Van conversions on various
base vehicles)

John Guest Speedfit Ltd,
Horton Road,
West Drayton,
Middlesex,
UB7 8JL
Tel: 01895 449233
(Push-fit plumbing couplings
and pipe)

Johnnie Longden Ltd,
Unit 24, Dawkins Road
Industrial Estate, Poole,
Dorset, BH15 4JD
Tel: 01202 679121
(Accessory wholesaler supplying
Henry GE water heater to dealers)

Just Kampers,
Unit 1,
Stapeley Manor,
Long Lane,
Odiham,
Hampshire,
RG29 1JE
Tel: 01256 862288
(VW Camper and Transporter
parts 1968–2004; accessories)

Labcraft Ltd,
22B King Street,
Saffron Walden,
Essex, CB10 1ES
Tel: 01799 513434
(Lighting and 12V products)

Lattoflex Bed Systems,
Thomas GmbH + Co.
Sitz- und Liegemöbel KG
Walkmühlenstrasse 93
27432 Bremervörde, Germany
Tel: 0049 4761 979138
(CaraWinx mattress support
systems)

Leisuredrive,
Unit 4, Fishbrook Industrial Estate,
Stoneclough Road,
Kearsley, Bolton,
Lancashire, BL4 8EL
Tel: 01204 574498
(Installer of high tops, van
converters, supplier of unit
furniture)

Leisure Plus,
Unit 5,
New Road Industrial Estate,
New Road, Hixon,
Staffordshire, ST18 0PJ
Tel: 01889 271692
(Wholesaler of adhesives,
delamination repair products,
sealants)

**Magnum Mobiles and
Caravan Surplus,**
Unit 9A, Cosalt Industrial Estate,
Convamore Road,
Grimsby, DN32 9JL
Tel: 01472 353520
(Caravan/Motorcaravan Surplus
Stock; bespoke building services)

Marquis Motorhome Centre,
Winchester Road,
Lower Upham,
Southampton, SO32 1HA
Tel 01489 860666
(Hire and buy scheme)

Maxview,
Common Lane,
Setchey,
King's Lynn,
Norfolk, PE33 0AT
Tel: 01553 813300
(TV aerials, satellite TV products,
free guidebooks)

Metrol Springs Ltd,
75 Tenter Road,
Moulton Park,
Northampton, NN3 6AX
Tel: (01604 499332)
(Gas struts with pressure-release
bleed valve for fine-tuning)

Middlesex Motorcaravans,
22 Station Parade.
Whitchurch Lane,
Edgware,
Middlesex, HA8 6RW
Tel: 020 8952 4045
(Complete and part-build panel
van conversions)

Miriad Products Ltd,
Park Lane,
Dove Valley Park,
South Derbyshire, DE65 5BG
Tel: 01283 586060
(Truma spares for heating, water
appliances and other accessories)

Morco Products Ltd,
59 Beverley Road,
Hull, HU3 1XW
Tel: 01482 325456
(Water Heaters, accessories)

The Motor Caravanners' Club,
22 Evelyn Close,
Twickenham,
Middlesex, TW2 7BN
Tel: 020 8893 3883

Motor Caravan Conversions (Reimo),
Collingham Street,
Off North Street,
Cheetham,
Manchester, M8 8RQ
Tel: 0161 839 1855
(Reimo conversions and supply of German parts)

Munster Simms Engineering Ltd,
Old Belfast Road,
Bangor,
Co. Down,
Northern Ireland, BT19 1LT
Tel: 02891 270531
(Whale water heater, compact space heater, semi-rigid pipework, pumps, taps and plumbing accessories)

Murvi,
4 East Way,
Lee Mill Industrial Estate,
Ivybridge,
Devon, PL21 9GE
Tel: 01752 892200
(Van conversion specialist)

The National Caravan Council,
Catherine House,
Victoria Road,
Aldershot,
Hampshire,
GU11 1SS
Tel: 01252 318251
(Trade association for caravans and motorhomes)

National Inspection Council for Electrical Installation Contracting,
(NICEIC)
Warwick House,
Houghton Hall Park,
Houghton Regis,
Dunstable,
LU5 5ZX
Tel: 01582 539000
(Certification of motorcaravan wiring for mains electricity)

The Natural Mat Company,
99 Talbot Road,
London,
W11 2AT
Tel: 0207 9850474
(Slatted sprung beech bed systems, anti-condensation underlay)

Noise Killer Acoustics (UK) Ltd,
103 Denbydale Way,
Royton,
Oldham,
OL2 5UH
Tel: 0161 643 8070
(Noise reduction systems for motorcaravans)

North East Truck+Van,
Cowpen Bewley Road,
Haverton Hill, Billingham,
Cleveland, TS23 4EX
Tel: 01642 370555
(Major chassis alterations: Air suspension installations)

Nu Venture Campers,
Unit 7, Actons Walk,
Wood Street, Wigan,
Lancashire, WN3 4HN
Tel: 01942 238560
(Motorcaravans built to customer specification)

Nu Venture Motor Homes,
Unit 2, Seven Stars Road,
Wallgate, Wigan,
Lancashire, WN3 5AT
Tel: 01942 494090
(Motorcaravans built to customer specification)

O'Leary Spares and Accessories,
314 Plaxton Bridge Road,
Woodmansey,
Nr Beverley,
East Yorkshire, HU17 0RS
Tel: 01482 868632
(Caravan/Motorcaravan surplus stock)

Osma rainwater products – *Sold through Builders' Merchants*
(Osma weld adhesive used for waste pipes and tank connections)

Parma Industries,
123 High Street,
Wickham Market,
Suffolk, IP13 0RD
Tel: 01728 745700
(Wheel trims, dashboard plastic veneer, general accessories)

Pleitner's PS Wohnmobil GmbH,
Laerstrasse 16,
33775 Versmold,
Deutschland.
Tel: 0049 054 23 20 40 0
www.pleitner.de
(Dealer linked with VW based Athano self build A Class)

Plug-In-Systems - *Contact your motorcaravan dealer*
(12V control components, water level sensors, gauges, electronic alarm)

Powerpart 230v accessories – *See BCA Leisure*

Propex Heat Source Ltd.,
Unit 5,
Second Avenue Business Park,
Millbrook, Southampton,
SO15 0LP
Tel: 023 8052 8555
www.propexheatsource.co.uk
(Propex compact blown air gas heaters; Malaga Mk II water heater)

Pro-Tow
Unit 1,
565 Blandford Road,
Hamworthy,
Poole,
Dorset, BH16 5BW
Tel: 01202 632488
(Car-a-Tow towing frames; Solar Solutions solar panels)

PWS,
Unit 5,
Chalwyn Industrial Estate,
Old Wareham Road,
Parkstone,
Dorset,
BH12 4PE
Tel: 01202 746851
(Racks, protector bars, custom-made tow bars)

Rainbow Conversions,
Unit 1, Algores Way,
Wisbech,
Cambridgeshire,
PE13 2TQ
Tel: 01945 585931
(Van conversions built to order; Vöhringer ply & accessories)

Regal Furnishings,
Unit 4,
Merlin Way,
Quarry Hill Industrial Estate,
Ilkeston,
Derbyshire,
DE7 4RA
Tel: 01159 329988
(Upholstery in a day, foam, bespoke curtains, overnight stays)

Reimo Motorcaravan Conversions,
Collingham Street,
Off North Street,
Cheetham,
Manchester,
M8 8RQ
Tel: 0161 839 1855
(High top roof installation, components, van converter, Reimo CD ROM)

Remis UK, - *Through accessory dealers*
(Remis blinds, flyscreens, roof windows)

RoadPro Ltd,
Stephenson Close,
Drayton Fields,
Daventry,
Northamptonshire,
NN11 5RF
Tel: 01327 312233
(Accessories, chargers, reversing aids, TVs)

Russek Publications,
Unit 6 29a Ardler Road,
Caversham,
Reading,
Berkshire,
RG45AE
Tel: 0845 0942130
(Vehicle repair manuals including Talbot Express models)

Ryder Towing Equipment Ltd,
Alvanley House,
Alvanley Industrial Estate,
Stockport Road East,
Bredbury,
Stockport,
SK6 2DJ
Tel: 0161 430 1120
(Electrical towing equipment)

Sargent Electrical Services, Ltd,
Unit 39,
Tokenspire Business Park,
Woodmansey,
Beverley, HU17 0TB
Tel: 01452 678987
(12V controls and panels)

Seitz Windows - *See Dometic*

The Self Build Motorcaravanners Club,
PO BOX 3345,
Littlehampton,
BN16 9FU
www.sbmcc.co.uk

SF Detection Ltd,
Hatch Pond House,
4 Stinsford Road,
Poole, Dorset, BH17 0RZ
Tel: 01202 645577
(Carbon monoxide detectors, LP Gas alarms)

Shield Total Insurance,
Floor 9,
Market Square House,
St James's Street,
Nottingham, NG1 6FG
Freephone 0800 39 30 33
www.shieldyourmotorhome.co.uk

SHURflo Ltd,
Unit 5, Sterling Park,
Gatwick Road,
Crawley, RH10 9QT
Tel: 01293 424000
(Water pumps)

Sika Ltd,
Watchmead,
Welwyn Garden City,
Hertfordshire, AL7 1BQ
Tel: 01707 394444
(Sikaflex cartridge sealants and adhesive sealants)

Silver Screens,
P.O. Box 9, Cleckheaton,
West Yorkshire, BD19 5YR
Tel: 01274-872151
(Insulated window covers)

Single Vehicle Approval Scheme (SVA) – *See Vehicle & Operator Services Agency.*

The Society of Motor Manufacturers and Traders,
Forbes House,
Halkin Street,
London,
SW1X 7DS
Tel: 0171 235 7000

Spinflo - *See Thetford (UK)*

Stoves plc,
Company name changed to:
Glen Dimplex Cooking Ltd,
Stoney Lane, Prescot,
Merseyside,
L35 2XW
Tel: 0151 426 6551
(Grills, Hobs, Ovens)

SVO (Calne),
Unit K, Stanier Road,
Porte Marsh Industrial Estate,
Calne,
Wiltshire, SN11 9PX
Tel: 01249 815141
(Power assisted steering,
adaptations for disabled users)

SvTech,
Chandler House,
Talbot Road, Leyland,
Lancashire, PR25 2ZF
(Specialist consultants on weight
up-grades and official weight plate
alterations)

Symonspeed Ltd,
Cleveland Garage,
1 Cleveland Road,
Torquay,
Devon, TQ2 5BD
Tel: 01803 214620
(Air assistance units and SOG
toilet system)

TB Turbo
(At time of re-print, Company
not trading)

TEK Seating Ltd,
Unit 32, Pate Road,
Leicester Road Industrial Estate,
Melton Mowbray,
Leicestershire, LE13 0RG
Tel: 01664 480689
(Cab seating, seat swivels, seat
bases and upholstery)

Thetford (UK),
4-10 Welland Close,
Parkwood Industrial Estate,
Rutland Road,
Sheffield, S3 9QY
Tel: 01142 738157
(Norcold refrigerators, toilets and
treatments, Spinflo cooking
appliances)

TOWtal,
Grove Road,
Stoke-on-Trent,
ST4 4LN
Tel: 01782 333422
('A' Frames, electric brake actuators,
trailers, scooter racks, tow bars)

Truma UK,
Truma House,
Beeches Park,
Eastern Avenue,
Burton-upon-Trent,
Staffordshire, DE13 0BB
Tel: 01283 511092
(Space and water heating
systems, gas components. See
Miriad Products for Truma spares.)

Trylon Ltd,
Unit J, Higham Business Park,
Bury Close,
Higham Ferrers,
Northamptonshire, NN10 8HQ
Tel: 01933 411724
(Resins, glass and guidance on
glass reinforced plastics)

**TVAC (Incorporating
Drinkwater Engineering),**
(TVAC, Leyland ceased trading in
January 2009. See VB Air
Suspension and NE Truck & Van
for air suspension product
information.)

van Aaken Developments Ltd,
Crowthorne.
(At the time of this reprint, the
Company was no longer trading.)

Van Bitz,
Cornish Farm,
Shoreditch, Taunton,
Somerset, TA3 7BS
Tel: 01823-321992
(Strikeback T Thatcham-Approved
security, gas alarm, Battery
Master)

Van Window Specialists,
Unit 4, Riverside Works,
Methley Road, Castleford,
West Yorkshire, WF10 1PW
Tel: 01977 552929
(Made-to-measure windows,
supply and fit, VW van
conversions)

VB Air Suspension,
Unit 13, Elder Court,
Lions Drive,
Shadworth Business Park,
Blackburn,
Lancashire, BB1 2EQ
Tel: 01254 848010
(Full air suspension systems
together with air assistance
products)

Vehicle & Marine Window Co.,
Victoria Street,
Birmingham, B9 5AA
Tel: 0121 772 6307
(Window manufacturers, fitters
and suppliers)

**The Vehicle & Operator Service
Agency,**
SVA Section,
91/92 The Strand,
Swansea, SA1 2DH
Tel: 0870 60 60 440
www.vosa.gov.uk/
(To apply for an SVA test and for
general enquiries. Detailed
information on the scheme also
on www.direct.gov.uk)

V & G Caravans,
107 Benwick Road,
Whittlesey, Peterborough,
Cambridgeshire, PE7 2HD
Tel: 01733 350580
(Replacement replica panels
in GRP)

Vöhringer Importers,
1 Butterwick Drive,
Herongate,
Shrewsbury,
Shropshire,
SY1 3XE
Tel: 01743 350580
(Stockist information for
lightweight decorative plywoods)

Waeco UK Ltd –
See Dometic Group
(Compressor refrigerators,
reversing aids, navigational aids)

Watling Engineers Ltd,
88 Park Street Village,
nr. St. Albans,
Hertfordshire,
AL2 2LR
Tel: 01727 873661
(Specially designed towing
brackets)

Webasto Products UK Ltd,
Webasto House,
White Rose Way,
Doncaster Carr,
South Yorkshire,
DN4 5JH
Tel: 01302 322232
(Diesel-fuelled heaters, water
evaporative air conditioners)

Whale –
see Munster Simms
(Water accessories)

Wheelhome,
Tip's Cross,
Blackmore Road,
Hook End,
Brentwood,
Essex,
CM 15 0DX
Tel: 01277 822208
(Specialist building compact
motorcaravans from MPVs)

Witter Towbars,
Drome Road,
Deeside Industrial Park,
Deeside,
Chester,
CH5 2NY
Tel: 01244 284500
(Towbars and cycle carriers)

Woodfit Ltd,
Kem Mill,
Whittle-le-Woods,
Chorley,
Lancashire,
PR6 7EA
Tel: 01257 266421
(Hinges, fittings, hardware, wire
storage baskets and catches)

Woolies,
off Blenheim Way,
Northfields Industrial Estate,
Market Deeping,
Peterborough,
PE6 8LD
Tel: 01778 347347
(Trim, accessories and window
rubbers)

W4 Ltd,
Unit B,
Ford Lane Industrial Estate,
Arundel,
West Sussex,
BN18 0DF
Tel: 01243 553355
(Mains 230v kits, socket testers,
ribbon sealants)

Young Conversions,
Unit 47,
Barton Road,
Water Eaton,
Bletchley,
Milton Keynes,
Buckinghamshire,
MK2 3BD
Tel: 01908 639 936
(Full or part conversions on any
base vehicle, stage payment
conversion, one-off designs)

ZIG Electronics, Ltd,
Saxon Business Park,
Hanbury Road,
Stoke Prior,
Bromsgrove,
Worcestershire,
B60 4AD
Tel: 01527 556715
(12V controls, chargers, water
level sensors and gauges)

Zwaardvis – See IMP
(High quality table support
systems and accessories)

**3M Co,
(Minnesota Mining and
Manufacturing Co.)**
To find local supplier
Tel: 0161 237 6130 or
check www.3m.com/thinsulate
(Manufacturer of Thinsulate
thermal insulation)

INDEX

Author Acknowledgements

A debt of gratitude is extended to the hundreds of people who have helped me build leisure vehicles and write books about caravanning. The following played a special part when *Build Your Own Motorcaravan* was being prepared:

- **The self-builders included:**
  Tony Brook (Mazda campervan)
  John and Alison Freame (Renault Trafic campervan)
  Mike Parker (Silver Screens, Bus conversion)
  Steve Rowe (VW Westfalia re-build)
  Roy Webb (Caravan to motorcaravan conversion)

- **Advice and technical assistance**
  Steve Barker (LCV Operations Manager, Fiat Auto UK)
  Barry Sharratt (Managing Director, AL-KO Kober Ltd)
  Barry Stimson (Designer and builder, Mystique body shell)

- **Photography**
  Anthony Butler (Image Photography – Cover photo)
  Motor Caravan Magazine (IPC Media Ltd, loan of photographs)
  Terry Watkins (Technical Manager, Sika Ltd, loan of photographs)
  Paul Stimpson (Loan of Beeny Box Photograph)

- **Project Management**
  Louise McIntyre and her colleagues (Haynes Publishing)

- Self-build Motor Caravanners Club (Project support)

- Guidance on products has also been gratefully received from countless people working in the component and accessory industries.

John Wickersham
20th January, 2006